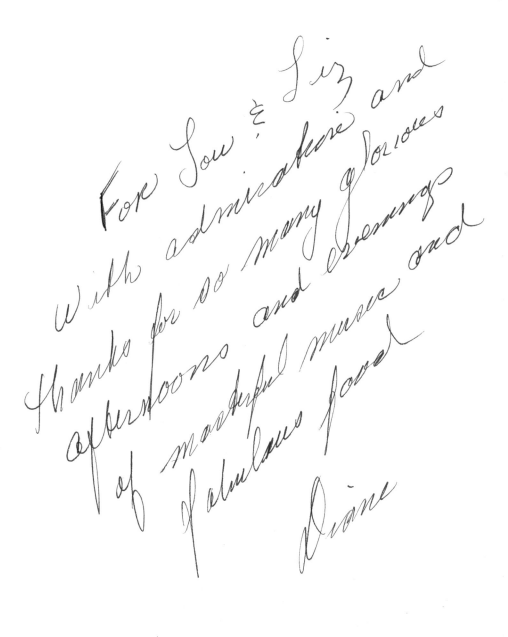

For Lou & Liz
With admiration and
thanks for so many glorious
afternoons and evenings
of wonderful music and
fabulous food

Diane

THE FABRIC OF SELF

The Fabric of Self

A Theory of

Ethics and Emotions

Diane Rothbard Margolis

YALE UNIVERSITY PRESS   NEW HAVEN & LONDON

Published with assistance from the Mary Cady Tew Memorial Fund.

Designed by James J. Johnson and set in Stempel Garamond type by Tseng Information Systems, Inc.
Printed in the United States of America by Vail-Ballou Press, Binghamton, New York.

Library of Congress Cataloging-in-Publication Data

Margolis, Diane Rothbard.
The fabric of self : a theory of ethics and emotions / Diane Rothbard Margolis.
p.   cm.
Includes bibliographical references and index.
ISBN 0-300-06990-1 (hardcover : alk. paper)

1. Self.   2. Self—Social aspects.   3. Emotions.   I. Title.
BF697.M32   1998
155.2—dc21   97-34298

A catalogue record for this book is available from the British Library.

The paper in this book meets the guidelines for permanence and durability of the Committee on Production Guidelines for Book Longevity of the Council on Library Resources.

10 9 8 7 6 5 4 3 2 1

In memory of my husband,
RICHARD JULES MARGOLIS,
for all reasons

Contents

Preface

THIS BOOK HAS TAKEN TOO LONG TO WRITE. When I began, I did not know how to articulate what I wanted to say. Perhaps I did not even know *what* I wanted to say, although the central thesis remained firm through all the book's drafts.

Along the way, I received many gifts. The first was a grant from the Center for the American Woman and Politics to study and compare women and men in local political parties. If, when I had published one paper based on that research, Ruth Mandel, director of the center, had agreed with me that it conveyed all I and the data had to say, this book would never have developed. In some sense, then, this is Ruth's book. She believed that there was more in the data and more in my head than had gotten into that paper. She urged me to continue.

With her recommendation and good words on my behalf from Wolf Hydebrand and Richard Sennett of New York University, where I had completed my graduate studies, the Bunting Institute at Radcliffe College accepted my application for a fellowship. It was a splendid year. I had time to think, to take James Davis's course in statistics, and to decide that I was on the wrong track in my search within social mobility theory for the variables that might explain why women were not climbing the ladder to career success in politics. Of all Bunting's and Harvard's riches — libraries, computer facilities, lectures, talks, and casual chats — the most valuable was a study group I joined with Naomi Chasan, Anne Costain, and Jane Roland Martin. Never before, and not since, could I so regularly and so fruitfully discuss developing ideas with colleagues.

Looking back, I think that the Bunting Institute's luxury of time and intellectual stimulation went to my head and led me to choose a task without regard to the resources I would need. By the time I left, I had listened and read enough to know that my findings of the differences between the women and men on the Town Committees were quite commonplace—similar differences between women and men appeared in virtually every social milieu where they worked side by side. But the explanations often proffered for those differences—patriarchy, power, unexplained variation—seemed to be labels rather than explanations. By the end of my year at the Bunting, my data and Harvard's luxurious intellectual environment had combined to send me down the path of theory.

Back at the Stamford branch of the University of Connecticut—where the regular teaching load of four courses and three preparations each semester left little time for thinking, reading, or talking—I made little progress. Fortunately, the university granted me a sabbatical leave, and James Davis agreed to sponsor me as a visiting scholar at the Harvard Department of Sociology. I thought I would finish my research that year. I didn't. As reviewers were beginning to say in response to the several applications I sent for other grants and fellowships, the project I had taken on in my year at the Bunting had become ambitious, and inchoate.

Fortunately, others whom I never met were completing parts of the project I had taken on. When Charles Taylor's *Sources of the Self* was published, I could stop trying to review the different moral orientations in Western philosophy that he had located so masterfully. Then I could focus on the much more congenial task of connecting those orientations to their social settings, something that Jean-Christophe Agnew had already done for the exchanger orientation. That part completed, the task was to understand how we could juggle all those moral orientations. Scholars working within the social construction of emotions led the way. All I needed then was to complete the knot between symbolic interaction and social constructionism that others had already begun to tie. My intellectual guides for this part of the journey are noted in the penultimate chapter.

Many colleagues and friends read chapters along the way and helped with encouragement, comments, and criticism: David Riesman, Myra Marx Ferree, Jerry Jacobs, Craig Calhoun, Kai Erikson, James C. Scott, David Franks, Randall Collins, Elga Wasserman, Sam Kaplan, and my son, Philip E. Margolis. With Louise Scott I discussed the concept of the sublime, which had been brought to my attention by Elizabeth McKensey at the Bunting Institute.

Thanks also to my editors at Yale University Press, John Covell and Jenya Weinreb. As manuscript editor, Jenya Weinreb rates a special thanks for her sharp eye, keen ear, and gentle corrections.

Although my turn toward theory and the close of the sabbatical year at Harvard sent me from the world of intellectual luxury, I could still bathe in uxorial comfort. Through all these struggles to articulate my thoughts, my husband, Dick, was there to embrace me and my ideas and, wonderful teacher, writer, and editor that he was, to help me find the voice with which to express this complex analysis. During the 1990–1991 academic year, the University of Connecticut granted me another sabbatical leave and another chance to finish. That year began with Dick's loss of kidney function due to the kind of medical neglect HMOs foster and ended with Dick's death after a kidney transplant.

No one could fill the void Dick left. Many, however, tried to dispel my loneliness and gave me the strength to go on with life and work. Among them are our sons, Harry and Philip; their wives, Susan and Susanne; their children, Anna, Isabel, Maya, and Jeremy Richard; my sister Skip and her husband, John; and friends Sally and Charlie Jacob, Bonnie and Kit Collier, Louise and Jim Scott, Elga and Harry Wasserman, Joan Larned, Jane and Stewart MacColl, Jane and Mike Martin, Sandy and Walter Mintz, Tim and Becky Blodgett, Carol Cerf, Joan and Roy Potter, and Joan Spade. The list of reachers-out reaches on. To all, my thanks; my gratitude is our bond.

In spite of all that help, the book remains imperfect; its flaws are my responsibility alone.

Introduction:
Not by Bread Alone

DURING THE MID-1970s, I conducted a study of women and men in local political parties. Its purpose was to determine why, in spite of an egalitarian ideology and legal guarantees of equal access to the political system, the political hierarchy in the United States was marked by a female presence that declined as status increased. I titled the first paper to come from that study "The Invisible Hands" because when I compared the work women and men were doing for their parties, the overriding difference was how difficult it was to see what the women were doing. Whatever they did, the men performed their work in more visible settings—at meetings rather than on the phone, at barbecue fund-raisers rather than at covered-dish-casserole fund-raisers, and at party headquarters rather than at home. Moreover, if rewards in terms of praise or position were not forthcoming, the men would stop contributing to their parties, whereas the women contributed in spite of criticism and small likelihood of personal or party success. Indeed, the less likely a successful outcome, the greater the difference in the proportion of men's labor to women's. And that difference was great: on average, the women gave three times as many hours to their parties as the men.[1]

I was perplexed: Why were the women working so hard without apparent reward? At the local level, work for political parties was voluntary, but popular explanations for women's lack of success at party work were similar to explanations for their relative lack of success in paid labor markets. The assumption was that if women weren't receiving rewards equal to those that men enjoyed, then women weren't performing as well as men. If they would only work harder, spend more time, be more "pro-

1

fessional," be more "assertive," they would earn all the career advancement and rewards men were getting. Contrary to this assumption, many studies, mine included, showed that the women were working at least as hard and as well, acting professionally, and being assertive. Still, once they reached a certain point in an organizational hierarchy, they hit what came to be known as the glass ceiling. Soon a new explanation for this phenomenon was introduced: women have not been pursuing these careers as long as men. When their experience and training equal the experience and training of men, their numbers in high office will come closer to the numbers of men in high office. But a Congressional study published in 1995 documents the continuing impassability of the glass ceiling. As years of experience increase, so does the gap between women's and men's rewards.[2]

After reading and thinking about these inequities for more than a decade, I concluded that explanations of inequality that focus on performance presume an egalitarian social structure that grants equal rewards for equal work. Although we often proclaim the benefits and existence of such a system — one that metes out rewards and punishments without regard to gender, race, ethnicity, or class — we do not live within such a system. The problem, and the answer to the question of why the women worked so hard for inequitable reward, is that in the United States today, several social structures, with several moral systems, and several ways of viewing ourselves guide our conduct simultaneously. All are part of our culture. All fashion the images we have in our minds of who we are, who we can be, who and what we should be, what we can and should expect from others, and how we should think of and treat each other. The reason women and men in the local political parties were acting differently and receiving different rewards is that they were following different moral systems. Moreover, everybody, including the women, expected the women and the men to be oriented to different views of themselves.

The orientation the women tended to follow is a system we depend on for our very lives. It sometimes receives sentimental support in idealized notions about the role of mothers or in angry pronouncements that family values are declining, but, for all the talk, it seldom receives clear, practical, easily perceptible support. The orientation the men tended to follow is our dominant system. It is so powerful a view in contemporary Western societies that it often appears to be the only view. Its conceptualization of the self is intensely individualistic, possibly the most individualistic moral system any culture has ever constructed. It projects an image of the self as an exchanger, a rational calculator balancing the quid pro quos of life. The belief that nobody gets or gives anything except in exchange for something else permeates this view of human nature and human behavior.

Unexpected consequences flow from the dominance of this view. Among other effects, this orientation has tended to enfeeble what Tocqueville called our "habits of the heart," by which he meant those bonds fostered by family life, religious traditions, and local politics. Tocqueville viewed such attachments as reins on opposite American tendencies—toward extreme individualism, on the one hand, and toward unthinking mass behavior, on the other.[3]

In a world of slackening ties, individualistic leanings tend to dominate the behavioral mainstream, and values that were once deemed central begin to look peculiarly borderline. Thus one political scientist, reflecting on the cynicism of our time, finds himself apologizing as he uses the expression "public spirit," which he concedes sounds "somewhat archaic" these days. Nonetheless he does use the term, because he believes it stands for a necessary approach to policy-making, one "that has tragically suffered a precipitous decline in recent decades."[4] This book joins two streams of contemporary thought. One critiques a society that appears to be flying off toward the two extremes Tocqueville warned against.[5] The other has been developing new understandings of culture and the social construction of emotions.[6]

Moral systems and views of the self go hand in hand. As Charles Taylor argues, "radically different senses of what the good is go along with quite . . . different notions of the self."[7] Because many moralities along with their associated views of the self guide our behavior (although most of the time we seem to be aware of only one view), my first project in this book is to examine current views of the self and bring them into a coherent whole. I do that by developing a typology of the diverse moral orientations and their attendant ways of conceiving the self.[8]

Each view offers a different way of imagining the self and its relation to others. The typology will provide a large mirror for collective reflection—one that can reveal the existence and the importance of such everyday, yet increasingly distrusted, motivations as public spirit and altruism. In this book I invite readers to reject single-track visions of the self. I suggest that to focus exclusively or even predominantly on people's predilections to narrow their relationships to exchanges, competitions, and rational choices is to underestimate the varied capacities of humans and to ignore many of the moral orientations that guide social life in the contemporary United States.[9] Humans do not live by bread alone. The true wealth of the species is its remarkable emotional and intellectual flexibility, its cultural inventiveness, and its ability to create all manner of social orders—and all manner of understandings of what it is to be a human agent, a person, or a self.[10]

The word *self* has many meanings in the United States these days. *Self* is a magazine whose authors think we should possess ourselves as a manufacturer might possess plastic. *Self* offers its readers advice on molding themselves so that, like any other well-handled commodity, they will bring great returns. This is one example of the orientation that I call the exchanger self.

Another popular view sees the self as something less malleable. This self is the essential quality of the person, the center of feeling and worth that each of us has at the core of our being. It is knowable, and we approach it in an attitude of discovery. This self cries out for expression. It is an example of the orientation I call the cosmic self.

In contemporary American culture, these two concepts of the self sit beside many other ideas of what a self is. My intention is not to champion any one of them but to define and analyze all of them. Contemporary political debate presumes underlying views of the self, but proponents of any given policy seldom clarify the view they hold. They seem unaware that different views of the self inform different political positions, and that all of us hold different and contradictory views of ourselves, the different views being brought to the fore in different social circumstances. We do not, nor can we, at the close of the twentieth century hold a single view of our selves, nor can we adhere to a single moral system.

Although the view of the self as an exchanger who makes rational choices has attracted the most scholarly attention and has been at the foundation of most recent social theory,[11] other views play a critical role in Western societies and in the daily lives of their peoples. My intention is to accord these other views the same analytic respect commonly reserved for theories of the self as a competitive, rational exchanger, and to examine each of these other views for its continuing influence on contemporary life. To say, as anthropologist Marcel Mauss did, that each society fashions its particular sense of what it means to be a person is to say that all views of the self are cultural products. Such ideas are created over time, reshaped and re-created in every act and comment that calls them forth. Further, to assert, as sociologist John Gagnon has, that ideas of the self "can be described as events in history" and analyzed in terms of the transformations that brought them to prominence, is to grant that each view emerged from a previous sense of the self, often one that had become inadequate for the kind of life and the kind of actor a changing society demanded.[12]

Gagnon takes a social constructionist stance toward the self, the same approach I shall take toward images of the self and the emotions. According to this approach, we view all images of the self as human inventions and parts of particular cultures. At some time in a culture's history, each image was invented, possibly first in some person's mind, or possibly in conversations among a group of people. Then the idea was promulgated, and eventually the image gained ascendancy through general adoption and sharing within the culture.[13] The now prevalent idea that the self is an *it* in *there* waiting to be discovered is a view that had a beginning and a development. The evolution of this concept will be the subject of Chapter 3.

Even the idea that there is something to call a self had origins in time, although, as Norbert Elias notes, those steeped in contemporary individualism may find that hard to believe:

> People to whom it seems self-evident that their own self (or their ego, or whatever else it may be called) exists, as it were, "inside" them, isolated from all the other people and things "outside," . . . cannot easily take account of facts which show that this kind of perception is itself limited to particular societies, that it comes into being in conjunction with certain kinds of interdependencies . . . that it is a structural peculiarity of a specific stage in the development of civilization, corresponding to a specific stage of differentiation and individualization of human groups. If one grows up in the midst of such a group, one cannot easily imagine that there could be people who do not experience themselves in this way as entirely self-sufficient individuals cut off from all other beings and things.[14]

Yet most of the world's people have not experienced themselves as separate. The individualistic, exchanger view of the self, a view that feels self-evident to many Westerners, is a relatively recent invention. Its ascendancy dates back to the eighteenth century.

As I develop typologies of prevailing views of the self, and note the history, the content, and the implications of each type, I shall use the term *self* in the context of a discussion of one or another image of the self. Within that context, *self* will refer to the self as that particular image sees it. Usually it will be associated with an adjective to denote the type under discussion—"exchanger self," "obligated self," "cosmic self."

When I use *self* in a more general sense, I shall use the term as George Herbert Mead did. Mead saw the self not as a stable object but as a process that occurs in human interaction. Mature persons have a reflexive capacity: they are able to see themselves as others see them and to look at themselves as objects, much as they might look at other people. In this process, they reflect on and evaluate themselves in terms of responses of others and in terms of an internalized store of cultural values Mead called the Generalized Other. The Generalized Other contains a culture's values, including appropriate feelings toward different types of persons and social events. It contains definitions of the kinds of situations in which we are likely to find ourselves, along with our appropriate attitudes and feelings toward those situations. It contains typifications of the kinds of people we may come across and how we ought to act toward them. It contains images of the types of person we might be or become and prescriptions for the way others ought to act toward us.[15] The typifications that concern us here are images of the self, ideas of what a self is and what a self can be, that most Americans have incorporated as components of the Generalized Other. We use these cultural images to imagine, construct, reflect upon, evaluate, and account for ourselves.

Not only is there no single *it* to be discovered deep within ourselves, there is no stable, unchanging idea that is the self. The self is process. It is ever changing. The images it uses in its reflections are many. Still, they can be grouped into types, as I have done in this book. Each image constructs a different boundary around the self, one that may encompass only a single individual or as many as all humanity or all creation. The boundary an image draws around the self that it constructs is one of the most significant aspects of the image. As we view ourselves with these images in mind, we see ourselves in many different ways, each of these ways shifting as we interact with others in different social situations.

One premise on which this book rests is that members of a society invent cultures, the chief ingredients of which are the visions they provide of what it is to be human. Our ability to reshape moral systems and definitions of the self is part of our ability to reshape human societies. Once we had evolved into creatures who could use language, emotions, and imagination to create flexible social orders that could be passed from one generation to another, we had also evolved into creatures who could be infinitely inventive about who we are.

For example, the exchanger image many Americans hold, which includes the idea that humans are naturally self-interested and competitive, is a view that was drafted during the Renaissance and elaborated on ever since. It is best suited to the times and places of its emergence. Back then, the earth was still rich with untapped natural resources, and most lives were passed within well-bounded communities whose social and physical walls prevented the growth of markets. As markets and market relationships transformed economic, political, and social life, a new, emancipated view of the self moved into center stage. Individualistic moral orientations and a view of human nature as self-interested were necessary for the development of market society. Nowadays, in a world transformed by markets—a world in which rationalistic, individualistic moral precepts hold the strongest sway—limitations of that view are becoming increasingly apparent.[16]

Older orientations, because they stand in contradiction to more recent ones, can sometimes become hidden. Nonetheless, they may continue to exert strong influences. My first goal is to organize moral orientations and conceptualizations of the self into a framework that illuminates the current power of each of them. This book is not, however, a comprehensive history of ideas about the self. The historical setting in which a view developed can suggest why a particular orientation emerged when it did, especially when we consider what it permits that was previously forbidden and what it forbids that was previously allowed or even required.[17] Attention to history can also help us to locate buried orientations, the ones overtaken by new constructions. Such views may exert powerful subterranean influences on our lives.[18] Sometimes, to use the words of Jean Baker Miller, they may incorporate the "crucial realms of the human experience" that psychoanalysis seeks to uncover.[19]

Arthur Koestler once envisaged "an instrument which would enable us to break up patterns of social behaviour as the physicist breaks up a beam of rays." With such a "sociological spectroscope," he imagined we would be better able to see "the rainbow-coloured spectrum of all possible human attitudes to life. The whole distressing muddle would become neat, clear and comprehensive."[20] In part, this book may be considered an attempt to realize Koestler's vision. I do not hope thereby to see all possible attitudes to life. My more modest goal is to begin by separating out for analysis three basic, or primary, views and three combined, or secondary, conceptualizations, much as a spectroscope breaks up light into the primary colors and their combinations.

In the next three chapters, our spectroscope will separate attitudes to life, or moral orientations, into three "ideal types": descriptions designed to magnify the most prominent characteristics of each. These ideal types are heuristic devices, portrayals separated here for analytic purposes like colors in a spectroscope. In daily life we find many blends and shadings waiting to be called to action as the situation demands. Our large repertoire allows us to act "appropriately" in different settings. Just as colors have many shadings, so do attitudes to life. Just as colors may be combined into plaids, stripes, paisleys, landscapes, or portraits while still maintaining their individual character, so too may moral orientations be combined into various patterns. Each moral orientation has a related image of the self. I call the primary, pure types "the exchanger," "the obligated self," and "the cosmic self."

The Exchanger

My analysis of ideal-typical cultural moral orientations, with their concomitant images of the self, begins in Chapter 1 with the one that currently overshadows all other conceptualizations: the self-interested, rational self—the exchanger. In this image, the self strives for emotional control; it appears to be perpetually balancing the quid pro quos of life. Here we see ourselves as unbound, free from obligations, able to choose commitments and make voluntary contracts. This orientation sees the self as alienable and fungible—that is, it treats itself as a commodity, with all the possibilities for exchange of commodities.

The historical growth of the exchanger orientation coincided in Western countries with the growth of markets; its design allows and encourages us to enter into market relationships. Such relationships draw boundaries around the individual; interactions are free from enduring entanglements.

At the time of its emergence, the idea of the exchanger was a liberating one. The feudal order from which it arose had entangled members in a web of social arrangements, a bondage of rigid family and communal boundaries. It had forbidden the very self-interest and pursuit of personal gain that Adam Smith argued would (like an invisible hand) propel resources toward their most valued use, enriching individuals and nations alike.

When the ring of coins sounded feudalism's death knell, a different approach to human nature and social relationships was welcomed, especially by members of the new class who could capitalize on their newfound freedom. Men, released from feudal obligations, were now on their own, which meant, in essence, that they were expected to be self-sufficient. In this new order, because no one needed protection, no one was required to be his brother's keeper. The bourgeoisie was not the only class to spring from the rubble of feudalism. By allowing the strong to neglect their traditional obligations toward the weak, market society saw a startling increase in poverty and homelessness. For many, feudal bondage had given way to capitalistic vagabondage.

The Obligated Self

Perhaps it was fear of loss and disorder aroused by the ravages of the market that induced social commentators of the nineteenth century to borrow a page from the feudal order. They took feudalism's central tenet, namely, that people were locked into particular niches in the social order, and used it to explain new social inequalities. The exchanger became a model for Western men. It is the orientation held by the middle-class white men in the local political parties I studied. People of other races or ethnic backgrounds were excluded from this image of the self: they were considered naturally designed for subservient places in the social order. Women, too, were excluded from those who might be imagined as exchangers. They were seen as helpmates, creatures guided by inscrutable, unaccountable intuition rather than rationality, and devoted to service and the nurturing of others rather than to self-interest. This is the model the women in the local parties followed and were expected to follow.

The idea espoused during the feudal period that God-given positions define and confine all persons within a network of obligations, and the modern notion that nature so defines and confines women and "lesser races," both fall within a view of what it is to be human that appears in many cultures. I call this image the "obligated self."

These days, the image of the self as a member of various groups within which we have obligations is obscured by the exchanger image of the self. Nonetheless, like the sun that makes all life possible even when concealed by clouds, the obligated self continues to be essential, contributing to human needs in ways that the exchanger cannot. Such philosophers as Rousseau must have sensed the void; they wrote mostly about men, but they also made a place for women. Rousseau knew that Emile needed Sophie.[21] Eighteenth- and nineteenth-century scholars assumed that Man the Exchanger needed Woman the Caregiver. For that they invented "women's sphere."

The conception and social construction of woman as the bearer of a finer sensibility and morality, and of nurturing as women's "natural" work, provided assurance that whatever essential work could not be organized according to market principles would nonetheless be performed. Women's sphere did for market society what the lower orders had done for feudal society: it provided for life's necessities with obligatory daily toil.

If we consider the labor that makes human life possible, even in market-dominated societies, we mainly find the labor that is presumed to come from women's very nature: bearing and raising children, keeping house, managing affective social relationships—in short, those labors that must be ceaselessly repeated, that have no definite beginning or end, and that could not be made scarce or left to rely on inconstant supplies of capital. Those labors became the women's work that is never done. They remain part of the definition of what it is to be a woman; they are the responsibilities that will be met regardless of the fickle fluctuations of markets. Quid pro quos are not enough; human survival requires a continual and unconditional transfer of life's necessities from person to person and from generation to generation. Chapter 2 will explore the obligated self.

The Cosmic Self

When Koestler imagined his sociological spectroscope, he thought that all possible human attitudes to life could be lined up along a continuum, as light is aligned from short to long waves. At the infrared end stands the Commissar, a type who believes that "logical reasoning is an unfailing compass and the Universe a kind of very large clockwork in which a very large number of electrons once set into motion will forever revolve in their predictable orbits. [At the] other end of the spectrum, where the waves become so short and of such high frequency that the eye no longer sees them, colourless, warmthless but all-penetrating, crouches the Yogi, melting away in the ultra-violet."[22]

Koestler's opposition of the commissar and the yogi, like most polar constructs, is too simple. It brings to mind Stephen Jay Gould's warning against dichotomies: in a world so full of things, we are forced to "categorize and simplify in order to comprehend." By creating enlightening epitomes, however, we risk "vulgarized distortion."[23] The concept of the obligated self, for instance, cannot be situated on Koestler's spectrum. Nonetheless, Koestler's commissar is very like the exchanger—an odd coincidence at first glance, because one thinks of the exchanger as a type suited to capitalism rather than to communism. What the two have in common is their reliance on rationality.

Koestler's yogi, meanwhile, is an example of the third orientation and view of the self that this book explores, the cosmic self. In this view, the self is continuous with spiritual existence and is incorporated into an organic universe. To use Koestler's words, this self is "attached to the all-one by an invisible umbilical cord."[24] In the cosmic view of the self, life is a never-ending search for oneness with the universe; this self has no boundaries. The modern cosmic self provides an escape from the two other primary views of the self. But it is an escape that leaves the other two views intact. Its sources lie in spiritual realms, first religious and later Romantic.

Gifts, Boundaries, and Emotions

After considering these primary, or pure, constructions of the self, I turn to the three combined forms, which I call the reciprocator, the called self, and the civic self. In Chapter 4 I shall describe these combined images, paying special attention to the way we build boundaries around selves. In this discussion of boundaries and combined images I shall draw from three major contributions to the literature on the gift. There are two reasons for this. First, we often use gifts to mark the boundaries we construct around the self. Second, when social scientists study values and behavior that do not fit the exchanger model, they often call those different social phenomena "gift exchange," or some other rubric with *gift* in it. The studies of the gift I shall use are Bronislaw Malinowski's seminal ethnography of the Kula Ring, Richard Titmuss's study of the British Blood Transfusion Service, and Lewis Hyde's exploration of gifts and art. Although all three authors use the word *gift* as if it denoted a single type of object involved in a single sort of relationship, they actually wrote about three different sorts of object, three different kinds of relationship, three different ways of conceiving selves, and three different moral systems. These correspond to the three combined images I wish to delineate. Malinowski's conceptualization of the gift combines characteristics of the exchanger and the obligated self into the type I label the reciprocator. Richard Titmuss's study combines characteristics of the cosmic self and the exchanger into the civic self, and Lewis Hyde's study of the artist combines characteristics of the cosmic self and the obligated self into the called self.

Philosophers, poets, novelists, and playwrights have all made contributions to the images in our minds of what it means to be a person, an actor, an agent, or a self. I will be borrowing from them, hoping thereby to infuse this analysis with what Martha Nussbaum calls a "language and forms . . . more complex, more allusive, more attentive to particulars" than sociology can afford.[25] Fictional characters, especially the more familiar ones, are part of culture and can serve as icons, helping shape popular ideas of what a person might be. Some may act as role models; others may be cautionary characters. All are selective mirrors of the self. They highlight certain features and reduce the contradictions and complexities in living persons. Thereby, they afford us a set of possibilities through which we can articulate ourselves and others. By interlacing expository statements from philosophers and social scientists with fictional portraits, I intend to combine direct explicit analysis with the more complex, suggestive, and allusive voice of art.

To illuminate the primary conceptions of the self, I will use three fictional characters. The exchanger will be drawn mainly from Galsworthy's portrait of Soames Forsyte, "the man of property" from *The Forsyte Saga.* For the obligated self, I shall draw on several sources, especially Gloria Naylor's *Women of Brewster Place.* The young Indian Siddhartha, taken from the novel of that name by Hermann Hesse, will help to construct the cosmic self. In choosing these examples, I selected characters that were simply portrayed and that would be familiar. Dramatic adaptations of the first two novels were aired on public television, and I provide a synopsis of the third.

The combined forms will be rounded out with a look at the correspondence between two poets, Leslie Marmon Silko and James Wright, gathered in a book titled *The Delicacy and Strength of Lace.* I will also use as examples actual persons whose media portraits have turned them into icons.

Cultures are complex, and where several moral orientations operate simultaneously, people are likely to find themselves responding to contrary rather than consonant precepts. We often think things through rationally and instrumentally, explaining and justifying our behavior to ourselves and others using what C. Wright Mills has called "vocabularies of motive." Recognizing that "motives vary in content and character with historical epochs and societal structures," Mills called for research that would locate motives in their historical epochs and specified situations.[26] Each image of the self I delineate incorporates a moral orientation, a component of which is a vocabulary of motive. But my analysis does not focus only on motives. Vocabularies of motive tend to be employed in the slow processes of cognitive reflection. Most of the time, we respond swiftly to social cues. The more illusive vocabulary of narrative and fictional characterization teaches a vocabulary of motive more illusive, ambiguous, and nuanced than the explanations of our cognitive accounts. The analysis in this book is an attempt to pin down the underlying emotional vocabulary that guides our swift response.

Thus the book will conclude with a theory of emotion. I shall argue that each view of the self sets a boundary around the person that may be singular, including just the individual, but which is more often plural, including groups of others. Emotions allow us to respond rapidly to the most subtle of signals. They let us know what is happening at the boundaries to the self, telling us when we are being joined to or separated from one group or another. We feel joy, for example, when we are joined to people with whom we want to feel at one, but we feel pain and grief when such connections are severed. We feel fear when positive relationships are threatened, but when we are joined to others against our desires we may feel disgusted and degraded. When our reflections on ourselves match an image we would like to have, we feel happy, but when we encounter interactions that call favored images into question or that reflect ignominious images, we feel defensive or angry. The particular feeling we experience will depend both on what is happening at a boundary and on which of the many images of our selves is currently foremost in our psyche. Just as our eyes respond to variations in light, so our emotions respond to variations at the boundaries we construct around our selves.

Emotional feelings are ubiquitous; humans have them in every society, just as humans in every society speak. But what they say differs, and what they feel under different conditions differs from one society to another and from time to time in the same society. Without the capacity for language and for feeling there could be no culture. Without culture there would be no more language than an infant's cries and no more feeling than the physical comfort or pain that induces a baby to coo or cry. A society such as ours, with multiple moralities and multiple images of selves, relies heavily on our emotional capacity. Emotions keep us attuned to what we are, what we are becoming, what groups we are joining, which ones we are leaving, and whether all these changes are good or bad for us. Identity is mercurial. It is, as Eduardo Galeano has said, "no museum piece sitting stock-still in a display case, but rather the endlessly astonishing synthesis of the contradictions of everyday life."[27] Conceptions of the self, of the person, the agent, the actor, have nudged each other and mingled with each other over the centuries as we arrange and rearrange ourselves into groups and societies. Those arrangements set the conditions for the ways we will organize our thoughts and feelings about who we are and what we may, must, and may not do. This book is, then, about culture and the moral ideas from which we develop images of selves in the contemporary United States.

CHAPTER ONE

The Exchanger

WHEN CONTEMPORARY AMERICANS collectively gaze into a mirror, the self they are likely to see is one suited to the marketplace, a persona fashioned from such sources as Thomas Hobbes's vain, mechanical man reckoning his worth in a marketplace of opinion, Adam Smith's Economic Man, with his "disposition to truck, barter and exchange," Charles Darwin's and Herbert Spencer's competitive man fighting for survival of the fittest, or Sigmund Freud's hedonic man guided by the pleasure principle.

Simplified for popular consumption, these complex images lent themselves to a view of the human as an exchanger and not much else. Exchanger views of the self provided a human counterpart for the market. They emerged in the sixteenth century when, according to historian Jean-Christophe Agnew, "boundaries separating market from other forms of exchange were rapidly dissolving." Traders and philosophers invented contracts, real and implied, to secure transactions that "an older, ceremonialized marketplace could no longer secure," and reference points for the self, once restricted to places in a feudal order, became "subject to the market's overarching rule of full commensurability" and to such detached, "impersonal abstractions as exchange value."[1] Unbound from land and lord, people became, like the market, placeless. Their bodies could roam, their characters could fluctuate. The self became property— a possession not much different from other commodities.

In this chapter I take Thomas Hobbes as a point of departure, because Hobbes early on sketched the character of the exchanger. But Hobbes's picture is abstract. To enliven the portrait of this central character of the modern world I turn to Soames Forsyte, John Galsworthy's creation of a "man of property."

Hobbes and the Concept of Man as Commodity

Thomas Hobbes helped usher in the modern era by broaching the notion that the self could alienate itself to create "artificial man"—that all-powerful, imaginary creature constructed of portions of diverse selves that he called the Leviathan, his term for the state or the commonwealth. *Leviathan,* Hobbes's masterpiece, was written to justify the monarchy for an age that had already begun to question the divine right of kings. Hobbes thought that it was not divinity but a combination of necessity and contract that made the monarch a legitimate ruler. Although Hobbes wanted to preserve the monarchy, his images of a man-made state created by a self-made man and of a self independent of superhuman forces were revolutionary ideas.[2]

The image of man that Hobbes began to craft, and which many others modified afterward, has many titles.[3] Some call it Bourgeois Man.[4] Others have called it, or something close to it, Market Man or Economic Man.[5] I shall call this version of the self the exchanger. That label helps to bring out his trading proclivities. Hobbes described him as a creature whose picture of the world comes from outside objects through his senses, not from some inner core. All men, he said, are much the same, distinguished only by "experience" and "passions." Experience renders some men more prudent than others. Prudence is "a *presumption* of the *future,* contracted from the *experience* of time *past."*[6] Passions (much like what we now call motivations) are "the more or less Desire of Power, of Riches, of Knowledge, and of Honor. All of which may be reduced to the first, that is Desire of Power. For Riches, Knowledge and Honour are but severall sorts of Power."[7]

"The Power *of a man,"* declared Hobbes, "is his present means, to obtain some future apparent Good."[8] These means are of two kinds: natural—faculties of body or mind, in which all men are essentially equal—and instrumental—"Riches, Reputation, Friends, and . . . Good Luck," in which men are unequal.[9]

Hobbes's belief that natural equality among men must perpetually clash against their pursuit of inequality led him to his famous declaration of the condition of man without benefit of the Leviathan state: a war of all against all, where "the life of man [is] solitary, poor, nasty, brutish, and short."[10] The state protects life and secures property so that mankind can safely follow its "general inclination": "a perpetual and restless desire of Power after Power (or, since it is essentially the same thing, riches after riches), that ceaseth only in Death."[11]

That ceaseless quest turns men themselves into objects of exchange — into commodities. To use Agnew's words, man became "a commodity self: a mercurial exchange value or 'bubble' floating on the tides of what attention others were disposed to invest."[12] For, said Hobbes, the "*Value* or Worth of a man" is "his Price . . . so much as would be given for the use of his Power." That price "is not absolute; but a thing dependant on the need and judgement of another. . . . not the seller, but the buyer determines the Price."[13] In short, a man is worth what the market will bear.

The coin of this market is the good opinion of others. This is a marketplace of honor, where, "out of an immensely large number of independent value judgments, an objective value of each man is established. It can only be so established because every man's power is regarded as a commodity, i.e. a thing normally offered for exchange and offered competitively."[14] The offering is often made through a presentation of the outward signs of the self — its body and material possessions. To win the good opinion of others, the exchanger makes a presentation of himself; he becomes a mannequin in a shop window.

Hobbes's doctrine, notes Canadian political scientist C. B. MacPherson, is clear, sweeping, and "widely disliked" — this last because "his postulates about the nature of man are unflattering."[15] But, argues MacPherson, these postulates are not meant to be universally valid. "Hobbes's state of nature or 'natural condition of mankind' is not about 'natural' man as opposed to civilized man." It is about how men whose desires and natures were "formed by living in civilized society, would necessarily find themselves if there were no common power able to overawe them all."[16] MacPherson's point is that Hobbes was saying not that humans are by nature greedy but that civilized society turns them into greedy creatures whose desire for riches after riches must be curbed by the state.

Modern literature is replete with Hobbesian characters.[17] In 1990, for example, the *New Yorker* published a story by Jim Harrison that featured a quintessential exchanger named Donald. For reasons I'll discuss later, most men of Donald's ilk (at least the fictional variety) have trouble keeping their wives. Donald is no exception. In Harrison's story, Donald's unhappy wife, Clare, wanders off into an Iowa cornfield, leaving him at a thruway oasis awaiting her return from the rest room. Clare spends a chilly night amid the alien corn, thinking about the man she has fled and their life together.

> In the nave of Notre-Dame he had whispered, "Remind me to make a call," as if he ever forgot. In the Uffizi he couldn't stop saying, "I wonder what this would bring at Parke-Bernet."
>
> The world itself was a marketing possibility. Before he had played his "tracking the Blues" tape [a weekly stock market report] in the car, he had interrupted a favorite Stravinsky passage to say that local acreage was recovering from the 1985 downturn. . . . A typical remark from him would be something to the effect that the black-walnut tree in their backyard was worth seven thousand bucks as furniture veneer, and that walnut-tree thieves were circulating through the Midwest, waiting for the innocent to go on vacation.[18]

Donalds are not universal, but they have sparked imaginations from Hobbes's time to ours. These images are not of merely greedy men and women. Greed makes people act like Midases, who try to turn everything into gold to be hoarded. Hoarding, however, is antagonistic to market principles. Riches, says Hobbes, must be "joyned with liberality."[19] Donalds are liberals—at least insofar as they trade liberally in their quest for power.

People modeling themselves on this image flourished in Victorian England. In Soames Forsyte John Galsworthy contributed a not very flattering view of such men: "upwardly mobile, acquisitive, new rich of peasant stock who made their money in the economic growth of London and England."[20] Galsworthy's *Forsyte Saga* is a trilogy that chronicles an Anglo-Saxon family over three generations, from its arrival in London in 1821 to its decline after World War I. The Forsytes made and were made by the Industrial Revolution. They were, in the words of one biographer of Galsworthy, "England's upper middle class, people who make money and property the measure of all things, and who value . . . the long steady family march toward riches, in which endurance is the cardinal virtue."[21]

The central plot of *The Forsyte Saga* concerns Soames Forsyte—the hard-nosed, controlled "Man of Property" after whom the first book in the trilogy is named—and his wife, Irene. She is a beauty, married against her desires, her resolve weakened by Soames's persistent importunities and her stepmother's complicity with Soames. The novel's plot follows Soames's attempts to possess this jewel, who feels no love for him.

Possessions are key to the Forsyte character. They are the quarry of

Soames's "restless desire for Power after Power." According to Hobbes, power and honor go hand in hand. Foreshadowing Thorstein Veblen's critique of the "conspicuous consumption of the rich and near rich," Hobbes pointed out that the possessions, actions, and qualities that convey power also bring honor: "Riches, are Honourable; . . . Covetousnesse of great Riches, and ambition of great Honours, are Honourable. . . . To be Conspicuous, that is to say, to be known for Wealth . . . is Honourable."[22]

Early on in "Man of Property," we get a taste of the Forsyte penchant for conspicuous display when the clan gathers in the dining room of Soames's uncle, Swithin Forsyte:

> A cut-glass chandelier filled with lighted candles hung like a giant stalactite above its center, radiating over large gilt-framed mirrors, slabs of marble on the tops of side-tables, and heavy gold chairs with crewel worked seats. Everything betokened that love of beauty so deeply implanted in each family which has had its own way to make into Society, out of the more vulgar heart of Nature. Swithin had indeed an impatience of simplicity, a love for ormolu; which had always stamped him amongst his associates as a man of great, if somewhat luxurious taste; and out of the knowledge that no one could possibly enter his rooms without perceiving him to be a man of wealth, he had derived a solid and prolonged happiness such as perhaps no other circumstance in life had afforded him.[23]

The Forsytes were "honorable." Sitting at Swithin's table was his twin, James, who, after being "engaged for fifty-four years . . . in calculations as to the exact pecuniary possibilities of all the relations of life," had come "to think purely in terms of money. Money was now his light, his medium for seeing, that without which he was really unable to see, really not cognizant of phenomena."[24]

One Forsyte, "young" Jolyon, son of "old" Jolyon (James's older brother), was far from being a pure exchanger. A painter, and the first Forsyte ever to leave his wife for a lover, young Jolyon was able to see the Forsyte world from a double perspective—with an insider's intimacy and an outsider's critical judgment. Galsworthy used him as an anthropologist uses an "informant"—as someone with one foot inside and one foot outside the culture under study. At one point young Jolyon explains the Forsyte character to his daughter's fiancé (later to become Irene's lover):

> A Forsyte takes a practical—one might say a common-sense—view of things, and a practical view of things is based fundamentally on a sense of property. . . . He knows a good thing, he knows a safe thing, and his

grip on property—it doesn't matter whether it be wives, houses, money or reputation—is his hall-mark. . . . the Forsytes are the middlemen, the commercials, the pillars of society, the corner-stones of convention; everything that is admirable! . . . My people . . . possess in a remarkable degree those two qualities which are the real tests of a Forsyte—the power of never being able to give yourself up to anything soul and body, and the "sense of property."[25]

The two qualities are related. A Forsyte cannot *give* himself up to anything because his soul and his body are property.

The Self as Property

There is much that can be said, and much that has been said, about the self as property. I shall stop here only to make a few points. First is the idea of alienation: the self that can be possessed is also a self that can be handed over to another. Second is the idea of the self as its own creation. From this concept, several facets of the exchanger self follow: the self is analogous to a machine—something that can make marketable goods, including itself, "out of the more vulgar heart of nature"; this self-authored commodity is in control of itself; and it is perfectible.

Art, the Self, and Alienable Property

In Hobbes's theory, a person's value is set as a commodity's value is set—in a competitive market. The fluctuation in its value gives us Man the Exchanger, questing insatiably for possessions that will impress others. That is a central feature of the exchanger image of the self, but it does not quite amount to Man the Commodity. Although, in Hobbes's view, the value of a person floats like a bubble on the attention others are willing to grant, Hobbes's self lacks one critical attribute of commodities: alienability.

To alienate an object, one must make it the full, no-strings-attached possession of someone else. Hobbes's image of the self was not the image of alienable property that the exchanger self would later become. True, Hobbes imagined a whole self put up for comparative valuation, that value floating on a market of opinion. The value, however, belonged to the exchanger—it did not become the property of another.

MacPherson argues that, from Hobbes's time to ours, our world has increasingly resembled a "possessive market society," a society in which labor is a commodity. A "man's energy and skill are his own, yet are regarded not as integral parts of his personality, but as possessions, the use and disposal of which he is free to hand over to others for a price."[26] In this model two things happen: (1) only a part of the self, its labor power, is marketed, and (2) that part becomes the property of another.

Hobbes laid the groundwork for partitioning the self and for its alienation with his theory of a commonwealth created from the power each member gives over to the state. And he did see a man's worth as something that was set in a market. But he did not quite turn the self into a commodity: the part of the self that was alienated—the power turned over to the state—was not the same as the whole self that was marketed.

It was Karl Marx who made the alienation and the marketing of labor power the centerpiece of his theory. Marx recognized that the market had created a sense of self even more radically altered than the view Hobbes advanced. Hobbes postulated a self that was in possession of itself. The critical aspect of that possession was a reputation—the honor and regard of others, a place in society. Hobbes traveled among the elite; he was writing a theory to legitimate the monarchy, and he seemed unaware of class.[27]

Marx traveled in different circles at a different time. He was an outsider looking in, and he wrote at the peak of the Industrial Revolution, when toddlers labored in factories for eighteen-hour shifts and the life expectancy in Britain's industrial cities had fallen below thirty years. Marx saw two classes: owners of the means of production, who could buy and sell everything, and workers, who had only their labor power to sell.

The owners of the means of production were like the selves Hobbes envisioned and Galsworthy illustrated. For them, life and trading were one: the whole world was a marketplace. The working class became exchangers of a very different sort. They became the thing exchanged. But although they had become commodities, they were not like other commodities; they were not slaves, even if Marx did use the term "wage slave." The owner of a slave bought the whole person; the owner of the means of production bought only a part, the labor power. Therefore, the slave owner might have more concern for the condition of the slave than the owner of the means of production would have for the condition of the worker. The slave owner had property to lose; the boss had nothing to lose. For their part, workers had to take whatever was offered—even if it could hardly provide the barest subsistence. If they did not, they would lose the only commodity they possessed—their labor power, that is, their lives.

Galsworthy's Forsytes were exchangers, not the exchanged. They bought and sold property, including the labor of others, but they did not sell their own labor. Their sire, the first Jolyon Forsyte, was a builder; his brother Edgar was "in jute." The men of the next generation included old Jolyon, a tea merchant, chairman of many companies; James, a solicitor, founder of the firm Forsyte, Bastard and Forsyte; Swithin, an estate and land agent; Roger, a "collector of house property"; Nicholas, who dealt in mines, railways, and house property; and Timothy, a publisher. When these Forsytes purchased the labor of others, they purchased only the labor power; they had no interest in the part not purchased. On the day the Boer War broke out, for example, Soames asked Warmson, the faithful family retainer, what he thought of the war: "The butler ceased passing a hat-brush over the silk hat Soames had taken off and, inclining his face a little forward, said in a low voice: 'Well, sir, they 'aven't a chance, of course; but I'm told they're very good shots. I've got a son in the Inniskillings.'" Soames was astonished: "'You, Warmson? Why, I didn't know you were married.'"[28] A slave owner would have known. In some ways the sale of labor power as a commodity creates relations between purchaser and seller that are harsher than those between master and slave. The master has some concern for the well-being of his property; the exchanger, trading just in labor power, has none. The life belongs to the worker, and the boss doesn't even want to hear about it; he wants to be free to make demands without compunction or concern.

Yet, some forms of labor cannot be separated from the life of the laborer. Such labors have always caused trouble in market society. The most obvious example is reproductive labor and its products. Another is artistic work. Soames's relationship with his wife, Irene, illustrates the first kind of trouble; his relationship with the architect Bosinney is an example of the second. The work of an artist cannot easily be segmented or alienated because the germ of creation emanates from an artist's personality—artists must give themselves to their work if a work of art rather than a commodity is to materialize.[29] Moreover, the commodity value of a work of art derives from the reputation of the artist, and such reputations—like the reputation (or "honour") of a Forsyte—cannot be alienated but remain the possession of the artist even when the work is sold.[30]

The first book of *The Forsyte Saga* hinges on a piece of art property. As kings, emperors, and robber barons have always known, artistic property makes one "conspicuous for power." It should come as no surprise, then, that the Forsytes were interested in art. "Flat-shouldered, clean-shaven, flat cheeked, flat waisted" Soames, a "sure trustee of the family soul," was "an 'amateur' of pictures." He "had a little room . . . full of canvasses stacked against the wall" that he would go to "on Sunday afternoons, to spend hours turning the pictures to the light, examining the marks on their backs, and occasionally making notes. . . . He noted the subjects of the pictures, the names of the painters, made a calculation of their values."[31]

Houses, too, figured prominently in the Forsyte quest after conspicuousness: Forsytes "would not be recognized, without habitats."[32] Indeed, "their residences, placed at stated intervals round the park, watched like sentinels, lest the fair heart of this London, where their desires were fixed, should slip from their clutches, and leave them lower in their own estimations. . . . There was old Jolyon in Stanhope Place; the Jameses in Park Land; Swithin . . . in Hyde Park Mansions; the Soameses in their nest off Knightsbridge."[33] From that nest off Knightsbridge, Irene was free to flit about London, fashioning a life and interests of her own. That freedom made Soames want to take more complete possession of her. To that end, he decided to build another house just outside London. He chose Philip Bosinney to be its architect. Bosinney was decidedly not a Forsyte: "he's one of these artistic chaps—got an idea of improving English architecture; there's no money in that," was uncle Nicholas's appraisal.[34]

Bosinney entered the Forsyte world as the fiancé of June, young Jolyon's daughter by his first wife. Further on in the passage I quoted earlier, as Jolyon explained the Forsyte character to Bosinney, he included an analysis of the Forsyte place in the world of art: "It's their wealth and security that makes everything possible; . . . it makes . . . art possible, makes literature, science, even religion possible. Without Forsytes, who believe in none of these things, but turn them all to use, where should we be?"

To this, Bosinney responded, "But I fancy there are plenty of Forsytes, as you call them, in my profession." Jolyon replied with a contrast between the types that I label the exchanger and the called person:[35] "The great majority of architects, painters or writers have no principles, like any other Forsytes. Art, literature, religion, survive by virtue of the few cranks [called selves] who really believe in such things, and the many Forsytes [exchangers] who make a commercial use of them."[36] Bosinney was one of the few cranks, Soames one of the many Forsytes. As Soames approached Bosinney's office to discuss the project of a house, "he fulfilled the inscrutable laws of his great class—of human nature itself—

when he reflected, with a sense of comfort, that Bosinney would be easy to deal with in money matters."[37]

As is often the case outside fiction, in Galsworthy's tale there was no ease between the architect and the exchanger—neither in money matters nor in anything else. The following Sunday the two went to look at a site Soames had chosen for his house. When Soames returned from bargaining with the estate agent, he found Bosinney "sprawled under a large oak tree" and "had to touch him on the shoulder before he looked up."

> "Hallo! Forsyte," he said, "I've found the very place for your house! Look here!"
>
> Soames stood and looked, then he said coldly: "You may be very clever, but this site will cost me half as much again."
>
> "Hang the cost, man. Look at the view!" . . .
>
> Soames looked. In spite of himself, something swelled in his breast. To live here in sight of all this, to be able to point it out to his friends, to talk of it, to possess it!

Later that afternoon Soames purchased the land with a view, but he wondered "how it was that this fellow, whom by habit he despised, should have overborne his own decision."[38]

Throughout construction, the Forsyte tried to keep costs down; the architect had other plans, and the house began to cost half as much again. Finally, when the house was ready to decorate, the owner and the architect had a showdown. Bosinney wrote to Soames: "If I am to go on with the business of decoration, which at your request I undertook, I should like you to clearly understand that I must have a free hand."[39] Soames responded: "I was under the impression that you had, and have had all along, a 'free hand'; for I do not recollect that any suggestions I have been so unfortunate as to make, have met with your approval. In giving you . . . this 'free hand,' I wish you to clearly understand that the total cost of the house as handed over to me completely decorated, . . . must not exceed twelve thousand pounds."[40] Bosinney countered: "If you think that in such a delicate matter as decoration I can bind myself to the exact pound, I am afraid you are mistaken. . . . I had better, therefore, resign." Soames equivocated: "I did not mean to say that if you should exceed the sum named in my letter to you by ten or twenty or even fifty pounds there would be any difficulty between us. This being so, I should like you to reconsider your answer. You have a 'free hand' in the terms of this correspondence, and I hope you will see your way to completing the decorations, in the matter of which I know it is difficult to be absolutely exact." [41] "Very well," replied Bosinney, and he completed the job, coming in four hundred pounds over the twelve thousand stipulated by Soames. Soames then sued to recover the cost overrun.

On their day in court, the architect's counsel argued that a " 'free hand' could not be limited, fettered, and rendered unmeaning." He pointed out that his client met his side of the bargain, carrying out the work "to meet and satisfy the fastidious taste of a connoisseur, a rich man, a man of property." Finally, he appealed "to the Judge, as a lover of the arts, to show himself the protector of artists, from what was occasionally . . . the too iron hand of capital." " 'What,' " said Bosinney's counsel, " 'will be the position of the artistic professions, if men of property like this Mr. Forsyte refuse, and are allowed to refuse to carry out the obligations of the commissions which they have given?' " [42]

The judge ruled in Forsyte's favor. At the book's end, the man of property possesses a house he will never inhabit; the artist, who could neither set a price on his labor nor cover the additional cost, is run over and killed by a horse-drawn carriage.

Bosinney, a modern-day Icarus, flew too high; he tried to decorate with a truly "free hand." Following the dictates of his muse, he had acted as if he owned the purse, indeed, as if there were no purse, no contract, no market to hamper his talent. Unable to alienate his labor, to surrender it to another's control, he suffered the ultimate alienation. In market society Bosinney's defeat was the likely conclusion to what Galsworthy calls a battle between "that eternal position of Art against Property." [43]

Viewing Bosinney's corpse, the inspector declared, "I don't believe in suicide, nor in pure accident, myself. It's more likely I think that he was suffering under great stress of mind and took no notice of things about him." Young Jolyon, who was there to identify the body of his daughter's fiancé, mused: "Concerning the cause of this death—his family would doubtless reject with vigour the suspicion of suicide, which was so compromising!" [44]

Like art, suicide brings out the limits of the self as an object of exchange. Exchangers like Soames might do all in their power to turn art into a commodity, to make another man's labor their own, to squeeze the utmost value from it; but they never intend to kill geese that lay golden eggs. If there is any delicacy or any art to exchange, it is in sensing limits— knowing when a market has peaked or bottomed, knowing when the artist is about to be pushed beyond endurance. Where the self has been too much treated as a commodity, the only recourse may be a suicide whereby the self repossesses itself to destroy the property of another. A historical example is that of the Indians of the West Indies who jumped en masse off a cliff. They were, according to John Collier, "driven to mass suicide, to mass infanticide, to mass abstinence from sexual life in order that children should not be born into horror."[45] The horror was the horror of slavery—the self as property of another.

For Marx, viewing the atrocities of the Industrial Revolution, the freedom to sell one's labor was in some ways worse than slavery. One might expect that only those threatened by poverty would accept a sense of self as nothing but a commodity. But present-day middle managers of major corporations commonly give so much of their time and minds to their jobs that not much life is left for their families or anything else. Although they have high salaries, they have hardly any independence from their corporations.[46] Class, or market position, is not the only factor that determines whether a person will adopt the view of himself as the exchanged or the exchanger, thereby entering into relationships that presume one of those stances. With Bosinney's death, however, Galsworthy seems to suggest that those who do not own the means of production must accept the position of the exchanged or die.

Of Men and Machines

Soames's attempt to possess Bosinney may have driven the architect to suicide, but Galsworthy leaves the line between suicide and accident blurred. Accidents do happen—even to Forsytes. In the world of markets, the purest exchanger may encounter inexplicable moments when things run amuck. But those are exceptions. They are happenings outside the sphere of the exchanger's vision—and outside the theory that frames that version of the self.[47]

For the most part, Forsytes are in control. They contrive the scheme of things. Their strength is a steady force—no heroics, no mysteries, just a dogged march forward. "They had only to keep their heads, and go at it steadily" is Soames's formula for realizing "the fecundity and elasticity of wealth."[48]

"Restraint, reserve"—to Soames these are "more dear almost than life."[49] He takes after his father, James, who, fearing that Soames's marital difficulties might bring scandal to the family, simply could not "grasp the possibility of people running any risk for the sake of passion. Amongst all those persons of his acquaintance, who went into the City day after day and did their business there . . . it would have seemed to him ridiculous to suppose that there were any who would run risks for the sake of anything so recondite, so figurative, as passion."[50] Forsytes, these cool, steely properties, were derived from a vision of the self forged in the same fires that had shaped markets. Passion had been beaten out of them. They had become unemotional, mechanical selves.

The chapters that follow will focus on human connections that are emotional, which is to say, all human connections outside the market. The negation of emotions that marks the exchanger orientation came in response to a time that suffered more than its share of violence and disorder, a time when people might welcome the idea of self-control as an escape from chaos.[51] From the late Middle Ages onward, specialized production for the market increasingly replaced production for subsistence. Fields were enclosed, fens were drained, forests were cut down. Modifications of the natural environment went hand in hand with changes in the social environment. Bankers and merchants became the new princes. Peasants became paupers. But the dispossessed did not stand idly by. Although they may not have called the tune, their discontents, expressed in frequent rioting, constituted a fundamental social and intellectual challenge.

Against that background of disorder, says Carolyn Merchant, "mechanism arose as an antidote to intellectual uncertainty and as a new rational basis for social stability." She points especially to the French mechanists—Marin Mersenne (1588-1648), Pierre Gassendi (1592-1655), and René Descartes (1596-1650)—who began around 1620 "to construct a mechanical philosophy that ultimately presented a solution to the problems of certainty, social stability, and individual responsibility." Their chief intellectual device was the machine as model for science, for society, and for the self. It provided then, and still provides, the "technological fix" that "mends ecological malfunction, . . . [and] maintains smooth functioning of industry and bureaucracy."[52]

Hobbes was a man of those times. He was a friend of, and for a short period a secretary to, Francis Bacon. He had met Galileo and was familiar with his work. When Hobbes fled to Paris in 1640 out of fear of reprisals from parliamentary leaders for his support of the monarchy, he was welcomed into the scientific group centered around Mersenne.[53] Biographer Arnold A. Rogow charges that "Hobbes characteristically was not one to give credit where credit was due," but he was influenced by these associates, acknowledged or not.[54] Evidence of that influence lies in his method, which he claimed to be an attempt to discover the laws of human motivation in much the same way that Galileo had discovered celestial mechanics.[55] The state of nature that he thought he saw, resembled the social disorder of his times: it was a state of chaos, anarchy, and fear brought about by the material appetites of each individual for competition, domination, and glory. His solution to disorder followed the predilections of his time: he "mechanized the cosmos by denying any inherent force to matter"; he reduced "the human soul, will, brain, and appetites to matter in mechanical motion"; and he argued that "nature, society, and the human body are composed of interchangeable atomized parts that can be repaired or replaced from outside." In short, the man whom Hobbes presents in the opening chapters of *Leviathan* resembles an automated machine: "What is the heart, but a spring; and the nerves, but so many strings, and the joints, but so many wheels, giving motion to the whole body?"[56]

Even today, that trope continues to be in active service. James Coleman, in *Foundations of Social Theory,* his monumental exposition of rational choice theory published in 1990, views the self as a "device" with two parts: "(1) a receptor of signals from the environment, and (2) an actuator which takes action toward the environment, using information from the receptor" with linkage between the two. Thus, as the twentieth century comes to a close, Coleman draws an image remarkably similar to Hobbes's seventeenth-century mechanical man, an image of the self that, in Merchant's words, "has built into it, equipment by which it alters its motion in response to differences in the material it uses, and to the impact and even the expected impact of other matter on it."[57]

Another metaphor, that of the world as stage and theater, figured heavily in Hobbes's thought and in social theory from his time to ours. Agnew uses the shifting meaning of this metaphor to show how contemporary views of the market, the theater, and the self were successively shaped in American and British thought during the two centuries between 1550 and 1750. "For the fifteen hundred years between its formulation by the Greeks and its revival by Renaissance Neoplatonists," Agnew observes, "the theatrical metaphor served as a reminder of the vanity of human achievements." At first, "individuals were to be understood as the mere playthings or puppets of God." Then, in response to the transformation of both the theater and the world, the emblem of the *theatrum mundi* was transformed. Hobbes and his contemporaries began to see the self as both an actor—"a *person*, is the same that an *actor* is, both on the Stage and in common Conversation"—and as playwright scripting his own parts and fashioning roles for the self.[58]

Self-authorship placed power and control in the hands of the self. It was yet another weapon in the arsenal against social turbulence, another mark of the times, and another feature of the self as commodity. As the market developed, and as feudal bonds loosened, people found that they could take possession of themselves, refashion themselves, make something of themselves. According to Margaret Strathern, self-direction constituted "an active proprietorship" of the self. It is the quintessential quality that makes the self a commodity: "Persons own their minds as well as their bodies, and their minds turn the proprietor of his or her own actions also into the author of them."[59]

As with a piece of cloth that one can cut and sew into the most marketable of garments, one can make oneself or remake oneself to suit the fashion of the times. Although it may seem far-fetched to link diet fads, contemporary joggers, or readers of *Self* magazine to seventeenth-century mechanistic philosophers, this is just the connection that philosopher Charles Taylor makes in his exploration of the roots of modern morality, *Sources of the Self: The Making of the Modern Identity.* Joggers, for example, seek to discipline and reshape their bodies—that is, to be the authors of themselves, body and soul. Behind this effort is a way of thinking of the self conducive to assumptions of self-control, self-discipline, and self-authoring that Taylor, like Merchant, traces to the mechanist philosophers.

Taylor makes more of Descartes and Locke, and less of Bacon and Hobbes, than Merchant does, because whereas Merchant focused on the idea of a mechanical self, Taylor focuses on the idea of a disengaged self, that is, a self that can stand apart from itself to be observer and creator. The idea of disengagement, articulated by Descartes and radically extended by Locke is, according to Taylor, "one of the most important developments of the modern era." Disengagement requires reflexivity, "the ability to take an instrumental stance to one's given properties, desires, inclinations, tendencies, habits of thought and feeling, so that they can be *worked on,* doing away with some and strengthening others, until one meets the desired specifications."[60]

Taylor calls this self-authoring, reflexive subject the "punctual self." It "has become a familiar modern figure . . . one way of construing ourselves. . . . To take this stance is to identify oneself with the power to objectify and remake, and by this act to distance oneself from all the particular features" of the self that are objects of potential change. We are not these features; we are the technician capable of molding the self. The "real self" in this vision is "the power to fix oneself as an object." [61] Such popular ideas as "it's all up to the individual" and "you can be anything you want to be" derive from the notion of the punctual self.

Forsytes were punctual selves. They believed that every feature of the self was owned property. Clothes, bodies, talents, and even passions and loves (if they admitted love) could be, and ought to be, fixed by the self. Thus, both Soames and his father James saw it as a failure of will and willingness when Irene did not take herself in hand and act the proper wife. Soames said to her, "I don't know what your idea of a wife's duty is. I never have known!" To which she, who subscribed to other views of the self and believed that gifts, such as love, could not be forced, replied, "I have tried to do what you want; it's not my fault that I haven't been able to put my heart into it." "Whose fault is it, then?" he asked. "The profound, subdued aversion" his wife felt "was a mystery to" Soames. "That she did not love him, had tried to love him and could not love him, was obviously no reason. He that could imagine so outlandish a cause for his wife's not getting on with him was certainly no Forsyte." [62]

A few weeks after that exchange, Soames's father, James, tried to take control: "Soames is very fond of you," he told Irene, "why don't you show him more affection?" Irene replied, "I can't show what I haven't got." "If you'd only . . . behave yourself," James almost said, but he changed it to "if you'd only be more of a wife to him." [63]

Culture, Vocabulary, and Axes of Variation

Behave is a word formed in the late fifteenth century from *haven* and the Old French *avier* and *avoir*, denoting having or possession. *Behave* or *behavior* in the modern West have to do with having oneself in control, with being self-possessed, according to John R. Wikse, who wrote about the "property-related" roots of some modern ideas of the self. Wikse wanted to uncover the "basic assumptions upon which [this] culture is constituted" in order to recover the unconscious and repressed "collective history" that is recorded in its language. Wikse follows Nietzsche, arguing that linguistic change does not just happen. "The origin of language itself" can be conceived as "an expression of power on the part of the rulers." Following this train of thought, one can imagine cool, controlled Forsyte prototypes, taking themselves in hand during the Renaissance and stiffening their resolve for the long trek up the social mountain. Stride by stride, they brought the language into step with their aspirations and their ideas of what life and selfhood could be.[64]

A wise man then and now is streetwise, says Wikse. He knows "the ways of his culture," *wise* and *ways* both deriving from the Old English noun *wise*, "which meant the 'ways,' manners, customs, and habits of a place"—its *fashion*, or "what is customarily done." "These ways," says Wikse, "are the facts of political culture, its products or artifacts, its moral heritage."

Facts, those darlings of the rational exchanger, are constructs of the powerful, according to Wikse, who puts a decidedly Mannheimean spin on his etymology at this point. The root of our word *fact*, he tells us, "is the Latin *factum*, past participle of *facere*, to do or make." Thus, "facts are made up by factions or political cults. . . . What is fashioned is fashionable: if 'it's just not done!,' then it's not a fact."[65]

One by one, Wikse lines up the words: *Property* and *propriety* are both "from the French *propriété*, meaning the fact of being one's own." "*Demeanor* derives from *demesne*, belonging to a lord," and is etymologically connected to *dominance* and *domain*. Thus "how one does relates to what one has." "*Deportment* . . . derives from Latin *portare*, to carry, in the sense of 'carrying oneself' or 'bearing oneself' (one's 'carriage'): ourselves are the property we carry." "*Conduct* derives from *conducere*, to collect or bring together, in the sense of 'Collect yourself!,' 'Get it together, man!,' that is, with the sense of self-control or mastery as in 'cool and collected.'"[66]

Irene Forsyte seemed cool and collected. Galsworthy used her calm, almost colorless, shimmering beauty as a leitmotif. She was a "tall woman, with a beautiful figure," which "swayed faintly, like the best kind of French figures; her dress, too, was a sort of French grey." Her "grave, charming face" seemed always under her control, and with Soames "she was ever silent, passive, gracefully averse; as though terrified lest by word, motion, or sign she might lead him to believe that she was fond of him." If "anyone had asked [Soames] if he wanted to own her soul, the question would have seemed to him both ridiculous and sentimental. But he did so want." This machinelike exchanger was neither so cool nor so free from the torments of emotion as he would have had it. In spite of himself, he desperately wanted something whose existence he denied, something that could not be owned, not even by a man of property.[67]

If we trace most words to their roots, observes psychoanalyst William Galt, we will find their meaning fluctuating between the opposing terms of a dichotomy, revealing a "preconscious sense in man of the basic identity between any two terms of a symbolic, moralistic dichotomy." Similarly, Kai Erikson notes that "whenever people devote a good deal of emotional energy to celebrating a certain virtue . . . they are sure to give thought to its counterpart. . . . Thus the idea and its counterpart become natural partners in the cultural order of things." He called this organization of counterparts "axes of variation," noting that "every human culture can be visualized, if only in part, as a kind of theater in which certain contrary tendencies are played out."[68]

In European and North American cultures, as they developed from the Renaissance to the present, in their language, metaphors, fiction, and in what they have taken for fact, contrasting tendencies of freedom and constraint were played out in the developing conceptualization of the exchanger. Control and possession pivoted on an axis of variation where freedom in its many forms often generated constraint in its many forms.

To conclude this chapter, I shall examine certain axes of variation, paying particular attention to five contrary tendencies in American culture. The first has to do with property, class, and possession. Self-possession is a critical feature in the conceptualization of the exchanger. It is a moral stance that simultaneously frees the individual and turns the self into an object. In this process, something curious happens: objects themselves gain power until *they* take possession of the self. Thus, both the self viewed as exchanger and the self viewed as the object exchanged give up life and freedom to property. Too complete an immersion in property and its increase can devour exchangers; too little property outside the self can render the exchanged powerless.

A second set of contrary tendencies is self-authorship and the crisis of identity. If freedom from the feudal barriers that defined people in terms of their social positions meant that people could make something of themselves, it also meant that they could make *anything* of themselves. With that freedom, a single, socially anchored identity was lost, leading to a plurality of selves and crises of identity.

The next set of opposing values is the converse of the protean self and its crises of identity. In a world where labor is marketed, people are judged and rewarded according to their merit—so people, like other commodities, must be measured against a single standard. This requisite of markets pulls against the promise of freedom and individuality, producing that characteristic of market society so frequently bemoaned—its demand for conformity.

A fourth contradiction emerges from concepts of rationality and self-interest. The belief from the sixteenth century onward that men were free to script their selves was balanced by limitations on how that drama might unfold, on which characters might be deemed sane, and on what actions might be considered appropriate. Freedom implied choice in markets and in politics, but the very markets that required freedom of choice whittled the choices to a precious few. Reason balanced freedom, commanding that a self act in its own interest, self-interest being the antidote to the very passion and disorder that self-authorship had come to abate.

Finally, I shall consider the social mobility of post-feudal society and the most limiting aspect of the exchanger self—its isolation. When feudal barriers fell and social distinctions evaporated, people were free to associate with anybody. To climb social ladders and at the same time avoid snobbery became the ideal. However, a new type developed: people who could get along with anybody but who lacked the emotional capacity to connect deeply with anybody. The affable exchanger, able to rub shoulders with the world, was incapable of holding anyone dear to his heart.

Class, Property, and Alienation

The exchanger is self-possessed yet depends for his worth on a marketplace of opinion controlled by countless others. Among the exchanged, the most significant possession of the self is labor power, a commodity that must be alienated if its value is to be realized. The architect Bosinney, for example, tried to win a free hand to control his labor, but he was not independent where it counted: "As far as the family had been able to ascertain his income, it consisted of two consulting appointments at twenty pounds a year, and . . . a private annuity under his father's will of one hundred and fifty pounds a year." The court's judgment against him for three hundred and fifty pounds plus costs was, as James put it, "a bad business for that young Bosinney; he'll go bankrupt, I shouldn't wonder." [69]

Irene's position was even more delicate. When James considered the possibility that she might leave Soames, he consoled himself that "luckily, she had no money—a beggarly fifty pounds a year! And he thought of the dead Heron [her father, a professor], who had nothing to leave her, with contempt." [70] That lack of property, it seemed to James and to Soames, not only kept Irene tied to Soames but forced her to trade in wifely services.

His wife's penury was all the more reason why Soames, who could only think in market terms, could not understand what Irene found wrong in him. "It was not as if he drank! Did he run into debt, or gamble, or swear; was he violent; were his friends rackety; did he stay out at night? On the contrary," Soames was a model husband. Irene was a woman extraordinarily "capable of inspiring affection . . . all the men were attracted by her; their looks, manners, voices, betrayed it." To be sure, Soames granted, "her behavior under this attention had been beyond reproach." And yet, "her power of attraction he regarded as part of her value as his property." He wanted the glow that lit the faces of other men to shine on him, yet "she gave him nothing!" Neither Soames nor James hesitated to remind Irene that she was not honoring her contract. The day James had words with her, he pointed out that "It's not as if you had anything of your own," a cutting reminder of her confining situation.[71]

Marriage, said Friedrich Engels, is a form of slavery: a wife sells her body "once and for all." In theory, the exchanger self was free to use itself as it would; in practice, if a person lacked the wherewithal to set herself free, then the bargains and contracts she was forced to make might rob her of independence. This was especially true for wives and artists, neither of whom could alienate their labor or segment and objectify themselves. They were forced into either total commitment or total alienation, the second being even more compromising than prostitution: as Engels observed, a prostitute only rents out her body "on piece-work as a wage-worker."[72]

At the other side of the class divide, property was no less commanding. "We are, of course, all of us the slaves of property," said young Jolyon on the day that he was trying to explain the Forsytes to Bosinney, "and I admit that it's a question of degree, but what I call a 'Forsyte' is a man who is decidedly more than less a slave of property."[73] The Forsytes, conspicuous for their fine possessions, were nothing but what they owned; property became them.

Self-Authorship and the Crises of Identity and Value

As property, the self floated toward the highest bid, its value. Its worth was calculated in opinions derived from its show of possessions or what others were willing to pay for its labor. Human value thus could be expressed as an equation: on the one side, the self; on the other, endless equivalents. This, says Agnew, is what sixteenth- and seventeenth-century merchants and thinkers had accomplished: in order to set man free for market choices and simultaneously to gain control, they had loosened the bonds of a feudal society where place and identity were one. Further, they had instituted a volatile and placeless market that "introduced into England's semifeudal society" a "social and political crisis of representation."[74]

Traditional social signs and symbols had "metamorphosed into detached and manipulable commodities." Selves had become slippery. "Just as London's [Stock] Exchange enforced an ideal of financial liquidity, so London's theaters enacted a vision of this new social and psychological fluidity. And why not, since the world was at once a market and a stage?" The power to shape one's self had rendered social identity precarious and "vulnerable to unexpected disruptions and disclosure." The self had become "deeply theatrical . . . a contingent, arbitrary, and instrumental affair, not a natural or supernatural calling."[75]

In this sense the theatrum mundi metaphor, resurrected and transfigured, came to express not only the self as author. It also "served playwrights as an ideal vehicle with which to convey the changing character of stage and society." As Agnew points out, the theatrical metaphor preserved "the older stoic melancholy" of Shakespeare's Jaques ("All the world's a stage") "while introducing the newer worldly aestheticism of a Richard II" ("Thus play I in one person many people").[76]

The value of individuals and the worth of life itself would fluctuate with business cycles. In good times, personages would bubble up from the masses, gaudy and honored in their newfound wealth. Sometimes, toward the end of a rising cycle, those bubbles would burst as opportunists became careless. Other times, failure would come with falling cycles. We see these effects today, as such fortunes as Michael Milken's and Donald Trump's rise and tumble with the market.

In less dramatic ways people of ordinary means also experience fluctuation in their fortunes. Good times might find them enjoying the enrichment of public works and social policies that testify to the high value of human life. Museums, schools, parks, and entitlements of all sorts provide a floor of support, preventing the lowliest from sinking too far. Bad times, however, find many sleeping on the street, as public funding and the worth of human life follow a downward market.[77]

Measure by Merit

Where values are as fickle as fortune, selves are seldom what they seem—at least not for long. And where the market is arbiter, a self is *merely* what it seems. Fluctuating selves reflect fluctuating markets when the price per pound of inorganic objects is balanced by the price per hour of labor.[78] Because standard measures facilitate the balancing of market equations, the market turns the face of the exchanger, like the face of any coin, into a facade without distinguishing features. This self, striving toward individual perfection, seeking its highest value, must mint itself according to the station of its aspiration. Where once de jure sumptuary laws forbade high cloth to low ranks, now de facto laws demand that we dress for success, investing in vestments to rise through the ranks.

In the market, craft has given way to mass production; incomes and positions, no longer birthrights, are doled out according to performances on standardized tests. As a result, freedom of expression comes to be expressed in a uniformity almost as unvarying as the uniformity imposed by feudal constraints.[79] The self-scripting self has become like scrip, a form of currency.

Interest and Rationality

Changing precepts governing money lending went hand in hand with changing ideas about the self. The usurer, notes Agnew, represents better than any other character the resemblance between the exchanger and currency. "The chameleonlike usurer bodied forth the ideal of full liquidity as a standard by which the inescapable costs and rewards of life could be measured." This fungible man, whose "self was effectively interchangeable with any or all" selves, "incarnated the characterlessness and 'infinite purposiveness' of the money he lent out at interest."[80]

Albert O. Hirschman tells us about the word *interest*. Derived from the French *intéret*, it was "originally pressed into service" in the late Middle Ages, as a euphemism "to make respectable an activity, the taking of interest on loans, that had long been considered contrary to divine law and known as the sin of usury." Machiavelli used *interest* politically. Advising the Prince to avoid such chivalric virtues as "the seeking of glory and other excesses" that were then being discredited, he proposed instead such formerly immoral practices as "cruelty, mendacity, treason, and so on," provided such behavior was pursued in the *interests* of the state. Some two-and-a-half centuries later, Adam Smith argued that careful adherence to self-interest should not be identified with such unsavory vices as "avarice" and "love of lucre." On the contrary, self-interest was a virtue so long as individuals acted "with a rational, calculating spirit that would often imply prudence and moderation."[81] Under the guidance of the Invisible Hand, interest would serve the general good.

Interest has been a slippery term, doing its share of euphemistic duty. Machiavelli and Smith used it to urge a freedom to act in formerly unacceptable ways. When combined with the idea of rationality, however, it limits the license it promises. Rationality presumes that, given freedom to choose, men would choose to act in accordance with a careful calculation of their own interests. These interests have often been construed so narrowly that Pistol's boast, "the world's mine oyster," has become little more than a shell game.

Under the skin of the exchanger, a character emerged from rationalist theory who has all the sensibility, imagination, and autonomy of a computer. *Reason,* Hobbes had noted, derives from the Latin word for account and "is nothing but *Reckoning* (that is, Adding and Subtracting)." Uncertainty is not an issue: with sufficient information, the rational, reckoning self zeros in on the single preference that best advances its interests. Correct reckonings produce singular results; truth is unitary. The Renaissance resurrected Plato's wisdom: to be ruled by reason means one is able to "give reasons," or to give "an account"—not a plurality of accounts, as today's postmodernists would have it, but a single bottom line. Plato, Taylor reminds us, considers plurality "error and imperfection." For Plato's twentieth-century disciples, the rationalists of social science, nothing has changed. True, the rational self may "not be wholly successful" in its "attempt to maximize utility," notes James Coleman. But that is because imperfect information or some pathology causes the exchanger to fall short of the decision "perfect intelligence" would demand. Only madness, lack of information, or stupidity would take the exchanger from the one choice that best advances his interests.[82]

From the freedom to choose where no rational alternative exists, defenders of rationality had one escape: the convoluted argument. For its defenders, there was almost no limit to the rhetorical machinations and rationalizations that could turn any social arrangement into a rational one. Observe, for example, the way Johann Gottlieb Fichte twisted ideas of self-interest and choice so that they could be made to seem the basis of a woman's willing submission to her husband. He claimed to yield to no one in championing women's legal rights, yet he argued as follows against gender equality:

> Woman is not subjected to her husband in such a manner as to give him a right of compulsion over her; she is subjected through her own continuous necessary wish—a wish which is the condition of her morality—to be so subjected. She has the power to withdraw her freedom, if she could have the will to do so. But that is the very point; she cannot rationally will to be free. Her relation to her husband being publicly known, she must moreover, will to appear to all whom she knows as utterly subjected to, and utterly lost in, the man of her choice.[83]

This is Soames's position precisely! And it is an argument Irene could, indeed must, understand: it ruled her life. But the rightness and naturalness of this sort of understanding have often been questioned.

Basically, Fichte and Soames use the arguments of exchange to buttress the arrangements of a system of obligation. Fichte takes Hobbes's notion that a person's reputation is everything and then says that if a woman's reputation depends on her appearance of submission and if her reputation matters to her, as it must, then her only rational position is to appear to be submissive. Far be it from Fichte to wonder why good reputations become the reward of patriarchal husbands and submissive wives. That's a question for the next chapter. First, we shall turn for a moment to the major shortcoming of the exchanger self—the reason why this orientation cannot be the only one a culture offers.

The Exchanger as Idiot

As the fences of the feudal world fell and social mobility became an honorable goal, men were made free to sell themselves to the highest bidder. To reach that goal, exchangers had to be careful not to let obligatory entanglements hold them back. They had to be free to move physically and socially wherever opportunity beckoned. Corporation managers who gladly accept the promotions that require them to transfer across the country or the world every other year are typical exchangers. So are upwardly mobile children who can no longer converse in mutually understandable terms with the parents who launched them. And the senior manager in his fifties or sixties who moves into a trophy house with a brand new trophy wife a decade or two his junior is a third example.[84]

All these exchangers pivot between what they have and what they want, careful lest insufficient intelligence or a moment of madness or attachment should induce a choice of less than maximum utility. The exchanger lacks an essential ingredient of human life: he cannot connect. Rational, cool, self-possessed, and calculating, the exchanger is a view of the self that, like reason, is a unity. Wikse calls him an idiot, taking his cue from the Greek root *idiotes*, meaning a private and separate person.

Wikse's book begins with memories of his childhood: stories of Lone-Ranger heroes saving communities and riding off into the sunset. These supreme individuals, idols of our time, are their "own persons"; they spurn attachments. Wikse believes that they exemplify modern ideas of the self, which emphasize "extreme individuation as the genuine foundation for being oneself." In separation from others, the rugged individual does "his own thing." [85]

Not that the Donalds and Soameses of this world don't make marriage contracts. They do. Nietzsche warned, "It is dangerous to be an heir"; one carries the madness as well as the reason of one's forebears. But for Forsytes, the danger lay in not having an heir. For them children were treasures, or, rather, treasuries—the one escape from having to give up life. Death was "contrary to their principles, they took precautions against it, the instinctive precautions of highly vitalised persons who resent encroachments on their property." Young Jolyon once said to Soames, "The other day I was calculating the average age of the ten old Forsytes, . . . I make it eighty-four already, and five still living. . . . We aren't the men they were, you know." Soames's only reply was a smile seeming to say, "Do you really think I shall admit . . . that I've got to give up anything, especially life?" [86]

Children were the primary hedge against death. The relations between Soames and his father, James, "were marked by a lack of sentiment peculiarly Forsytean, but for all that the two were by no means unattached. Perhaps they regarded one another as an investment." Still, it touched James to his emotional depths "to have creatures who were parts of himself, to whom he might transmit the money he saved, was at the root of his saving; and, at seventy-five, what was left that could give him pleasure, but—saving? The kernel of life was in this saving for his children." [87] If you could not take with you the possessions that made life worth living, you could at least leave them to offspring. One could not exactly bank on one's children—one never did know how they would turn out—but one could always bank *with* them. Finally, then, the chief paradox of the exchanger self is that without coupling it ceases to exist.

In order to couple, at least in market societies, rationality must be tempered with emotion. The emptiness of life reduced to the exchanger self inspired frequent criticisms of the exchanger view of the self. "The simplest reason for doubting the omnipotence of rationality," notes Randall Collins, "is that different proponents of rationality often disagree among themselves." "Specialists without spirit, sensualists without heart," was Max Weber's censure,[88] a rebuke echoed by T. S. Eliot in "The Hollow Men" (1925):

> Shape without form, shade without colour
> . . . gesture without motion
> . . . the hollow men
> the stuffed men
> . . . Waking alone

Because the exchanger orientation is designed for human relationships that can be more fleeting than sand sculptures, market-dominated societies necessarily enjoy other moral orientations. Members of these societies construct and reconstruct themselves from a full palette of images as they move from one social context to another. In the chapters to follow we shall be looking at other versions of the self. Although they were not necessarily designed as antidotes, they seem to have been suggested by voids and contradictions in the exchanger view of the self, for they have in common two features absent from the exchanger orientation: they all see the self in terms of connections to others, and they all focus on human emotions.

CHAPTER TWO

The Obligated Self

"WE ARE ALL BEING MARKED by each other all the time, classified, ranked, put in our place, and I see no escape from that," declared Robert Frost.[1] He was talking about teachers and the grading they do, but grading is not a teacher's monopoly. As Frost said, we are all always grading each other. The criteria change with the situation—or at least we believe they should. We consider it wrong, for example, when teachers are guided by a child's physical appearance, but not when model agencies are. Teachers are supposed to base their grading on students' performances alone. Studies show, however, that students' gender and race often influence teachers' evaluations.[2] Gender and race are different criteria from performance; they are what Ralph Linton called ascribed characteristics. Performance, by contrast, is an achieved characteristic. Ascribed statuses, says Linton, "are those which are assigned to individuals without reference to their innate differences or abilities. They can be predicted and trained for from the moment of birth. The *achieved* statuses are, as a minimum, those requiring special qualities, although they are not necessarily limited to these. They are not assigned to individuals from birth but are left open to be filled through competition and individual effort." Linton noted that societies are structured so that in some settings ascribed characteristics matter and in other settings achieved characteristics matter.[3]

Ideally, teachers mark students on the basis of achievement alone, and mothers give all their children the same status, caring for each according to his or her needs. In reality, teachers and mothers do a bit of both kinds of grading. Pitirim Sorokin argued that societies could be sorted into two types: "open societies," in which most statuses are achieved, and "closed

societies," in which most statuses are ascribed. He observed that with industrialization and modernization, societies become more open.[4]

My comparisons of the activities of women and men in local political
parties revealed that Linton had touched on something much larger than
just the organization of society into achieved or ascribed statuses. Often
some types of people entered a status on the basis of achievement criteria
while others entered, or were excluded, on the basis of ascriptive criteria.
If Harvard University favors the children of its alumni, for example, then
they will win acceptance on ascriptive criteria while most other students
are accepted on achievement criteria.

The same sort of thing was happening on the Town Committees.
The assumption was that Town Committee membership was based on
achievement—on competition and individual effort. Once members had
been chosen, the expected behavior, or role, of every member should
have been the same regardless of whether the incumbent was a woman or
man. However, my study showed several differences between women and
men: the criteria for membership were different, what was expected of
them as members was different, and their central orientations once they
had become members were different. The women and the men tended to
see women as part of a social order that obliged them to perform a set of
duties whose end was the preservation of their party. They tended to see
the men as individuals who needed to be personally rewarded in order
to keep them involved in their party because they were free to come and
go as they chose. Of course, these were tendencies, not clear-cut differences. The women and men varied in how they expected themselves and
others to act. Nonetheless, in general, the women and men appeared to
follow different orientations. That is why the women worked so many
more hours for so many fewer rewards, and why so much of what the
men did was done onstage while so much of what the women did was
done backstage.

Nothing in these findings was new. Both the different orientations
and their connection with gender had been noted by Jessie Bernard. In
her book *The Female World,* she reviewed some common "polarities,"
such as Linton's ascribed and achieved statuses and Sorokin's open and
closed societies. Sociologists have developed many similar dichotomies
to describe social evolution from preindustrialized to industrialized societies. Bernard concludes that although the polarities "were not identified
as sex-based by their proponents," the term used to describe the preindustrial world characterizes what she calls the female world, whereas

the term used to describe the modern world characterizes what she calls
the male world:

> To use Maine's conception, the female world has indeed been a status-
> organized world and the male, a more contract-organized one. The
> female world has indeed been a more kin- and locale-based one, reflect-
> ing the "Blut-und-Bod" (blood and soil) character of the Gemeinschaft;
> the Gesellschaft or capitalistic world has indeed been an exchange world,
> peopled primarily by men. . . . Kropotkin's mutual aid may indeed be
> viewed as representing the ethos of the female world and Spencer's sur-
> vival of the fittest as illustrative of the rugged individualism characteristic
> of the male world.[5]

Other dichotomies do not take an explicitly evolutionary tack. Still,
Bernard sees in them a contrast between the world according to male experience and the world according to female experience:

> Ruth Benedict's characterization of the Apollonian and Dionysian is in-
> deed consonant with the conceptualization of the female world as con-
> servative and tradition-bound and the male world as violent. . . . The
> female world can indeed be characterized by Parson's ascription, diffuse-
> ness, particularism, collectivity-orientation, and high affectivity and the
> male world, by achievement, specificity, individualism, muted affect, and
> universalism. . . . And finally, although Boulding does not specify the in-
> tegry as a female world, a good case can be made for the conception that
> historically the integry has indeed been a woman's world or rather, per-
> haps, that it has been "manned" by women.[6]

These polarities, then, most of which are intended as descriptions of
two different types of society—one pre-urban, the other urban and industrialized—can also be used to describe the worlds of women and of
men in contemporary industrialized society. The question remains, Why
does the social order that analysts expected to diminish, and even dis-
appear, continue to guide the lives of women?

The whole idea of ascription, and even of ranking people and putting
them in their places, makes Americans uncomfortable. The political,
social, and economic revolutions that paved the way for markets and
brought the exchanger to prominence were supposed to wipe out distinctions based on ascription and replace them with distinctions based on
achievement. Equal respect for all persons, a cornerstone of democracy,
became what Charles Taylor calls a "hypergood," a value "incomparably

higher" than others.[7] To mesh with that new morality, the "closed" societies of feudalism, with their impervious boundaries surrounding estates, should have given way to either "open" or "classless" societies.

That did not happen. Instead, equality and inequality have become poles on a salient axis of variation in American culture. At one end are the prizes or punishments—the riches or poverty—that come from competitions won and lost. We make much of marketplace success. The conspicuous consumption Veblen wrote about is portrayed in magazines and in such television shows as *The Lifestyles of the Rich and Famous.* We believe that each individual should be able to rise to the highest level his or her talents and hard work command. Most important, people who do well should be able to give their children "every advantage."

There is the rub. At the other pole is a strong belief that "every advantage" should be extended to all children so that competitions can begin with everybody on a "level playing field." This axis sometimes is argued, especially by conservatives, as if "equality of opportunity" lies at one pole and "equality of results" lies at the other. They say that they support equality of opportunity but not equality of results. And yet, unless the state supports the highest quality of all the resources that produce opportunity—schools, parks, health care, and so on—inequality of results quickly translates (through providing one's children "every advantage") into inequality of opportunity.

Another axis on which the values of exchange and obligation conflict has, as one pole, Americans' pride in the ethnic and racial diversity of our nation, and, as the other pole, the sometimes violent activities designed to keep our residential neighborhoods racially and ethnically pure. We don't believe in ascribed statuses, but with every gesture, every word, every act we put ourselves and our fellows in social places using the clues of ascription—race, ethnicity, last names, age, and gender.

Societies in which the exchanger became the dominant idea of what it is to be human are built upon underpinnings of ascription and obligation much as a new house might be built upon the foundation of an older one that had burned down. Although birth as a Rockefeller cannot today crown life the way birth as a Plantagenet once did, it still does turn heads and open doors. Those who have seen others fly by on wings of privilege are more likely to acknowledge feudal remnants than those who have been lofted on a legacy. (An open gate is hardly noticeable, a closed one cannot be ignored.)[8] Perennial complaints in the United States that "it's not what you know but who you know" signal the continuing relevance of social ascent by biological descent.

Nonetheless, and in spite of much evidence to the contrary, people continue to believe that identities based on such ascribed characteristics as family background have lost their salience. Roy F. Baumeister, for example, interpreted the extraordinary popularity of the television series *Roots* during the mid-1970s, and the "major obsession" with genealogical research that followed, as an example of "misguided attempt[s] to gain self-knowledge by reviving an obsolete feature of identity." "Unfortunately," he proclaimed, "one's ancestry is no longer a vital part of one's identity. It now usually makes very little difference who your great-grandfather was. . . . And since useful self-knowledge failed to emerge from the study of individual ancestries, this fad died an early death."[9]

The crowds that flock to the newly opened Ellis Island Museum or to the Israel Museum in Jerusalem do not seem to know that they are out of style. Both museums offer opportunities to search family backgrounds. Their popularity demonstrates a strong and continuing urge to connect one's biography to a larger family history. That inclination to learn something of one's self by knowing something of one's people derives at least in part from the continuing importance of family background. As Charles Taylor says, "My self-definition is understood as an answer to the question Who I am. And this question finds its original sense in the interchange of speakers. I define who I am by defining where I speak from, in the family tree, in social space, in the geography of social statuses and functions, in my intimate relations to the ones I love, and also crucially in the space of moral and spiritual orientation within which my most important defining relations are lived out."[10] Family trees have not been cut down; their roots continue to nourish a sense of the self based on ascriptive characteristics.

Still, Baumeister only exaggerates. The freedoms concomitant with the idea of the exchanger have been extending gradually to a larger and larger proportion of people. For centuries, one social movement after another has been animated by the hopes of a new group of still excluded people that they too might enjoy boundless opportunities for self-fulfillment and self-realization—those much-lauded goals that accompanied belief in the exchanger. Most recently, with the civil rights and the women's movements, black people in the United States and women worldwide have enjoyed some greater freedom to travel where their talents might take them. That should not, however, blind us to the ways in which people are still defined, and their lives still shaped, by their place in a social order imposed on the basis of ascribed, not achieved, characteristics.

In every known society, people are assigned to some places in the social order based on ascribed characteristics. Depending on these assignments, people are defined by others and by themselves. In a particularly sharp example of such categorization, Booker T. Washington told of a former slave who was asked how many were sold with him. "There were five of us," he responded, "myself and brother and three mules." [11]

Although only market-related or, more precisely, marketable differences among individuals are supposed to influence positioning in contemporary Western societies, the religious, ethnic, and racial identities of their families in addition to their own gender still play a large part in determining where people stand in the social order, what they may do, and what they may not do. In other words, different moral orientations are applied to people of different genders and of different religious, ethnic, and racial backgrounds. They are treated differently, and they are expected to view themselves and act differently.

Often those who recognize the continuing significance of race, gender, and family background consider the enduring potency of these factors a flaw in an otherwise just society, calling it discrimination and prejudice. They favor attempts to use the law, education, and other forms of persuasion to fight against prejudice and discrimination and against those groups powerful enough to impose subservient identities on others. However, attributing the continuing importance of ascription entirely to the self-serving actions of the powerful merely skims the surface. It ignores the social contribution and importance of systems of obligation.

Below the surface of discrimination and prejudice lies a way of ordering the life of a society so that activities and relationships essential to human life continue. The battle against discrimination and prejudice cannot be won if social reform merely widens possibilities to play the exchanger. Obligations to care for others—obligations that are currently assigned to only a few classes of people: women and minorities—need to be widened to pertain to all adults. Classification based on ascribed characteristics permeates all sectors of Western societies, even though such classification is inimical to the basic social ideologies of the exchanger orientation. That happens because ascription puts people into relationships that guarantee the performance of essential work—work that cannot be marketed. If we do not find new ways to guarantee the care that humans need, attacks on discrimination and prejudice, such as legislation against the grossest manifestations of systems of obligation (no court or legal system could possibly touch their finer points), will not be able to rid a society of a structure essential to its existence.

This does not mean that the particular ascriptive assignments the world now suffers are necessary. Indeed, their dissonance with virtually every other Western sense of what it is to be human is precisely what makes Westerners deny the continuing existence of these assignments. In this chapter I shall explore that dissonance by comparing the exchanger orientation with the obligated orientation. My goal is to show, first, what social obligation achieves that the freedom of an exchanger loses and, second, that the system of obligation developed in Western countries during the Industrial Revolution has outlived its usefulness.

Soames Forsyte is white and rich. In a world of exchange, he and his brothers have feathered their nests. The women in Gloria Naylor's novel *The Women of Brewster Place* are black and poor. In a world of obligation, they struggle to make a nest that might withstand the tempests of an unfriendly society. Naylor chose a neighborhood for her book's title. In urban societies, the geographic map often reflects the social map. Brewster Place had been home to Irish immigrants and then to Italians before it contained the "multi-colored 'Afric' children" Naylor writes about. They came to Brewster Place "because they had no choice and would remain for the same reason."[12] Brewster Place is a far cry from the Hyde Park and Knightsbridge neighborhoods inhabited by Forsytes, and more than an ocean and a half-century separates the Forsytes from Brewster Place women. But what London's best addresses were to the Forsytes, Brewster Place was to Naylor's women: a home for their families and an indicator of their place in the social world.

What Constitutes a Unit? Individuals and Members

One point Galsworthy made was that Soames had trouble bonding to anyone but his daughter Fleur, to whom he related as property. As Forsyte family fortunes rose, their emotional bonds attenuated, so that even as Soames tried to couple in order to have an heir, he guarded against attachments as if they were dangerous. By contrast, Naylor portrays her women as people who are always reaching out, offering love and accepting love.

The first characteristic of the obligated-self orientation that distinguishes it from the exchanger orientation is the assumption that the self does not stand alone.[13] Obligated selves are members, or parts, of a larger whole. There are several ways of thinking of persons as parts of a larger whole. One is a confounding of identities, so that, like a raindrop that has fallen into a lake, the individual cannot be distinguished from the whole. That is a characteristic of the cosmic self, which will be examined in the next chapter. Members in systems of social obligation, however, can be distinguished one from another. They are like leaves on a tree. Like a tree's leaves, the members are viewed as parts that would dry up and die if they were detached from their life-giving source. The Laplanders, for example, use the same word for people and reindeer. Because the people could not exist without the reindeer, they are linked in life and word.[14]

That the self can not be whole in itself is a difficult concept for Westerners, especially Americans, to grasp, but it is a common idea. One anthropologist after another tells us that to view the person as part of a larger whole is the prevailing conception in most cultures.[15] Incorporation into a larger whole seems as obvious and as natural to most of the world's peoples as self-interest and individualism seem to Westerners. Westerners are so steeped in the individualism of the past five centuries that only a strong conscious effort will bring to mind an idea of the self merged in a social body. Where the coming of age is signified not by a moving in (to places vacated by one's elders) but by a moving out (to places of one's own), where the major challenge of psychological development is said to be separation, imaginations need fierce stretching to contemplate many selves merged into one.[16]

A. R. Radcliffe-Brown makes a distinction that may help us understand the differences between individuality and collectivity. "Every human being," he says, "is two things: he is an individual and he is also a person. As an individual he is a biological organism. . . . as a person [he] is a complex of social relationships."[17] Note that Radcliffe-Brown, who chose his words carefully, says not that the person is *in* a complex of social relationships but that the person *is* a complex of social relationships.

Another way to illustrate the idea of the person as a complex of social relationships is to turn to the early Roman family. Henry Maine tells us that an essential difference between ancient and modern society is that the unit "of a modern society is the Individual," but in the ancient system, there were no individual qualities: "the moral elevation and moral debasement of the individual appear to be confounded with . . . the merits and offenses of the group to which the individual belongs." The patriarch didn't merely represent the family in civil society; he *was* the family. The household was the basic social unit, and within it, the eldest male ruled supreme. Over his children he had "the power of life and death . . . of uncontrolled corporal chastisement; he can modify their personal condition at pleasure; he can give a wife to his son; he can give his daughter in marriage; he can divorce his children of either sex; he can transfer them to another family by adoption; and he can sell them."[18] The paterfamilias "disposed absolutely of the persons and fortune of his clansmen." It was through him that the members of his clan were connected to the larger society, and he was answerable for any malfeasance by the clan's members—although to satisfy claims against them he "possessed the singular privilege of tendering the delinquent's person in full satisfaction of the damage." In short, the paterfamilias controlled his clan's members as the prophet Matthew advised disciples to control their own members: "if thy right hand offend thee, cut it off and cast it from thee."[19]

The Organismic Metaphor and Social Systems

Although Matthew's unit in this instance was the single individual, it is a small step, often taken, to think of persons as members of the social body much as limbs are members of the physical body. The organismic metaphor is robust; it has served diverse cultures.[20] It trains the mind on the whole as it suggests the image of society as a creature greater and more important than its parts. Ideas of system maintenance and pathology, maturation and decay, are common components of descriptions of society as an organism. Justifications of obligations that are part of selfhood in these systems often emphasize the different functions of body parts (the organs of the organism) and the contribution of each to a harmonious whole.[21]

An often cited example is the Hindu Laws of Manu, which codified a strict obligatory status system based on an image of society organized into castes, each of which emanates from a different part of a spiritual body: "For the sake of preserving this universe, the Being, supremely glorious, allotted separate duties to those who sprang respectively from his mouth, his arm, his thigh, and his foot."[22] Westerners often cite the Hindu caste system as the epitome of what I am calling an obligated-self orientation because they think that their own social world is free from such confining ideas.[23] But Westerners don't have to turn East for examples. In the twelfth century, John of Salisbury, churchman and close friend of Thomas Becket, argued for centralized government and against feudal suzerainty by describing the commonwealth as

> a certain body which is endowed with life by the benefit of divine favor. ... The place of the head in the body of the commonwealth is filled by the prince, who is subject only to God ... even as in the human body the head is quickened and governed by the soul. The place of the heart is filled by the Senate, from which proceeds the initiation of good works and ill. The duties of eyes, ears, and tongue are claimed by the judges and the governors of provinces. Officials and soldiers correspond to the hands. Those who always attend upon the prince are likened to the sides. Financial officers and Keepers ... may be compared with the stomach and intestines.[24]

For Europeans the organismic metaphor projected daily life. It emphasized the interdependence of estates and the "subordination of individual to communal purposes in family, community, and state." This was the metaphor Charles I used to undergird his power during the English Civil Wars, and according to Caroline Merchant, it was the image against which Hobbes, Descartes, and Bacon had cast their mechanistic analogy.[25]

Close cousins to the organismic metaphor are comparisons of human systems of obligation with the ordered societies of social insects. "As bees in early summer ply their toil/ . . . the work goes hotly forward," wrote Virgil.[26] Likewise, Shakespeare's Bishop of Canterbury explains in Henry V that heaven divides

> The state of man in divers functions,
> . . . : for so work the honey bees;
> Creatures that, by a rule in nature, teach
> The act of order to a peopled kingdom.
> They have a king, and officers of sorts:
> Where some, like magistrates, correct at home;
> Others, like merchants, venture trade abroad;
> Others, like soldiers, armed in their stings,
> Make boot upon the summer's velvet buds . . . [27]

Venerable examples these; their progeny is prolific and survives to this day.[28] During the Industrial Revolution, social science, and sociology in particular, married the principles of science to the organismic metaphor in order to generate an influential theoretical tradition called positivistic organicism. Positivistic organicism is an oxymoron, a combination of scientific standards and fanciful metaphor, whose internal contradiction, noted Don Martindale, should be "immediately obvious." Nonetheless, it has survived decades of criticism, which led Martindale to add, "The learned world will not overlook contradiction unless it has good reasons for doing so."[29] One good reason to overlook the contradiction between positivism and organicism is that the organismic metaphor supports those at the top of the hierarchy it envisions, while the appearance of science bestows legitimacy.

Another good reason to overlook the contradiction between positivism and the organismic metaphor is that the organismic metaphor provides a powerful tool to preserve social systems of obligation by making them appear to be beyond human control. They seem a part of nature or of a divine order, unalterable in history and absolutely resistant to human will or intervention. Because humans in fact are not physiologically different in ways that predetermine any but their reproductive behavior, social differentiation and inequalities must depend on powerful belief systems. As Yi-Fu Tuan observes about the organismic metaphor, "Society thus conceived encouraged submission and discouraged radical criticism because its hierarchical orders were understood as part of the overall harmony of nature."[30]

Organismic and hymenopterous metaphors buzz by, emphasizing the naturalness of social inequality and the importance of obedience. So long as the different types of human being constructed by these schemes accept their place and work in society as uncritically as social insects accept theirs, society can roll along as smoothly as summer's velvet buds. All can live in the comfortable knowledge that God made kings or that it would be as absurd to expect a man to nurture an infant as to expect a hand to breathe.

Each culture has its mythmakers. The most effective develop explanations for the way people experience social life. Aristotle, for example, claimed that nature "recognizes different functions and lavishly provides different tools, not an all-purpose tool like the Delphic knife" but one tool for each purpose, and "any human being that by nature belongs not to himself but to another is by nature a slave . . . [a] tool or instrument . . . useful for the purposes of living. . . . [I]t is both right and expedient that they should serve as slaves . . . as between male and female the former is by nature superior and ruler, the latter inferior and subject."[31]

Rulers don't usually depend on the power of the word alone. They add physical force to maintain such myths and punish deviations in word or deed. Those who question systems of obligation often suffered severe punishments. Joan of Arc is a famous example. But she is not the only one to burn for dreaming that her talents needed expression in a social status from which her body was barred. Aristotle, and the church fathers who tied the Maid of Orleans to the stake, claimed, as most defenders of systems of obligation do, that the social order was of superhuman design. Beliefs that people are what they are and do what they do because they could not be or do otherwise, undergird systems of obligation. The designer may be God or nature; the design is immutable. Free will is foreign to systems of obligation.

Families and Mortality

Free will is also foreign to human mortality, and that is key to the tenacity of social systems of obligation. Conceptualizations of the obligated self are part of a culture's design to deal with death, birth, and the succession of generations. Although the modern West tries to control even death, using elaborate medical technology in the attempt, humans remain mortal. Conceptualizations of the exchanger self conceal death and dependency as they fashion the human being into a self-creating, self-directing, self-controlling thing. Such views hardly bother with dust-to-dust or whence we came and whither we go.

Soames, the exchanger par excellence, fancied that he would not have to give up life. Indeed, the whole *Forsyte Saga* can be read as a struggle against inevitable death. The women of Brewster Place, by contrast, do not battle against certainties. Their foe is the power of men to unravel the bonds women weave. Naylor's women are cast-offs. Abandoned by angry fathers, inconstant lovers, and weak sons, they yearn to reconnect what men disconnect. The difference between Soames and Naylor's women reflects the difference between men and women that nineteenth-century thinkers designed when they invented separate spheres for women and men. Women's sphere anchored women (half the adult population) to the home and gave them obligations to the family, especially children. Meanwhile, it freed men for exchange relationships and the market. The current trend in the United States toward single-parent households, in which children are raised by only their mothers, is an unexpected, but not surprising, continuation of the social pattern that freed men from obligation while preserving, through women, the obligation of one generation to care for the next.

Anthropologists have been trying for almost a century to find a universal definition for the family. Some now agree that any relatively stable arrangement for the care of infants and children should be called a family.[32] That definition is useful here. It redirects analytical focus from the pinnacles of systems of social obligation (from the patriarch in the ancient Roman family, for example) to their foundations. It shows what a contemporary teenage mother and her child have in common with the ancient Roman family: through them both, children are cared for—at least sufficiently for life to go on.

Life goes on, because in every culture some types of person are defined as those who take care of others. Exchange views that reduce relationships to the economic conceal most forms of dependency.[33] Such views spawn popular concepts like the "self-made man," which give the appearance that independence (biological, economic, or social) is humanly possible and desirable. By contrast, conceptions of obligated selves are part of designs for interdependence. They build obligations to care for others into the very definition and identity of some humans.

In a famous passage from *The Elementary Structures of Kinship,* Claude Lévi-Strauss describes a young man he saw in a central Brazilian village. The man crouched "for hours upon end in the corner of a hut, dismal, ill-cared for, fearfully thin, and seemingly in the most complete state of dejection." Intrigued, Lévi-Strauss "asked who this person was, thinking that he suffered from some serious illness." His interlocutors laughed at Lévi-Strauss's ignorance as if the cause of the man's condition should have been self-evident. Then they explained that the man was a bachelor. Lévi-Strauss interprets: the abject unhappiness of bachelors works "to prevent those two calamities of primitive society . . . namely, the bachelor and the orphan."[34]

Because it is impossible to completely escape the meaning systems of one's own culture and the language it uses, assumptions that anthropologists make sometimes tell as much about their own cultures as their ethnologies tell about the cultures they study. Lévi-Strauss, the Western anthropologist, was astonished by the abject, barely-alive bachelor, dependent on the grudging kindness of relatives. Note, however, that Blanche, the single woman dependent on the kindness of strangers in Tennessee Williams's *Streetcar Named Desire,* is a character whose existence surprises no one. In Western cultures, women's dependency is assumed and emphasized, whereas men's is made virtually invisible. (A good example is the invisibility of the work that women did on the Town Committees.) According to Western folk wisdom, bachelors, instead of appearing ill-cared-for and dejected, are carefree and happy. That image fits the ideological hegemony of exchange, giving off the impression that the breadwinner's economic independence is tantamount to independence in general.[35]

Western assumptions concerning women and dependency inform the work of another anthropologist: Colin M. Turnbull, who brought the Ik to the attention of the West.[36] The Ik were a Ugandan people, close to extinction because they had been removed from their hunting lands to make way for a nature preserve. As Turnbull analyzes the Iks' response to their dire condition, he inadvertently reveals some of the Western assumptions about mothering that prevent us from understanding the cultural constructions that ensure the care of children.

Turnbull stressed the lack of love and caring among the Ik. "Anyone who cannot take care of himself is a burden and a hazard to the survival of others," he observed. "Children are useless appendages, like old parents." He further reported, "The mother throws her child out at three years old. She has breast-fed it, with some ill humor, and cared for it in some manner for three whole years, and now it is ready to make its own way. I imagine the child must be rather relieved to be thrown out, for in the process of being cared for he or she is carried about in a hide sling wherever the mother goes, and since the mother is not strong herself this is done grudgingly."[37]

Under the conditions of near-starvation to which the Ik had been reduced, life itself was often slapstick. Almost the only spark to laughter was someone else's pain. Thus a child's death could have pie-in-the-face elements: "Whenever the mother finds a spot in which to gather, or if she is at a water hole or in her fields, she loosens the sling and lets the baby to the ground none too slowly, and of course laughs if it is hurt. Then she goes about her business, leaving the child there, almost hoping that some predator will come along and carry it off." Once a leopard did take an infant. Turnbull reported, "The mother was delighted."[38]

The Western anthropologist was horrified. Most Westerners would be. In the Western scheme of things, where dependency of husbands on wives is invisible, the dependency of children on their mothers is assumed to be met by a maternal bond or "instinct" so universally "natural" that a normal mother could no more fail to love, protect, and nurture her young than she could fail to breathe.[39] Turnbull seemed to be a typical Westerner in this belief. Thus he was hard-pressed to explain the mother's delight in the predator's choice of dinner. He tried a couple of explanations from his exchanger orientation. First, he opined that Ik mothers care for their young so that they themselves would receive care when they are old. But the Ik cared so little for their elderly that when Turnbull comforted a dying old man with a sip of water, the others were infuriated at his waste of a scarce resource. Second, he attributed to the Ik the idea that children might be helpful if there were "a good year in the fields during which the family . . . finds mutual advantage in cooperation." This was, he claims "the only reason conceivable to the Ik." But he added, in his own voice, "The family, otherwise, is for the insane, for it spells death, not life." [40]

In exchange terms, the family *is* insane (in any society). To understand why sane Ik women nurse their infants, grudgingly or not, for what must be three excruciatingly long years of near starvation, we need to move away from biology and rational choices and toward the powerful systems of obligation that maintain most societies. Turnbull does not do this. Instead, he presumes quite the opposite, writing about a "broken" culture. Or he takes the instinctual compulsion to nurture for granted and wonders disapprovingly why the care isn't better.

Analysis that focuses on social obligation suggests a different question and different answers. The question is not why Ik women didn't take better care of their young but why they cared for them at all. Why did mothers carry their infants wherever they went? Why in a sling? Why for three years? [41] Answers lie not in female chromosomes, nor in implicit or explicit exchanges, but in an Ik culture that was not broken. What is missing from Turnbull's ethnography, which I think he would have found if he had been looking for it, is a definition of women that would have denied mothers a social existence of any sort if they failed to nurse their infants for the obligatory three years. There must have been many rules these women were following. These were the rules of their culture that assured a succession of generations under even the harshest conditions.

This does not mean that human biology has no effect on human behavior. What has come to be called the nurture-or-nature debate is not a question of whether biology has an effect on human behavior and social arrangements. Almost everyone agrees that it does. The question is what kind of effect. The position expressed here—one common among social scientists—is that human biology makes us a plastic animal without programmed instincts. Our linguistic capacity, our emotional capacity, and our intellectual capacity all combine to allow humans to have a culture as the guide to behavior. Where other species act by instinctive direction, we act by cultural direction. Enormous cultural variation in child rearing and in every other response to biological necessities indicate that although the problems to be solved are biological and universal, the solutions are cultural and highly variable.

Although the relatively long period of human infancy is universal, for example, the means of providing the care that infants need is extremely varied. In some societies infants are suckled by their mothers for three years and longer. In other societies almost no contact takes place between mothers and their children. Lloyd deMause reports that "of 21,000 children born in Paris in 1780, 17,000 were sent into the country to be wet-nursed, 3,000 were placed in nursery homes, 700 were wet-nursed at home, and only 700 were nursed by their own mothers."[42] Those who claim that mothering is instinctual need to explain how genes that are constant can transmit the highly variable, sometimes rapidly changing, and complex behavior involved in mothering. Compare, for example, the food gathering of the Ik mother with the behavior required of a contemporary mother in the United States—behavior such as dealing with landlords, doctors, grocers, and welfare workers. Moreover, although sexually differentiated genes for mothering have yet to be discovered, sexually differentiated definitions of humans and sexually differentiated socialization practices are easily observable. Until the discovery of genes that can account for caring behavior in some females (usually of the serving class) but not in males (or wealthy females), the simplest explanation for the caring behavior exhibited by most females remains the one that is easily observed: cultural definition.

Moral systems that guarantee care for children return us to the question of units. Exchange theories treat the individual as the unit; systems of obligation treat intergenerational social groups, usually the family, as the unit. When extinction threatens, the family spells death for the individual, especially the individual mother, who may be weakened beyond survival by burdens of child care. Then the obligatory patterns, to which no alternative is even thinkable, show their power. They force one generation to sacrifice itself to the next. In the ineluctable social definitions of the obligated self we would find the reason Ik mothers care for their offspring. Those definitions work by denying social existence (and thus life itself) to those who fail to fulfill the caregiving inherent in their identity. Failure to care becomes as unimaginable as sailing beyond the horizon in a world believed to be flat. Enforcing such definitions is a matter of tossing offenders beyond the pale. Like Lévi-Strauss's Brazilian bachelors, they will be neglected, or worse, like Joan, they will be burned.

That is one reason why, with her own death looming, a mother might still care for her young. But that is also why she is likely to feel more emancipation than grief when a predator snatches her infant. The Ik mother has fulfilled her obligation and now, through no fault of hers, she is relieved of it. Similarly, in the contemporary West, when death has long tarried over a sickbed, people often greet the final demise of their loved one with some relief. There is nothing shocking or horrifying about either the Ik or the Western sense of deliverance.

Motion by Emotion

The exchanger view of the self recognizes emotions, but mostly as impediments, deceptive traps, or diversions from our rational pursuit of self-interest. All other views of the self treat emotions as a human endowment, a means through which we interpret and respond to our environment that is not deceptive, dangerous, or an indication of moral weakness. Conceptualizations of the obligated self interpret feelings as motors that drive persons toward the obligations they should fulfill. The particular feelings that are said to motivate people vary from culture to culture and from time to time. Ancient cultures, such as patriarchal Rome, emphasized awe, fear, and reverence. But those feelings did not mesh well with exchanger ideals of equality, freedom, and independence. So, as the market expanded and free will replaced obligation, love became the ruling emotion.[43]

Love works well in a culture dominated by the exchanger image of the self because it can combine the exchanger's rational self-interest with the obligated self's lack of choice. In the alchemy necessary to explain obligation, especially asymmetrical obligation, in a society that strongly values choice, equality, and freedom, the things we do because we are obligated to do them can, with the invention of love, be interpreted as the things we cannot avoid doing because we are possessed by love. Thus, if once kings ruled by a divine authority flowing through their blood, now women will care for their children, their husbands, and their elderly parents out of "natural" feelings of love and devotion. Acting according to our natures is, of course, desirable. Therefore, moving right along from irrational nature to rational self-interest, the things we do because it is our place in society to do them become the things we *want* to do because they make us feel good. Women care for children, this story goes, because mothering makes mothers feel good.[44]

In this way, beliefs, such as Aristotle's, that servitude is in the slave's nature and subordination in the woman's, are reinforced with the added belief that joy flows from the innate adoration and love that motivates devoted service. Within this framework, caregiving, generosity, self-sacrifice, and altruism lose their moral value. What credit could attach to behavior as unavoidable as breathing?

Albert Hirschman traces changing attitudes toward caregiving in changing meanings of the verb "to meddle." Not until the eighteenth century, he says, did it "firmly acquire its present-day derogatory sense. Previously these terms had a neutral and sometimes even a positive con-notation: after all, to meddle is to care for somebody or something outside of one's own immediate circle or area of interest, an attitude and activity that became offensive only in an era when to mind one's own business had become enthroned as a general rule of conduct."[45] Over the years, the value of caregiving has declined to the point where today, according to Sister Marie Augusta Neal, altruism is often considered "at best a uto-pian ideal, at worst a foolhardy endangering of the species."[46]

Altruism is a troubling phenomenon in a society dominated by ideas of the exchanger orientation. Why would anyone put the interests of another before one's own? Or, to put the question in the terms E. O. Wilson uses to frame the central problem of his candidate for new dis-ciplinary status, sociobiology: "How can altruism, which by definition reduces physical fitness, possibly evolve by natural selection?"[47]

The solution offered within every discipline that has turned its atten-tion to this problem has been to argue that altruism only *appears* con-trary to self-interest. Sociobiologists working within the theory of natu-ral selection have developed a subtheory called kin selection. Within this framework they devised complicated equations to show that behavior that seems to be altruistic is, in fact, self-interested because it indirectly increases the survival chances of the altruist's genes.[48]

Political scientists, at pains to explain cooperation, have worked out elaborate experiments to show that cooperation is in the best interests of the cooperator as long as both sides anticipate frequent interaction.[49] Anthropologists studying the reciprocal gift exchange that takes place in many simple societies emphasize that givers expect to receive, and social controls are in place to see that they do receive a return on their gift—

albeit after some delay and without precise calculations of the worth of the gift and its return. Finally, psychologists argue that altruists' return is in emotional coin—it makes them feel good. In these analyses, emotions become the functional equivalent of a commodity, and self-interested calculations are said to direct the self toward that which increases good feelings and avoids bad feelings. Anna Freud, for example, points out that the satisfaction that caregivers derive from helping others belies the selflessness of their acts.[50]

Such arguments may seem as convoluted as Fichte's explanation of wifely subordination. But remember Martindale's observation: "The learned world will not overlook contradiction unless it has good reasons for doing so." The contradiction here is between views of the self as exchanger and views of the self as obligated. By overlooking the contradictions between these two orientations, a society can enjoy the benefits of a social order based on obligation while simultaneously relieving some persons from responsibilities in order to get on with the business of a market economy. By insisting that there is no essential difference between behavior that preserves the human species and behavior that furthers the individual, and by reducing altruism to its opposite—self-interest—altruism and the contradiction between the exchanger self and the obligated self are both made invisible. In this way, the idea of the exchanger as the one and only correct view of the self survives along with obligated-self social controls that force some persons to serve and save the group even at their own expense.

In order to maintain social arrangements inimical to market relationships while simultaneously expanding markets into almost every corner of social life, modern cultures used the paraphernalia of science to create myths as irrational and as powerful as totemism or any other supposedly primitive belief at which Westerners scoff. But science did not do the job all alone. Theories that are deceptively rational, such as positivistic organicism, could not by themselves produce the modern chimera—obligated selves who appear to enjoy all the rights of an exchanger but are as hamstrung by their passions as peasants were constrained by obligations to their lords. For such a self to become believable, the Western world needed art. The novel, invented alongside the market, produced images of exchangers, such as Soames, but its more important productions were characterizations of modern obligated selves, many of them struggling to be free of their obligations and some of them succeeding, but with mixed results.

The exchanger self could not a society make. The new social order, no longer arranged by the hand of God, needed heroes and heroines who, no longer fueled by duty, would be propelled by a force more potent than obligation—else there would be no new generations. Novels furnish the modern imagination with fantasies of love, a force strong enough to make exchangers happily relinquish their autonomy. They tell family stories, focusing especially on the moment when individuals fall madly and passionately in love and so join another individual to take a family to its next generation.

As love edged out awe, fear, and loyalty as the overwhelming emotions in systems of obligation, the novel—with its everyday, romantic, loves-me, loves-me-not questions—could captivate readers just as epic poetry had once engrossed listeners with its heroic passions and quests for fame and renown. The new stories were about the new class that grew from the market: burghers (like the Forsytes) and their daughters and sons replaced royalty and heroic archetypes. Attachments shifted from such immense abstractions as God, Principle, and Country to particular persons. Settings changed too: from the open, public battlefield to the closed, private bedroom. The political became private.[51]

From the eighteenth century onward, fiction reveled in sentiment and revealed familiar private lives. It could show how characters as different in life circumstances as the Forsytes and the women of Brewster Place were driven by the same life force. Naylor's women know what Soames could not understand. They are poor where he is rich, and rich where he is poor; but these opposite types struggle toward the same goal: an endless family line. We have already seen how Soames struggled for an heir. Now see how Naylor inflates a bowl of oatmeal to epic proportions as Mattie watches her son at breakfast: "The oatmeal . . . was moving through his blood and creating skin cells and hair cells and new muscles that would eventually uncurl and multiply and stretch the skin on his upper arms and thighs, elongate the plump legs that only reached the top rung of his chair. . . . Her own spirit . . . pushed and struggled to make all around them safe and comfortable."[52] Gold might run through Forsyte veins and oatmeal through the veins of Mattie's boy, but the plots all agree: love is the fuel, and a family's lasting and rising place in the world is the destination.

According to Peter Brooks, the nineteenth century's obsession is "with questions of origin, evolution, progress, [and] genealogy," which is why plots become important. "From sometime in the mid-eighteenth century," he says, "through to the mid-twentieth century," Western societies created plots—in fiction, history, philosophy, and the social sciences. "As Voltaire announced and the Romantics confirmed, . . . the question of what we are typically must pass through the question of where we are, which in turn is interpreted to mean, how did we get to be there?"[53]

Fathers figure as prominently as lovers in these plots, reflecting the lingering power of patriarchy. But more than patriarchy gives these men their power. The modern novel is about love, sometimes love between fathers and their children. This love can run deep, regardless of the class, country, or decade of the story. In *The Forsyte Saga,* James Forsyte discovers as he approaches death that "the kernel of life was in saving for his children." Similarly, Mattie's father, Sam, "lives and breathes" for his child.[54]

Typically, however, a father's love finds expression in market terms: James Forsyte builds a fortune. Sam struggles to wrest a little more for his daughter than a rural black girl usually gets. When Mattie wanted a pair of patent-leather pumps, Sam "hired himself out in the sweet potato fields for a month of Saturdays" to get them for her. And when she had scarlet fever, he "neglected his farm and insisted on sitting by her bed every day—all day—while the life was burning and sweating out of her pores. It became a legend in those parts, and even her mother never knew how he had gotten the white doctor from town to make that long trip to the house for her. Sam never mentioned it, and no one dared ask."[55]

There is nothing these fathers won't do for their daughters—except let them marry below their station. Romantic love is a wild card that fathers struggle to tame. One of the earliest novels, Rousseau's *La nouvelle Héloïse,* established the theme with a tragic tale of forbidden love between Héloïse and her tutor. Following in that tradition, Naylor's story begins with a seduction scene between Mattie and Butch Fuller, the "no-'count ditch hound" who, according to her father, Sam, "no decent woman would be seen talking to."[56] When Mattie gets pregnant with Butch's child, her father banishes her.

Most plots pursue the question of who will marry whom. Usually the heroine's (and sometimes the hero's) march down the church aisle is a climb up the social ladder. For women, who could only lose place if they entered labor markets, marriage markets are everything. Thus Samuel Richardson's poor but honest heroines marry and become mistresses of the manor, and Jane Austen's heroines "improve their purses," and usually their statuses too, through marriage.[57] Seductions and marriages are the denouement of most novels.

But birth figures, too, for such writers as Thomas Mann and Galsworthy, who follow families through generations. Soames's moment of ecstasy, or at least as close as he can come to an exalted feeling, arrives when he views the infant who was such a disappointment because she was female. "Suddenly his heart felt queer, warm, as if elated. . . . The sense of triumph and renewed possession swelled within him. By-God! this—this thing was *his.*" With this possession Soames escaped the tragedy of an end to his line. His daughter, Fleur, was his ticket to eternity. Even Soames, the quintessential exchanger, could be moved by the core feature of societies based on obligation—continuance of family lines. However, even as Galsworthy included an ingredient of the obligated self in Soames, he remained faithful to the image of an almost pure exchanger by transforming social obligation into a form of individualized property—"By God! . . . this *thing* was *his.*"[58]

Time

Galsworthy's narrative is about generations, but his characters are isolated exchangers whose time begins with their birth and threatens to end with their death. Only their own aging or imminent death forces their ruminations to range beyond the moment. Forsyte men, possessing much, dream little. The women of Brewster Place possess little, but dream across eons. On the bus that took her from home with Butch's baby in her belly and her father's rage in her ears, Mattie tried to imagine that she could "suspend time, pretend that she had been born that very moment on that very bus, and that this was all there was and ever would be. But just then the baby moved, and she put her hands on her stomach and knew that she was nurturing within her what had gone before and would come after. This child would tie her to that past and future as inextricably as it was now tied to her every heartbeat."[59]

Naylor, writing about obligated selves, knew that time in this orientation stretches as far back as a group's memory and as far forward as its hope. The exchanger self, disconnected from others, is disconnected as well from past and future. It is a thing of the moment; its relationships are ad hoc, rational, quick, unemotional, but also, according to Hobbes and Durkheim, competitive and antagonistic. Reflecting Hobbes, Durkheim wrote that "where interest is the only ruling force each individual finds himself in a state of war with every other since nothing comes to mollify the egos, and any truce in this eternal antagonism would not be of long duration. There is nothing less constant than interest . . . such a cause can only give rise to transient relations and passing associations."[60]

Emotions of attachment take time to develop. We generally assume that given time and proximity, affections will develop.[61] Frank O'Connor made the connection between time and feeling in his story "Guests of the Nation," which is about a couple of British captives held by the Irish. At a point in the story where the captives have been held for so long that their Irish guards have become fond of them, one of the guards, the narrator, learns from his commander that his charges are hostages: "If they shoot our prisoners we'll shoot theirs," says the commander. The guard complains that he and the other guard were never warned. "You might have known it," says the commander:

> "We couldn't know it, Jeremiah Donovan," says I. "How could we when they were on our hands so long?"
> "The enemy have our prisoners as long and longer," says he.
> "That's not the same thing at all," says I.
> "What difference is there?" says he.
> I couldn't tell him, because I knew he wouldn't understand. If it was only an old dog that was going to the vet's, you'd try and not get too fond of him, but Jeremiah Donovan wasn't a man that would ever be in danger of that.[62]

Jeremiah Donovan, like Soames Forsyte, wasn't a man likely to slip from the isolation of exchange to the connectedness of obligation. Most other people must guard against getting too fond of a dog, a prisoner, or anything else that they will have to treat as a commodity. That is one reason exchanges are usually consummated in short order.

Systems of obligation build lasting connections. For the obligated self, time is neither a commodity nor a possession; it is a dimension within which human lives and relationships mature and decay.[63] The obligated self moves within a hierarchy of responsibilities and demands for attention. Activities are taken up not according to a plan or a clock but according to how needs present themselves. In a sense, exchangers command time, and obligated selves are commanded by life within time. They meet obligations according to natural requirements.

Naylor's women struggle to maintain life's flow and ward off decay. One narrative features a middle-class activist who comes to Brewster Place with do-gooder projects in mind. She calls herself Kiswana, an African name chosen to symbolize rejection of her people's forced subjection in the United States. About a week after she moves onto Brewster Place, her mother visits. They argue: "I'd rather be dead than be like you—a white man's nigger who's ashamed of being black!" Kiswana cries. Her mother leaps from her chair and grabs the girl by her shoulders, bringing her "so close to her mother's face that she saw her reflection, in the tears that stood in the older woman's eyes."

> "My grandmother," Mrs. Browne began slowly in a whisper, "was a full-bloodied[64] Iroquois, and my grandfather a free black from a long line of journeymen . . . and my father was a Bajan who came to this country as a cabin boy on a merchant mariner. . . . I am alive because of the blood of proud people who never scraped or begged or apologized for what they were. . . . When I brought my babies home from the hospital, my ebony son and my golden daughter, I swore before whatever gods would listen—those of my mother's people or those of my father's people—that I would use everything I had and could ever get to see that my children were prepared to meet this world on its own terms, so that no one could sell them short and make them ashamed of what they were or how they looked—whatever they were or however they looked. And Melanie, that's not being white or red or black—that's being a mother."[65]

There it is: the image of a mother, the quintessential image of an obligated self in the contemporary United States. When such authors as Naylor draw a picture of an impassioned woman who thinks of herself as part of a long line that she will foster with everything she has, they are not just portraying someone in a role that some women might play as one might play the role of uncle or streetcar conductor—or father, for that matter. Mrs. Browne stands for a moral order. Galsworthy would never have made Soames passionately invoke the long lines that connected one generation to another. That would have been out of character because Soames operates from an exchanger orientation that sees time in terms of the nuclear family at most. For Mrs. Browne, time links generations.

Contemporary images of the obligated self include a broad assortment of characters, from a father who sits watching while sweat pours out of his child's fevered forehead, to children who struggle with the obligation to be obedient to their parents, to married couples who struggle with the obligation to be faithful. But the paragon of the obligated self is the modern mother. She counterbalances the exchanger self most powerfully. Fathers can proudly turn their backs on trouble, forbidding degrading liaisons and banishing fallen daughters, but mothers must find ways for life to go on, discovering meanings in the present that offer possibility for the future. Lewis Hyde notes that although cultures face both forward and backward, "most artists seem to face themselves in a primary direction, toward either the past or the future. The *fils à papa* (the father's son), say the French, has the spiritual attitude that serves the past, while the *fils à maman* is in love with emerging life."[66]

When Mattie becomes pregnant, Naylor follows the tradition of the male parent looking backward while the female parent looks forward. Mattie's father throws her out—she has shamed the line; she must be expunged. Her mother, by contrast, offers saving words. Mattie says, "I'm so ashamed." Her mother responds: "Ain't nothing to be shamed of. Havin' a baby is the most natural thing there is. The Good Book call children a gift from the Lord. And there ain't no place in that Bible of His that say babies is sinful. The sin is the fornicatin', and that's over and done with . . . what's going on in your belly now ain't nothin' to hang your head about—you remember that."[67]

In this tradition, a mother's moral orientation is as different from a father's moral orientation as a mother's orientation to time is different from a father's orientation to time. Without regard to clocks, and with no concept of overtime in their approach to work, mothers find time for what needs to be done. They maintain the seamlessness of time in a world transformed by the second-to-second splintering of time that has accompanied the development of market society. Markets, and all activities that regularly bring large numbers of strangers into coordinated interchange, require a regular way of ticking off time into discrete, regular intervals, such as weeks and hours.[68] The mechanical clock, says David S. Landes, "made possible urban life as we know it, promoted new forms of industrial organization, and enabled individuals to order their life and work along rational, more productive lines."[69]

The obligated self struggles against clocks. Although attempts to put infants on rigid schedules recur often in market-dominated societies, babies' noisy complaints usually give such fads swift riddance. Most attempts to make sickness and other organic events conform to clocks are similarly brief. Caregiving and attention-giving work do not transform easily into the paid labor of an industrialized society. Emergency workers at hospitals and fire departments can handle heroic moments, but needs for everyday care and responsibility are not easily met in the market. The Victorian idea of women's sphere, with its ideal roles of wife and mother, was a cultural answer to the human need for continuous care.

Such ditties as "A woman's work is never done" recognized that women's obligatory work did not conform to clocks or even sunsets. By the mid-twentieth century, when the second wave of the women's movement was gaining strength, that saying, if invoked at all, tended to confer only a trivial observation on the boundlessness of women's work, because there was a general assumption that housewives did not work. The question "Do you work?" was taken to mean "Do you work for pay?" Therefore, one of the first efforts of the consciousness-raising phase of the movement was an attempt to establish the belief that raising children and maintaining households involved work, and that even if women did not punch time clocks or receive salaries, their caregiving efforts were work. Mothers often complain about the common assumption—made especially by teachers and other child caregivers—that mothers have all the time in the world, or at least as much time as their children need. As a result of this assumption, mothers, including those who work full time outside the home, are usually the parent called when the child is hurt or becomes ill at school.[70]

Where mothers are concerned, there is supposedly no scarcity of time or of anything else. Lewis Hyde and Marshall Sahlins observe that scarcity was invented for markets. The Law of Scarcity, says Hyde, is a principle so basic to market economies that both Paul Samuelson and Milton Friedman begin their economies with it. Marshall Sahlins states that "modern capitalist societies . . . dedicate themselves to the proposition of scarcity," adding that "inadequacy of economic means is the first principle of the world's wealthiest peoples."[71]

For the exchanger, time, like money, is scarce. It is homogeneous, objective, measurable, and infinitely divisible. Because it can be consumed by a plethora of activities, its scarcity is intensified. Scarcity in turn enhances its worth.[72] Thus it behooves the exchanger self to be always busy, even to the point of using time simultaneously in as many different ways as possible.[73] Activities that are paid for become more highly valued than activities not paid for, and finally, even when the activity is not remunerated, we think metaphorically of the time it takes as money: "How do you *spend* your time these days? That flat tire *cost* me an hour. I've *invested* a lot of time in her. . . . You need to *budget* your time."[74] For the obligated self, by contrast, whatever is, must suffice. Time is simply there, an endless circle punctuated by life events set in endless seasons.

Bound Identities

As market forces demanded segregation and segmentation of daily activities, time became a boundary—a way not only to order activities but also to locate conceptions of the self. There was family time for the obligated self, work time for the exchanger, and other times for other senses of the self. Contemporary life, however, is not so well ordered that the boundaries are impregnable. A world with many possibilities and much scarcity offers fertile soil for boundary invasions.[75] "Stress," a sense of being overextended, overwhelmed, and overburdened, has become a common complaint in the United States. Sometimes, though, complainers sound more like boasters. For time, like all other boundaries in the exchanger's world, is experienced as an impediment, a challenge, something to overcome or at least manage.

Strutting "stressed-out" dilemmas is one way we can show how good we are when we are thinking of ourselves as exchangers. Each year, advises a popular career guidebook, your vita—literally, your life—should change. Otherwise, you are in a rut. Time should be used, according to this advice, for the accumulation of resources to fashion a future persona better able to exploit time and other resources than the one at hand. The exchanger, living in a world of becoming, measures success against improvements in the property called the self.[76]

The obligated self is more of a fixed thing. In order to contrast modern industrial society with the societies he studied, Robert Redfield created another of those dichotomous ideal types that Jessie Bernard says describe not only the different societies their authors intended but also the worlds of women and men. Redfield's contrast was between "folk" and industrialized societies. In folk society, a person may occupy "just [one] position in a system of relationships which are traditional in the society." In modern Western societies, where "gender roles," or, more accurately, "gender identities,"[77] are very similar to total identities in folk cultures, a person's position in a system of relationships is "in large part fixed at birth; it changes as he [or she] lives, but it changes in ways which were 'foreordained' by the nature of his [or her] particular society."[78]

Where people are bound by the god-given or nature-given obligations their type of person must fulfill, personal change is strictly limited and social boundaries identifying each person's place in society tend to be definite and strong. Historians of biography and literature observe that when women and men are fixed in status, truth, "even the whole truth about an individual, existed in what was stereotypic rather than what was unique . . . people were not seen in their complexity, but in the accomplishment of their role in society. . . . The whole message of culture is to remind people of their place in society and to warn them that only sorrow can result from any attempt to break the chains that tie them to family, trade, religion, and class."[79]

Social devices that maintain boundaries around selves may be as subtle as a glance, or they may be tangible, such as stone walls or doors that lock. Time is one kind of manifest barrier; the built environment is a more apparent example. Medieval towns were walled to keep strangers out. But within the great halls of medieval castles, few physical demarcations separated function from function or person from person. People knew their own place and everybody else's, and they addressed each other according to social station. Then and now, people construct walls with slight but impenetrable gestures of everyday life. Tone of voice, smiles and frowns, attention paid and notice not taken, the averted eye and the glance that pierces, open arms and turned backs, kisses, handshakes, slaps, and bows —all these were, and remain, the commonplace gestures of notice and disregard that indicate a person's place in the social order.[80]

Gestures can also tear down social walls. An "uppity" person knows but rejects her place as something below her. *Uppity* is a word seldom applied to men or to high-status women (they have no place to go but down). Etta, a woman of Brewster Place, was uppity: "Etta spent her teenage years in constant trouble. Rock Vale had no place for a black woman who was not only unwilling to play by the rules, but whose spirit challenged the very right of the game to exist. The whites in Rock Vale were painfully reminded of this rebellion when she looked them straight in the face while putting in her father's order at the dry goods store, when she reserved her sirs and mams for those she thought deserving, and when she smiled only if pleased, regardless of whose presence she was in."[81] The white people of Rock Vale, a rural town, knew how to punish uppity black girls and maintain invisible walls by creating cautionary trouble. In urban centers, stone walls and wrought iron fences are often erected to take the place of the invisible social boundaries that were broken down by the demands of free commerce.

Walls and fences figure prominently in Naylor's novel. In the planning stage, "Brewster Place was to become part of the main artery of the town."[82] Then its first inhabitants moved out, the neighborhood was filled "with people who had no political influence; people who were dark haired and mellow-skinned," and City Hall powers built a wall that turned Brewster Place into a dead-end street, blocking it from the growing prosperity of the rest of the town. The wall symbolizes the social barriers that repress Naylor's women. It stood "only six feet from Mattie's building," blocking the light, starving her plants.[83]

Walls have reasons. They forcibly separate different types of people from one another. Markets have no external walls, but only the exchanger portion of the self is allowed in; other aspects of the self are kept out (recall Warmson in *The Forsyte Saga,* who had a son in the army before his employer even found out he was married). Strangers who come to trade in cities are limited, one-dimensional men and women.[84] Possession of commodities is all they need and is all an exchanger is supposed to take into consideration when trading. Although the exchanger orientation emphasizes individualism, in practice it demands uniformity. One dollar looks like another, and one seller or buyer is supposed to be the same as another. Often charges of prejudice and discrimination follow when other characteristics are brought into an exchange interaction. One more axis of variation has, at one pole, the uniformity demanded of exchange performances counterposed, at the other pole, by our fascination with individuality. In the world of exchange, failure to perform well is met with dismissal. In the world of obligation, we are stuck with whoever fills a particular status, so that much anxiety is reflected in cultural pressures for people to perform the duties of statuses they fill. A bad accountant can be fired; a bad mother must be endured.

Differences between the times and places appropriate to the exchanger and the obligated self are often described as differences between private and public worlds.[85] The key to those differences is the concept of the self that ought to be operating. Where these two worlds collide, confusion and contradiction prevail. One such place is the home—at once the site of many obligatory relationships and the object that represents most people's greatest economic asset. At this tangible juncture between the world of obligation and the world of exchange, brokers separate buyers and sellers. Here also, special laws define what makes a home a house. When drafting the Civil Rights Act of 1968, Congress had to determine just how many rooms the fictitious Mrs. Murphy could rent before her rooming house was transformed from a home in which she could choose her guests freely to a commodity where the only distinguishing characteristic to mark persons for admission or exclusion could be their ability to pay the rent.[86]

Naylor catches the difference when she describes Mattie's search for a place to live: "As the evening approached" and "her legs were starting to tremble from . . . the heavy load she had carried around all day," Mattie circled the same block twice. A woman called to her. Mattie "remembered passing that old white woman just minutes before. She must have wandered into one of their neighborhoods again." But when the woman called to her, Mattie heard a black voice. "She hesitantly approached the fence and stared incredulously into a pair of watery blue eyes."

The woman was to be Mattie's salvation, but salvation does not come on the wings of exchange relationships. Naylor therefore has these two negotiate the boundary between obligation and exchange in the only scene in her literally told story that is tinged with illusion and disorientation: "Mattie saw that the evening light had hidden the yellow undertones in the finely wrinkled white face, and it had softened the broad contours of the woman's pug nose and full lips." The woman asked a lot of personal questions (too many and too personal for exchangers). Then she invited Mattie past the fence and into the house: "You might as well come on in and get that boy out the night air. Got plenty of room here. Just me and my grandbaby. He'll be good company for Lucielia."

Mattie obeyed. She followed the woman into the "huge living room overcrowded with expensive mahogany furniture and china bric-a-brac" through a dining room where "a yellowing crystal and brass chandelier hung over an oak table large enough to seat twelve people." This table was not as opulent as Smithen Forsyte's, but it signified the same thing: a place in the world.

Mattie was confused. She sensed that the line between worlds of exchange and obligation was being crossed, but she didn't know what to make of it. " 'I don't even know your name!' Mattie stammered. 'That mean you can't eat my food? Well, since you gotta be properly introduced, the name of what's in the kitchen is pot roast, oven-browned potatoes, and string beans. . . . And the crazy old woman you're sure by now you're talkin' to is Eva Turner. . . . People 'round here call me Miss Eva.' " [87]

To say "People 'round here call me Miss Eva" is to say that one is known; one has a reputation. In prisons, armies, and other total institutions where initiates are stripped of clothes, hair, and other possessions in which self-feeling is invested, the most significant loss is not physical at all. It is the loss of one's full name. More than any other loss, says Erving Goffman, the loss of their names forces inmates to suffer "a great curtailment of the self."[88] What is curtailed is not the whole self. The exchanger, the self that counts time and money, can nonchalantly accept identification by number. It is not diminished by being identified by number in a total institution any more than by being identified by a credit card number. It is the obligated self, the self whose name signifies a place in the world, that is destroyed in total institutions, for that is the aspect of the self that the total institution tries to possess totally.

Names tell a lot about a person's place in social structures. Sometimes the names of people and the names of the places they occupy are the same. Marcel Mauss gives an example from the Zuni, among whom certain names are passed down through generations. "What is at stake in all this," he says, "is the very existence of [the chief and the clan] and of the ancestors reincarnated in their rightful successors, who live again in the bodies of those who bear their names, whose perpetuation is . . . only guaranteed by the perpetuating of the names of individuals, of persons."[89]

Western societies practice a vestigial naming of a similar sort. Examples are juniors who bear their father's or mother's names and the Ashkenazi Jewish prohibition against naming a child after a living relative, as if two cannot occupy the same name—the same place—at the same time. Some old names reflect descent (Richardson, Peterson); others reflect occupation (Cooper, Collier, Barber). But the most important information that names give us now is about race, ethnicity, and gender. These are categories that figure heavily in contemporary systems of obligation: Jane O'Neil is probably female, of Irish descent, and Catholic; David Schwartz is probably an Ashkenazi Jewish male.

Once Mattie learns Miss Eva's name, she feels compelled to give her own. Then the two begin a negotiation not of the price of the place but whether the place will have a money price at all. Naylor continues the scene in which Mattie and Miss Eva negotiate the boundaries between exchange and obligation: "Mattie hurried behind Eva and Basil into the kitchen. 'I meant no offense, Mrs. Turner. It's just that this was all so quick and you've really been kind and my name is Mattie Michael and this is Basil and I don't even know how much space you got for us or how much you want to charge or anything, so you can see why I'm a little confused, can't you?'" Miss Eva was not at all confused. She wanted a relationship between two obligated selves: "'I ain't runnin no boardinghouse, girl; this is my home.'"[90]

Mattie stayed on for many years, and the two women helped each other raise Ciel and Basil. They became like family, each filling places left vacant by parents, would-be husbands, and children. Whenever Miss Eva ventured too far with her advice, Mattie held the line by asking the price of room and board.

There is no money price in the world of obligation. One precept in the world of exchange is that rewards should be based on merit; rewards and responsibility rise and fall together. But in systems of obligation, especially those that support market societies, the opposite is true: the vital responsibility of caregiving is the work of low-paid or nonpaid low-ranking people, mostly women. Such responsibilities, if they fall to upper-class people at all, belong to the women.

Galsworthy, whose trilogy is about families and their regeneration, tells precious little about the caregiving work that goes into the project of bringing a family from one generation to another. That is probably because he does not write well about women. Irene, for instance, a key character in his story, is hardly more than a shimmering phantom. Nevertheless, we do get a whiff of an upper-class woman meeting her caregiving responsibilities when we find James "neat in his high hat and his frock-coat, on which was the speckless gloss imparted by perfect superintendence. Emily saw to that; that is, she did not, of course, see to it— people of good position not seeing to each other's buttons, and Emily was of good position—but she saw that the butler saw to it."[91] Position, or place, determines what one superintends and what one actually does— especially where care and responsibility are concerned.

But lack of money can have the same effect as its abundance. Both extremes separate the one responsible for the care of family members from the one who actually does the work. Poor women in market societies often do the caregiving work that middle- and upper-class women superintend, while their own caregiving work is performed by some other woman—a relative or someone who is paid even less. So it was that before she met Miss Eva, Mattie "found an assembly-line job in a book bindery, and she paid Mrs. Prell, an old woman on the first floor, to keep him during the day. . . . Mattie would walk the thirty blocks back to the boardinghouse to see the baby during her lunch break. She had just enough time to rush in, pick him up, see if he was wet or marked in some way and then go back to work."[92]

Whatever their class differences, Emily and Mattie occupied the same position in the family. Systems of obligation tend to follow a similar structure. Most are arranged into three major tiers. At the top is a set of high ranks for full adults. In the middle are two sets of intermediate ranks: one is made up of training positions designed to prepare individuals for promotion to the highest ranks; the other is composed of positions designed for system maintenance and service to the lowest ranks. These middle ranks are often filled by biologically mature adults who are, by social definition, barred from the top ranks. The lower levels are for the immature and the biologically incapacitated. They may be ranked according to both age and the likelihood of entrance into the intermediate ranks of training or service.

Describing the intermediate ranks in early Roman society, Henry Maine wrote:

> [The law] enfranchises a son or grandson [middle, training rank] at the death of his Parent . . . to become himself the head. . . . But a woman, [middle, service rank] of course has no capacity of the kind. . . . There is therefore a peculiar contrivance of archaic jurisprudence for retaining her in the bondage of the family for life. This is the institution known to the oldest Roman law as the Perpetual Tutelage of Women, under which a Female, though relieved from her Parent's authority by his decease, continues subject through life to her nearest male relations, or to her Father's nominees, as her Guardians.[93]

Those in the highest ranks generally control decision making, distribution of material resources, and admission to all positions in the system. They may be obliged to protect everyone in the system. They issue commands to those in lower ranks from whom they receive deference and service. Often they demand prodigious service from those in the intermediate-training ranks. They may also receive some service from those in the intermediate-service ranks, but most of the obligations of these ranks are to those in the lowest echelons.

Systems of obligation may be nested, with the pattern repeating itself as the levels descend, each structure mirroring the larger scheme of the major ranks like a set of Russian dolls. For instance, in those Asian cultures where the new bride and the mother-in-law are both in the intermediate-service sector, the relationship between them may mimic the relationships between top and middle-training positions. Similarly, mothers superior in convents exercise power over novices, middle managers exercise power over subordinates, and senior classmen lord it over freshmen, although all of them are subordinate to others in higher ranks.

Moreover, in any society several systems of obligation may exist side by side, each discrete system of relationships following a similar pyramidical shape.

Instinct or Instruction

Equality or inequality of persons is one of the great divides among ideas about the self. According to the obligated orientation, people are as different as queen bees, drones, and soldier bees. As in bee hives, only a certain number of individuals can occupy some ranks—usually, the higher the rank, the fewer the incumbents. Nature, according to this belief, designs incumbents with the qualities necessary for the functions they must perform.

That explains how the obligated self lands in its social positions and how it is able to perform the tasks associated with those positions. The exchanger orientation does not present the assignment of people to social positions so simply. Many treat modern industrialized societies as places where freedom and equal opportunity prevail. According to the exchanger view, social inequalities flow from difference in human capital or merit—innate talents, education, experience, and especially motivation. Rewards are said to motivate individuals to get the training they need to use their individual talents in ways most beneficial to society.[94]

Differences between obligated and exchanger views of social inequality boil down to the difference between "can" and "may." "Can" indicates ability to do something, whereas "may" expresses permission to do it. According to most obligated-self accounts, there is a wonderful coincidence between innate capacities and social placement, between the "cans" and the "mays" of social life. According to exchanger-self views, position is achieved and assignment depends on motivation and training —although innate differences do play a role. In this view, there is always room at the top, and innate deficits in talent can be overcome through effort. We might call this extreme exchanger doctrine the "one percent inspiration, ninety-nine percent perspiration" school. It holds that you *can* do whatever you set your mind to; there are no *mays* about it. Following this line of reasoning, believers often heap opprobrium upon those who suffer low status, blaming victims of systems of obligation for the degraded social positions they cannot escape.[95]

Only the exchanger orientation puts such extraordinary emphasis on the idea of a level playing field, and no society presents its members with one, although some societies where exchange values predominate come closer to that ideal than others. Evidence flowing from recent civil rights and women's movements indicates that the United States is not as far removed from feudal and caste societies as its citizens would like to believe. Once these liberation movements had broken down a host of "may nots" that had masqueraded as "cannots," women and black people discovered how easily they could perform activities that once had been deemed beyond their capacity. Female and black doctors, lawyers, governors, and supreme court justices show that most activities that once appeared to depend only on innate ability in fact depended largely on permission.

One way to solve the problem of contradictions between evidence and belief is to retreat from the extreme meritocratic position and acknowledge that the social world is not an entirely open marketplace. Ralph Linton, who introduced the concepts of ascribed and achieved statuses, noted that "the majority of the statuses in all social systems are of the ascribed type and those which take care of the ordinary day-to-day business of living are practically always of this type." Based on his broad knowledge of scores of cultures, he especially noted, as have many other anthropologists, that "the ascription of occupations along sex lines is highly variable."[96]

In other words, although every society assigns statuses according to sex, the work attached to a status is not strongly related to physiological differences between the sexes. In one society women perform most of the economic functions while men perform spiritual work, spending most of the day in prayer.[97] In another society those functions are reversed. In one society the men dance and giggle and adorn themselves while the women bargain in the market. In another that work is reversed. One society has strict prohibitions against women and men doing each other's work. In another society there is hardly any differentiation.[98] What this variation tells us is that physiology has little to do with status ascription by sex: highly variable phenomena (ascription of occupations along sex lines) cannot be explained or caused by an invariable phenomenon (genetic differences between males and females).

Linton's view is the opposite of Aristotle's. According to Linton, nature has indeed designed an all-purpose tool like the Delphic knife for the ascribed statuses—those that are assigned according to a system of obligation. Stating this view in extreme terms, the behaviorist psychologist John Watson crowed, "Give me a dozen healthy infants, . . . and I'll guarantee to take any one at random and train him" to be able to enter any occupation "regardless of his talents, penchants, tendencies, abilities, vocations, and race of his ancestors."[99]

Maintaining Boundaries

Because humans are not morphologically different in ways that would determine the division of any but reproductive labor, societies must have other equally powerful ways to keep people in their places. In small relatively permanent settings where everybody is known to everybody else, such as Redfield's folk societies, and in small groupings, such as families, there is little problem: everybody usually shares ideas of what each person is and where he or she fits. But when societies grow, when markets bring strangers together, something else is needed. We thus find such boundary-maintaining mechanisms as the sumptuary laws enacted during the fourteenth and fifteenth centuries in England, which regulated dress and diet by rank, thereby marking status distinctions and preventing what the market was threatening to permit: a confusion of social place.[100] Although sumptuary laws were so contrary to free trade and markets that they did not last long, costumes have continued to reflect custom. Examples range from involuntary stigma, such as Hester's *A* in *The Scarlet Letter* or a prisoner's stripes, to such voluntarily marked garb as the zoot suit. People often invest in mink coats, for example, so they can appear to occupy places to which they aspire. Advice to "dress for success" follows a long tradition of expert instructions in the art of sartorial boundary crossings.[101]

But no society can long afford to have its important boundaries so easily crossed. To keep essential services flowing, people in statuses with obligations necessary to the day-to-day maintenance of life in a society must be confined by impassable barriers. Rape can be a powerful restraint. It is almost as common a theme in novels as romantic love and patriarchal power. Thomas Hardy's Tess, George Eliot's Hetty, and Paul Scott's Daphne all learned the hard way that if they did not love within the boundaries of their station, they would be raped or banished. Even Galsworthy's upper-middle-class tale includes a brush with spousal rape, as Soames makes a desperate attempt to possess Irene by forcing sex on her. Naylor's book, too, begins with a seduction that leads to banishment and ends with the fatal rape of a lesbian. These stories reflect and critique a society that uses rape to keep women in their places. Democratic Western societies seldom impose curfews and other restrictions, but women's vulnerability to rape accomplishes the same thing, which is one reason a major focus of the women's movement is on violence against women.

There are more effective, pervasive, and resilient means of restraining women than violence or dress restrictions. These are the myths about the differences between women and men that are attributed to nature and biology, but that are in fact part of the social construction of gender. They define what a woman is, where she may be, and where she may safely go. Current Western myths are a Victorian heritage. Some of the ideas they contain may reach back to antiquity; they are old wine. During the nineteenth and early twentieth centuries the particular definitions of sex and gender that contemporary Western cultures live by were poured into new bottles designed to complement ideas of the exchanger self. I shall close out this chapter by describing sociology's contribution to the ideas of gender that guide our lives.

Market success empowered the new business class exemplified by the Forsytes, but their burgeoning wealth could not buy what they craved above all else: high status. For that, they had to denounce old rigidities based on lineage (their origins were humble, not noble) and replace them with new certainties about human inequalities. Not God and the church, but nature and the academy, stepped in to grant authority to modern systems of obligation. Along with academics in the fields of biology, theology, education, and philosophy, some of the most impressive contributions to the cultural grounding of the new obligated self were made within the new field of sociology.

August Comte, originator of the term *sociology*, envisioned the field as a supreme and general discipline under which all the others would take their specialized places. Its mission would be to reveal the workings of society by applying to it the scientific methods that were working so well in the natural sciences. As did most other mid-nineteenth-century scholars, Comte assumed that the social world was guided by natural forces. Just as natural science begins by systematically observing and then explaining the physical world in order to manipulate and change it, the goal of sociology would be to observe and explain the social world so that "the order of things instituted by man" might "be simply a consolidation and improvement of the natural order."[102]

In his *System of Positive Polity*, Comte laid out the place of women in the natural order: "We find it to be a natural law that Woman should pass the greater part of her life in the family."[103] He also stated, "Different as the two sexes are by nature, and increased as that difference is by the diversity which happily exists in their social position, each is consequently necessary to the moral development of the other." [104] Woman, according to Comte, was naturally without self-interest: "In the most essential attribute of the human race, the tendency to place social above personal feeling, she is undoubtedly superior to man. Morally, therefore, . . . she merits always our loving veneration, as the purest and simplest impersonation of Humanity, who can never be adequately represented in any masculine form." [105]

For all women's moral superiority, Comte thought that their heads were full of air: "Women's minds no doubt are less capable than ours of generalizing very widely, or of carrying on long processes of deduction. They are, that is, less capable than men of abstract intellectual exertion." [106] Because their minds are deficient, women should, as Aristotle claimed centuries earlier, be subordinate: "Woman's life should be concentrated in her family . . . even there her influence should be that of persuasion rather than that of command." [107]

Comte was merely echoing the common and learned assessments of his day. [108] Later in the century, sociologists, most notably Gustav LeBon (the French founder of social psychology whose study of crowd behavior is still cited and respected), argued that intelligence was directly related to cranial size and that the differential between women and men increased with civilization:

> In the most intelligent races, as among the Parisians, there are a large number of women whose brains are closer in size to those of gorillas than to the most developed male brains. This inferiority is so obvious that no one can contest it for a moment; only its degree is worth discussion. All psychologists who have studied the intelligence of women, as well as poets and novelists, recognize today that they represent the most inferior forms of human evolution and that they are closer to children and savages than to an adult civilized man. They excel in fickleness, inconstancy, absence of thought and logic, and in incapacity to reason. [109]

Such myths harnessed women to the home and caregiving. These myths enjoyed hallowed treatment—as if they were as well founded as the theories that allowed other scientists to harness power from steam. Sometimes they were done up in numbers like LeBon's cranial measurements, but often, especially in the infant disciplines of psychology and sociology, which were just beginning to acquire experimental and statistical grounding, "casual observation, anecdote and folk wisdom" filled in where data was lacking. As Cynthia Eagle Russett notes, the state of their art was "readily apparent in the frequency of comments such as 'no one can question,' 'it is a matter of universal recognition,' and 'everyone admits.' "[110]

Lack of any real scientific basis did not weaken the power of these myths. Even Emile Durkheim, generally agreed to be among the brightest stars of sociology's founders, was taken in. So impressed was he by LeBon's measured skulls that he used them to support his own theory of the division of labor in society. This theory argues that as societies develop, differentiation increases. Durkheim's seminal case was sexual differentiation:

> The further we look into the past, the smaller becomes this difference between man and woman. The woman of past days was not at all the weak creature that she has become with the progress of morality. . . . Dr. LeBon has been able to distinguish directly and with mathematical precision this original resemblance of the two sexes in regard to the . . . brain. [He] has shown . . . that with the progress of civilization the brain of the two sexes differentiates itself more and more. . . . The difference which exists, for example, between the average cranium of Parisian men of the present day and that of Parisian women is almost double that observed between male and female of ancient Egypt. . . . Thus though the average cranium of Parisian men ranks among the greatest known crania, the average of Parisian women ranks among the smallest observed.[111]

There were some notable nineteenth-century dissenters—John Stuart Mill, for one, and Friedrich Engels, for another—but, by and large, the second half of the nineteenth century found almost everybody who was anybody agreeing that nature was as immutable a deequalizer as God ever had been. Cynthia Russett, Stephen Jay Gould, and several others have painstakingly gathered the evidence to prove that LeBon and his cohorts misused the paraphernalia of science to create the powerful myths of racial and sexual difference that formed the foundation of contemporary systems of obligation. The question is, why, at the dawn of science, was science so flagrantly abused?

The answer once again follows Martindale's maxim: the learned world will not overlook contradiction unless it has good reasons for doing so. The good reason for falsifying the evidence in order to restrict women and "lesser breeds" to positions in society that cater to human needs for care is that the exchanger view of the self and its social environment, the market, cannot meet these needs. As the household was converted from a relatively self-sufficient productive unit to one dependent on markets, as moral standards changed to make way for the exchanger, these scholars must have sensed the threat to life itself from a world peopled only by exchangers. Their powerful myths of racial and gender difference provided a social type that stemmed the upheaval accompanying the West's escape from feudalism and softened the agony of transformation from a feudal to an industrial society. Social theory spread the idea that nature itself demanded the new order, especially the separation of women and men into different social spheres.

Such individuals as Soames are a particularly modern type. They had no place in the feudal scheme, where a person's position in the family and the family's position in the larger society ordered life. Then, deviation from the path set by one's parents' rank—even imaginings of such things—was sacrilege. But technological change, such as the power loom that turned wool into a valuable exchange commodity, also turned almost everyone from their feudal obligations. The landed gentry proclaimed a new freedom to hedge the commons and expel peasants in favor of sheep.[112] Peasants, in turn, were freed from obligations to serve their lords. Cast from the commons, they became, in Karl Marx's words, "the untrammelled owner[s] of [their] capacity for labour."[113] With that freedom, the cornerstone of capitalism, they were able to exchange their labor in the marketplace. Often that meant weaving the lord's wool for starvation wages.

Be that as it may, the social order based on community, on obligation, and on the presumption of sacred inequality was on its last legs by the watershed year, 1776, when Adam Smith championed economic man. Although Smith had a larger view,[114] his legacy was an all-pervading, exchange-driven interpretation of social life. That theory meshed well with Charles Darwin's theory of biological evolution and with Herbert Spencer's concept of the survival of the fittest.[115] All these theories of human nature focused on self-interest and competition. They are not scientific theories. They are ethical theories, ideas not about what is but about what should be. They clothed moral prescription in scientific language, making it appear as though the qualities they wanted to sanction were the ineluctable human qualities nature demanded. Gain, writes Karl Polanyi, is "a motive only rarely acknowledged as valid in the history of human societies." Never before the nineteenth century was it "raised to the level of a justification of action and behavior in everyday life. The self-regulating market system was uniquely derived from this principle."[116]

Gain and self-interest achieved moral ascendance because those motives were in the self-interests of the developing entrepreneurial class and
also of those theorists who advanced such virtues. As the market took on
increasing importance, European men were increasingly governed by the
social order of exchange. European men also dominated the marketplace
of ideas. In such treatises as Comte's, men were assigned their place and
obligations as leaders of society and as natural competitors for places in
increasingly specialized labor markets. A new morality was invented so
that men would narrow their interests and motivations and become competitive and self-interested for the good of society. Women were assigned
their place in the family and were told that they could not be other than
altruistic, for that was their nature.

Such stories were told over and over again in evolutionary dichotomies that were very popular at the time. These were then-and-now tales
that contrasted the preindustrial with the industrialized world and that,
as Jessie Bernard noted, actually described the newly separated spheres
of women and men. Most of these social evolutionary theories postulated succession—replacement of one type of society by another. Thus,
they led us to believe that the Industrial Revolution effected a near-total
eclipse of one social order by another. They thereby helped to hide the
world of women, to make it invisible.

Even theories that argued most strenuously for complementarity between women and men conceded that the older forms were vestigial.
Sometimes the newer forms were praised.[117] Often the older forms were
mourned.[118] But whatever their moral disposition, these evolutionary
theories made the same underlying assumption: earlier communal social
orders—what I have been calling systems of obligation—had been overtaken and, according to some theories, virtually obliterated by the later
individualistic social systems—the market society.[119]

These descriptions of society before and after industrialization helped
to institute a new system of obligation, located in the family and link-
ing the family to the "all-important" market through the work of men.
A system of obligation with the family as its unit, with functions ascrip-
tively assigned, was designed so that men would devote themselves to the
market while women, free from the market's demand for scarcity, would
attend to the care of the young, the old, and those of ages in between
whose impaired capacities prevented their competition in the world of
exchange.[120]

As the market gained societal dominance, women's sphere maintained those aspects of human life that commercial markets, and social structures modeled after them, tend to ignore. The conception and social construction of the home as a sanctuary over which women presided, of woman as the bearer of a finer sensibility and morality, and of nurture as women's "natural" work, gave assurance that social life would be ordered so that essential actions that do not lend themselves to commercial exchanges would continue to be performed. As men (and some women, too) were inventing the mechanical, economic, political, and psychological machinery that would bring the world toward market domination, they also created that congeries of expectations and relationships called women's sphere. It was the vehicle that preserved a system of obligations in order to preserve life itself.

Moral differentiation accompanied this division of labor. The early nineteenth-century creation of women's sphere can be interpreted as the gendering and transformation of identities that paralleled the economic transformation from family or estate-centered production and local markets to industrial production and international self-regulating markets.[121] Psychic differences that psychologists have found between men and women reflect the different moralities of the exchanger and obligated-self orientations. Carol Gilligan's study of the different moral development of girls and boys presents these differences. She argues that boys develop a morality based on abstract principles while girls develop a morality based on relationships and responsibility for others.[122] Although these different moral developments tend to be associated with gender in the contemporary United States, they actually reflect the different moralities of the obligated self and exchanger self. Justice based on the equality of persons is a principle well suited to exchange, to a sphere of free and open competition exemplified by an image of Justice blindfolded so that she cannot see the particulars on her scales: she can only weigh them and find for balance. Justice based on differences in needs and in responsibilities is a principle on which the ethics of obligation rests.

Eighteenth- and nineteenth-century political revolutions proclaimed and established an equality of persons and a justice and morality that would be different from the justice and morality of monarchies, those families writ large. It was the equality of citizens. Regarding the state, all citizens would have equal rights, equal access to resources, and equal obligations. Since then, the modern state has grappled with the contradictions between citizen's equality and the different kinds of inequality connected with the ethics of exchange and the ethics of obligation—the class inequalities generated by markets and the natural inequalities of human biological difference.

We are not born equal. We are born with a broad range of strengths and weaknesses in our physical, mental, and psychological makeup—and we are born dependent. Without an ethic of protection and care, market-dominated societies would be depopulated in a lifetime, for there would be no social basis, neither motor nor motive to bring new generations to life and adulthood. Our natural dependency and inequality, along with inequalities stemming from markets, have forced citizens of the modern state to depart from nineteenth-century egalitarian and laissez-faire liberal roots in order to pass legislation that curtails the free play of markets (such as the graduated income tax and anti-trust legislation) and institute categorical protections (such as child labor laws).

Societies without strangers may get on without markets; but no society, not even one dominated by market exchange, can get on without a system of obligation that assigns caregiving responsibilities. Some analysts note the way many household functions have been turned into market processes. They point to such things as the clothes we no longer spin and sew at home but buy ready-made; the food prepared on assembly lines, not in kitchens; and the nursing homes that care for our elderly and infirm. These observers speculate that the functions remaining in the household stay there only because we have not yet devised the technology to turn them into commodities. But with the possibility of renting out wombs, now that fetuses can be transplanted and then gestated by women who are not their biological mothers, it should be evident that virtually all goods and services could be commodified.

An insufficient technology is not what preserves contemporary ideas of obligation. Systems of obligation are necessary because the market and modern technology cannot provide the moral grounding for relationships necessary for human survival. Paradoxically, advertisements for commodities often promise precisely what a commodity cannot provide: a place in society where you will be noticed, cared for, and, perhaps, be cared about as well. Advertising copywriters know what we want. Unfortunately, it cannot be bought.

Rational choice theorists contend that even the family is structured like a market where members balance costs and benefits. But, like Fichte's century-old explanation of a wife's "free" choice, their argument usually includes some presumption that the care motivated by obligation makes the caregiver feel good. They are right: we do feel better when we meet our obligations. Although social scientists have focused on loss of instincts and gain of linguistic capacity as the biological basis for the cultures and societies that make human survival possible, our emotional capacities are at least as important. Social systems are enforceable because we feel good when we act in concert with the moral precepts of our cultures and we feel bad when we do not. Because several moral systems operate simultaneously in contemporary societies, the precepts of one moral system frequently contradict the precepts of another. In his book *The Sociological Imagination,* C. Wright Mills explained what happens when moral systems lose their coherence: individuals become troubled, and they experience feelings of apathy and anxiety. Societies seem to fall apart.

When Mills wrote his book, at the close of World War II, it seemed that only one moral system was operating in the United States and that it had lost its power. What I am arguing here is that then, as now, more than one moral system directed our lives and their precepts often contradicted each other. From her study of several Native American cultures, Ruth Benedict concluded that cultures tend toward consistency, each one exhibiting a central ethos.[123] It may be that the difference between what we have been calling simple and complex cultures is that the first operate under a single ethos with one set of moral precepts, whereas in the second, several cultures and moral systems operate simultaneously. In most Western countries, as the culture of exchange gained ground, exchange and obligation became gendered, and exchange became the moral system to guide men's lives most strongly while obligation remained the moral system that guided women's lives most strongly. Before World War II, obligation remained a powerful system for men as well as women. That power was reflected in such social phenomena as stable nuclear families with low divorce rates, increasing quality of schools, and federal deficits that remained relatively low because it was argued that one generation did not have the right to impoverish the next. Following World War II, however, the strength of exchange grew so great that systems of obligation lost their power, especially in the lives of men.

Social movements are diverse and have many causes. The women's movement that gathered steam in the 1960s was fueled in large part by a decline in the power of the system of obligation. Young women in the civil rights and student movements complained that they were degraded and not accorded respect by the men in these movements. Betty Friedan reported that older middle-class women were complaining of a "malaise without a name."[124] It was similar to the lack of energy, the apathy, that

Mills thought many were feeling at the close of World War II. People lose moral energy when social support for their way of life, their moral system, is in decline.

Women, especially middle-class women, responded to the degradation they were experiencing by adopting the exchanger orientation. These women argued that if men were honored by doing well at their careers, then careers were what women needed, too. They got them, and many did well at them. But that has not solved the problem—not for most women, not for most children, and not for American society. What needs to be addressed is the system of obligation under which we still operate. Most systems of obligation define adulthood as a time when biologically maturing individuals take on responsibilities for the well-being of others. By pretending that we have no system of obligation, our society has, almost by default, developed an absurdity: the less well educated and emotionally mature a girl is, the more likely she is to be burdened by motherhood at a young age. Men, by contrast, are increasingly relieved of responsibility for the children they father. Nobody who thinks about this situation is happy with it. Hardly anybody recognizes that the problem is neither "raging hormones" nor people who won't "assume responsibility for themselves." The problem is a market morality that enjoys a strength far out of proportion to its contribution to the well-being and survival of the world's people.

Humans are flexible precisely because they are not hardwired with instincts. Our reliance on culture instead of instinct allows us to suit our values to our situation. Perhaps the system of exchange will weaken its hold enough to allow the creation of a new system of obligation, one that can complement rather than compete with the exchange orientation. Perhaps change will come from another quarter, from the orientation we often call spiritual. That orientation is the subject of the next chapter.

CHAPTER THREE

The Cosmic Self

MEISTER ECKHART, the fourteenth-century Christian mystic, envisioned a split between our corporeal body and our eternal, divine spirit, or soul. The body is debased, the soul is exalted; their conjunction, life, is a brief phase in the soul's wanderings, during which it resides in the body. In this vision, the soul is imprisoned, and life is a penance best endured by detachment from things of this world. "The soul," says Eckhart, "is not perfectly beatified until she casts herself into the desolate Deity where neither act nor form exists and there, merged in the void, loses herself; as self she perishes, and has no more to do with things than she had when she was not. Now, dead to self, she is alive in God."[1]

That view, still influential among some believers, has had rough sledding since the Enlightenment. Science, secularism, humanism, and rationality made such abstract ideas of God and the soul seem suspect at best, absurd at worst. How could the rational mind countenance a God, much less an eternal soul? Where was the proof, the empirical evidence that modern reason demands?[2]

An influential answer came from the Romantic Revival. Beginning in the last quarter of the eighteenth century, led by Johann Wolfgang von Goethe and Friedrich von Schiller in Germany, the movement spread through England and France. Its chief exponents were John Keats, Lord Byron, William Wordsworth, Percy Bysshe Shelley, Samuel Taylor Coleridge, and Sir Walter Scott in Britain, and André Chénier, Alphonse de Lamartine, Alfred de Musset, and Victor Hugo in France. Transcendentalism was its American cousin; Ralph Waldo Emerson its chief advocate.

Romanticism offered a cosmic vision of the self that could satisfy a post-Enlightenment culture. Rather than renunciation, its goals were a unity with nature achieved by tapping into the innermost core of one's being, there to find an infinite, universal voice. Emerson called this voice that "portion of truth, bright and sublime," that "lives in every moment to every man." Proof of its existence were brief glimpses of that "divine principle lurking within."[3]

This chapter groups under the rubric "cosmic self" conceptualizations ranging from ideas of renunciation to ideas of the self as an essential, unique core of one's being. At one extreme, exemplified by Eckhart, the self disappears into a higher order; at the other, exemplified by Emerson, the self appears as an inmost essence of a higher, spiritual order. In all versions, the self melds into something universal.

However a culture crafts its image of the cosmic self, every culture seems to have one. At least that is what anthropologists tell us. Perhaps the cosmic self answers a critical human need. Humans, along with losing instincts and gaining a capacity for language and culture, seem to have developed a need to imbue life with higher meaning. Perhaps we create cosmic selves for the same reason we create images of obligated selves: because we are mortal. The obligated self takes care of the practical and social work needed to replace one generation with another. Cosmic images ease the suffering of separation from things of this world by offering something eternal. Whatever the reason, a spiritual, otherworldly self that gives life and death their explanations and their value seems to be a cultural universal.

Like modern views of the obligated self, Romantic ideas of the cosmic self filled vacuums left by conceptualizations of the isolated exchanger self. The exchanger leaves a void where connection and emotion are needed—a vacuum revealed by a large literature on the modern psychic dilemma. Not only Max Weber's "sensualists without sensibility" and T. S. Eliot's hollow men (quoted at the close of Chapter 1) but also a host of philosophical and psychological works characterize the modern self as vacant, suffering from "ego loss" and "a sense of emptiness, flatness, futility, lack of purpose or loss of self-esteem." Such descriptions as René J. Muller's "Marginal Self," Robert J. Lifton's "Protean Man," Erich Fromm's modern man "escaping from freedom," Christopher Lasch's narcissist and "minimal self," and David Riesman's "other-directed" man typify this critique.[4]

Durkheim's theory of anomy provided an archetype for these analyses. Modern societies, he said, suffer chronic social anomy—a condition in which social guides and constraints are weakened, leaving the individual detached from society and the direction it provides. Before the modern era, "a whole system of moral forces" exerted discipline. But those forces prevented market formation and, over time, all institutions were subverted to the market. Government became a tool and servant of industry. So did religion, as it consoled poor workers, taught them contentment with their lot, and assured them that Providence had ordered their place in society and would reward them in a better world to come. Religion also helped constrain rich masters by reminding them "that worldly interests are not man's entire lot."[5]

Durkheim believed that the market was taking over the whole of life; its demands were becoming the dominating morality. Thus industry, "instead of being . . . a means to an end . . . [became] the supreme end of individuals and societies alike." Appetites, "freed of any limiting authority," were "sanctified" and placed "above all human law." Restraint became "a sort of sacrilege." Greed was aroused along with a thirst "for novelties, unfamiliar pleasures, [and] nameless sensations, all of which lose their savor once known. Henceforth one has no strength to endure the least reverse . . . and it is seen that all these new sensations in their infinite quantity cannot form a solid foundation of happiness to support one during days of trial." Further, "inoculated with the precept that their duty is to progress," men find it hard to "accept resignation." Thus, "the entire morality of progress and perfection" becomes "inseparable from a certain amount of anomy."[6]

Anomy, generated by freedom, lack of regulation, and the belief in infinite progress and human betterment, makes people search frantically for new pleasures, each of them barren once acquired. With nothing higher than the individual, nothing worth more than the next fad on the market, life itself loses its value, and suicides increase.

Durkheim was one of the first to analyze the contemporary dilemma in those terms; Charles Taylor is among the most recent. Taylor sees the problem as the democratization and leveling of values. In the modern world, many moral systems compete for our allegiance. We value such things as "rational mastery, or a rich conception of family life, or expressive fulfillment, or fame."[7] But, says Taylor, we need to make qualitative distinctions among competing values and to attribute greater importance to what he calls hypergoods. Hypergoods are "not only . . . incomparably more important than others," they "provide the standpoint from which [others] must be weighed, judged, decided about." They tell us what makes life worth living and answer the kinds of questions about the meaning of life that moderns, without hypergoods, consider sophomoric, confused, and irrelevant.[8]

Taylor believes that despair and psychological disorder are the price we pay for degrading values that once stood as hypergoods. Riches, or "questing after them," to use Hobbes's words, are surely not enough, but neither, according to Taylor, was the intense individualism of the Romantic movement. It allowed people to claim "an individual and private source of meaning as a basis for actions (the source of this meaning could be labelled as a genius, a vision, the imagination, a unique biography or collection of experiences) which was greater than the sum of meanings and actions justified by one's social obligations," but it did not provide a sufficient corrective to the Enlightenment.[9]

The Romantic movement is often interpreted as a reaction against the empty, icy indifference of the Enlightenment's free, disengaged self, which was guided by mind. Romantic conceptualizations of the self, like all cosmic conceptualizations, offered something more spiritual, something larger than the rational individual. Unlike the older, renunciatory cosmic conceptions of such oracles as Eckhart, the idea of the Romantic self meshed extraordinarily well with the exchanger self. Both the exchanger and the Romantic cosmic orientations are intensely individualistic, the Romantic cosmic even more so. Their chief difference is that while the exchanger self seeks riches as evidence of its worth and rights to recognition from others, the Romantic cosmic self seeks itself—that "ineffable something," that unique, original "abstract of . . . pure . . . natural laws."[10]

In addition, the Romantic version of the cosmic self offered an escape to the downtrodden from the pain of low class position and low status in a society that was increasingly coming to blame such misfortunes on individual faults rather than God's will.[11] Not only did the idea of an interior truth oppose the Enlightenment's insistence that truth is something objective and external to the individual—truth being *out there*—it also offered opposition to systems of obligation that sometimes made people seem to be nothing more than role-players or status enactors whose value was equal to their station. The "true self" was interior, not a mere enactor of roles.

John Gagnon makes the same point, saying that over the centuries following the French and American revolutions, an increasing number of persons felt that instead of being composed of a limited and coherent bundle of socially given roles that would change slowly over the course of their lives and being judged primarily by the competence of their public performances, [they] began to experience the relationships which they had with others, what we would call 'the roles that they were required to play,' as increasingly detached from or alien to whom they truly were or what they really wanted to be. A proto-self was being detached from roles, a proto-self that would change though not isomorphically, as the roles that were played changed, a self that would decide what was inside and what was outside, what was self and what was other.[12]

This self—interior, not reduced to social roles, obligations, or relationships but instead soaring to spiritual heights—became the subject that Americans have in mind when they say they are trying to "find themselves" or when they talk about their "real" or "true" selves. It is the strongest contemporary cosmic image of the self and is therefore the one I shall have in mind in the discussion that follows.

Siddhartha: The Last Romantic of the Western World

Whereas I picked *The Women of Brewster Place* and *The Forsyte Saga* out of many possibilities that presented themselves as illustrations of the exchanger self and the obligated self, Hermann Hesse's *Siddhartha* seems to be an obvious choice to illustrate the cosmic self. American ideas of the cosmic self are drawn from sources as diverse as the medieval traditions of Meister Eckhart, the religious traditions of the indigenous peoples of the Americas, various ecology movements, and Eastern religious traditions, especially Buddhism.[13] *Siddhartha* fits into the last category, Hesse having figured prominently in several of the West's twentieth-century infatuations with Eastern philosophies, most recently in the mid-1960s when his work gained a sizable cult following.[14] Steeped in two major sources of the American cosmic vision—German Romanticism and Eastern spiritualism—Hesse was well situated to bring them together. His parents were missionaries in India, and his maternal grandfather, also a missionary in India, was an accomplished linguist and scholar of Indian lore.

Siddhartha is an enigmatic, spiritual legend.[15] It tells the story of Siddhartha's search for Atman, the Only One. One possible reading is to interpret the book as a tour through the three unmixed visions of the self—the obligated self, the exchanger, and the cosmic self. Siddhartha, like Emerson, knows from the start that the unity he seeks can be found only "within the Self, in the innermost, in the eternal which each person carried within him."[16] His search begins in the world of the obligated self, in his parents' house, where "the handsome Brahmin's son grew up with his friend Govinda." From the vantage of an obligated orientation, Siddhartha appears to be close to his appointed station when the novella begins. He has passed through the lowest level, childhood, and is doing well at the second, the apprentice level: "Siddhartha had already long taken part in the learned men's conversations, had engaged in debate with Govinda and had practiced the art of contemplation and meditation with him."[17]

Siddhartha was, in short, the apotheosis of a young Brahmin. His father was happy because Siddhartha showed all signs of completing the course set for him. He was "growing up to be a great learned man, a priest, a prince among Brahmins." His mother was proud of her "strong, handsome, supple-limbed" son who greeted her with "complete grace." When he "walked through the streets of the town . . . love stirred in the hearts of the young Brahmin's daughters." Siddhartha "delighted and made everybody happy," just as a youth who fulfills all his obligations would.[18]

"But Siddhartha was not happy." He could see his life stretch out before him in this world of tradition and he "had begun to feel that the love of his father and mother, and also the love of his friend Govinda, would not always make him happy, give him peace, satisfy and suffice him." This world rotating round the daily cycles of offerings and ritual, revolving also around the generational cycles of succession, would not bring him peace. Even his father, "the blameless one," did not "live in bliss" but must "wash away his sins and endeavor to cleanse himself anew each day."[19]

Siddhartha decides to leave the world of his father, in which life is ordered by the authority of elders and the duty of youngers, where life as it will be repeats life as it had been. He approaches his father, asking permission to join the ascetics: "I wish to become a Samana." His father responds: "There is displeasure in my heart. I should not like to hear you make this request a second time." A showdown between generations begins. Through the night and into the next day, Siddhartha remains "silent with folded arms." Finally, his father, realizing that Siddhartha will stand thus until he dies, releases him: "You will go into the forest . . . and become a Samana. If you find bliss in the forest, come back and teach it to me. If you find disillusionment, come back, and we shall again offer sacrifices to the gods together."[20]

In the next chapter, Siddhartha joins the Samanas and experiences the renunciatory cosmic self. Much as Meister Eckhart might have recommended, he has nothing more to do with the things of the physical world. He fasts fourteen days, then twenty-eight days: "The flesh disappeared from his legs and cheeks. Strange dreams were reflected in his enlarged eyes. . . . Silently he crouched among the thorns. Blood dripped from his smarting skin, ulcers formed, and Siddhartha remained stiff, motionless, till no more blood flowed, till there was no more pricking."[21]

Even with the Samanas, even as he renounces all the things of the body, the cycles of life and his place in the world of the obligated self hold him back. Unsatisfied, Siddhartha and Govinda renew their quest. This time they seek out the true Buddha, Gotama, the Illustrious One, whose expression is "so full of goodness and peace." When they find him, they separate. Govinda joins the Buddha. Siddhartha continues on his own way. In terms of the structure of systems of obligation, Govinda remains at the middle level, always a follower. Siddhartha graduates to the uppermost level of systems of obligation and becomes fully adult. "Something was no longer in him, something that had accompanied him right through his youth and was part of him: this was the desire to have teachers and to listen to their teachings." Now his goal is "not to seek another and better doctrine . . . but to leave all doctrines and all teachers."[22]

At each turning point in his highly structured novella Hesse inserts a soliloquy through which Siddhartha reviews and critiques the road already taken. This device gives Hesse a chance to critique each view of the self that Siddhartha experiences. At this point, Siddhartha reviews the paradox of the renunciatory cosmic self. He "wanted to rid" himself "of the Self, to conquer it," but he "could only fly from it." And in those efforts "nothing in the world [occupied his] thoughts as much as the Self." He reasons that he remains ignorant of himself because "I was afraid of myself, I was fleeing from myself. I was seeking Brahman, Atman, I wished to destroy myself, to get away from myself, in order to find in the unknown innermost, the nucleus of all things." Then, bridging the renunciatory and the Romantic cosmic selves, he thinks: "I sought Brahman, I wished to dismember and unpeel my Self in order to find in its known interior the kernel of all shells, Atman, Life, the Divine, the Ultimate. But in doing so I lost myself." He looks around, and Hesse gives us a good whiff of German Romanticism when he has Siddhartha notice that "the world was beautiful, strange and mysterious. Here was blue, here was yellow, here was green, sky and river, woods and mountains, all beautiful, all mysterious and enchanting, and in the midst of it, he, Siddhartha, on the way to himself."[23]

This whisper of the Romantic cosmic self presages things to come. Ontogeny will repeat phylogeny as Siddhartha follows the historical path of Western cultures from a strict obligatory order to a renunciatory cosmic self to the exchanger, ending finally with a Romantic cosmic sense of the self. But regressions and portents occur along the way. Now, having parted from Govinda, Siddhartha will experience the exchanger self. First he must liberate himself completely from the world of the obligated self.

When the novella began, Siddhartha was just leaving the lowest rung, the place for children, and entering the middle level of a system of obligation. When he rejected Gotama and all teachers, he became an adult and entered the highest station his birth had ascribed to him. Now Hesse will free him entirely from obligations with a scene of rebirth. "I have indeed awakened and have only been born today," Siddhartha thinks as he begins another soliloquy:

> When he left the . . . grove of the Illustrious One, . . . it was his intention and it seemed the natural course for him after the years of his asceticism to return to his home and his father. Now . . . this thought also came to him: I am no longer an ascetic, no longer what I was, I am . . . no longer a priest, no longer a Brahmin. . . . Previously, when in deepest meditation, he was still his father's son, he was a Brahmin of high standing. . . . Now he was only Siddhartha. . . . Nobody was so alone as he. He was no noble man, belonging to any aristocracy, no artisan belonging to any guild and finding refuge in it, sharing its life and language. He was no Brahmin, sharing the life of the Brahmins, no ascetic belonging to the Samanas. Even the most secluded hermit in the woods . . . belonged to a class of people.

At that moment, with no obligatory status, Siddhartha "began to walk quickly and impatiently, no longer homewards, no longer to his father."[24] Book 1 ends here.

Unfettered, with no social place and no ties, Siddhartha is ready to enter the world of exchange. He passes a day and a night in contemplation. This is a liminal period between the world of following and the world of owning. Victor W. Turner is the contemporary authority on liminality. He follows Arnold Van Gennep, who first studied *rites de passage,* the ceremonies that accompany changes in status, such as confirmations, graduations, marriages, and funerals. These ceremonies have three phases:

the first phase, in which individuals are detached from their former status (when, for example, the father walks his daughter to the altar and leaves her there); the liminal period, when the passenger has no status, is no longer what she was and not yet what she will be (the moments at the altar); and the third stage, when the passengers have completed their journey and arrived at their new status (husband and wife leave the church).[25]

Siddhartha's liminal moments, which come between the different selves he experiences, occur by a river, which he crosses every time he travels from one self to another. Rivers are good metaphors for liminality, and many writers have used them that way. Rivers can be like mirrors, reflecting the image that looks into them; they are fluid; they follow a set course; sometimes they flow slowly and calmly, but sometimes they are turbulent; and they can carry passengers or drown them.[26] Now Siddhartha comes to the river and meets Vasudeva, the humble ferryman who, at the book's end, will guide him toward his final integration of selves. With Vasudeva, Hesse follows another Western literary convention—the true teacher will not appear to be a teacher; unlike the Buddha, who occupies the highest ranks, Vasudeva is a worker, a lowly boatman.

Siddhartha sleeps in the ferryman's straw hut by the side of the river. The next morning he asks the ferryman to take him across, ending this liminal period. Once again he is reborn, this time into the world of physical delights. His teachers are the courtesan Kamala and the merchant Kamaswami (both names are based on the Sanskrit root *kama,* meaning "love" or Kama, the god of desire).[27] At first Kamala rejects Siddhartha, telling him he "will need much money" if he wants to be her friend.[28] She introduces him to the rich merchant Kamaswami so he will learn how to obtain the things he needs—or, in terms of the images of the self that I have been developing, so he will learn to be an exchanger. Soon Siddhartha (who excels at everything he does) becomes rich enough to be Kamala's friend and lover. He adds constantly to his possessions: "Siddhartha had learned how to transact business affairs, to exercise power over people, to amuse himself with women; he had learned to wear fine clothes, to command servants, to bathe in sweet-smelling waters. He had learned to eat sweet and carefully prepared foods, also fish and meat and fowl, spices and dainties, and to drink wine, which made him lazy and forgetful. He had learned to play dice and chess, to watch dancers, to be carried in sedan chairs, to sleep on a soft bed."[29]

Siddhartha spends twenty years cultivating his senses, learning and enjoying their pleasures.[30] But gradually the exchanger's malaise, which

Durkheim and others identified, overtakes him. He feels distant from himself: "Like a player who plays with his ball, he played with his business, with the people around him, watched them, derived amusement from them; but with his heart, with his real nature, he was not there. His real self wandered elsewhere, far away." He slips farther away from the feelings of "glorious, exalted awakening," which he had experienced as a youth: "Slowly, like moisture entering the dying tree trunk, slowly filling and rotting it, so did the world and inertia creep into Siddhartha's soul; . . . made it heavy, made it tired, sent it to sleep. . . . Slowly the soul sickness of the rich crept over him. . . . the clear inward voice that had once awakened him and had always guided him in his finest hours, had become silent." When he had reached the summit of life as an exchanger, "the world had caught him; pleasure, covetousness, idleness, and finally also that vice that he had always despised and scorned as the most foolish—acquisitiveness. Property, possessions, and riches had also finally trapped him. They were no longer a game and a toy; they had become a chain and a burden."[31]

After a period of internal emptiness, reflecting the flatness, futility, and lack of purpose that so many other social critics have seen in the exchanger self, Siddhartha enters another liminal period. Thinking of how low he had fallen, he contemplates suicide as he wanders through the forest. Soon he reaches "the long river in the wood, the same river across which a ferryman had once taken him when he was still a young man." He sleeps, and upon awakening "he looked at the world like a new man. . . . Perhaps he had really died, perhaps he had been drowned and was reborn in another form." He thinks: "I stand once more beneath the sun, as I once stood as a small child. Nothing is mine, now I am beginning again like a child . . . Siddhartha was transitory, all forms were transitory, but today he was . . . a child—the new Siddhartha—and he was very happy."[32]

Here Hesse takes the opportunity to issue a soliloquy on the self Siddhartha was leaving, the exchanger. Siddhartha "had to go into the world, to lose himself in power, women, and money; . . . to be a merchant, a dice player, a drinker and a man of property, until the priest and the Samana in him were dead." Born again, Siddhartha is ready to move toward a final integration of selves. This culmination will take place by the river that "has many voices: the voice of a king, of a warrior, of a bull, of a night bird, of a pregnant woman and a sighing man, and a thousand other voices . . . the voice of Being, of perpetual Becoming."[33]

Having experienced the three kinds of self in isolation, Siddhartha is ready to live *on* the river, which suggests that the state to be achieved is a liminal one, a state of perpetual becoming, not being. This time Siddhartha will not reject his other selves. He will not destroy the exchanger, as he had the Samana. Instead he will bring his selves back to integrate them: "It was worthwhile listening to them [the mind and the senses,] to play with both, neither to despise nor to overrate either of them."[34] And, having cut himself off from the world of obligations, he must now return to that world as well.

Siddhartha's return to the world of the obligated self begins with the realization that he has not yet experienced love as "ordinary people" do. "He envied them the one thing that he lacked that they had: the sense of importance with which they lived their lives, the depth of their pleasures and sorrows, the anxious but sweet happiness of their continual power to love. These people were always in love with themselves, with their children, with honor or money, with plans or hope."[35]

Siddhartha's lessons in love will bring him back to the world of obligation, the world of generations. Unbeknown to him, Kamala had been pregnant with his son when he left her. When the boy is twelve years old, she goes with him on a pilgrimage and comes to the river where Siddhartha is living with Vasudeva. A snake bites her, and Siddhartha comes upon her as she lies dying. He learns that he has a son and promises Kamala that he will take care of the boy.

Fatherhood teaches Siddhartha the joys and pains of love. His son is a disobedient and angry adolescent, and it is not long before he flees. Siddhartha, having enjoyed love, suffers its corollary, loss:

Siddhartha . . . could not give up his son. He allowed the boy to command him, to be disrespectful to him. . . . Once, when the boy's face reminded him of Kamala, Siddhartha suddenly remembered something she had once said to him a long time ago. "You cannot love," she had said to him and he had agreed with her. He had compared himself with a star, and other people with falling leaves, and yet he had felt some reproach in her words. It was true that he had never fully lost himself in another person to such an extent as to forget himself; he had never undergone the follies of love for another person. He had never been able to do this and it had then seemed to him that this was the biggest difference between him and the ordinary people. But now, since his son was there, he, Siddhartha, had become completely like one of the people through sorrow, through loving. He was madly in love, a fool because of love. Now he also experienced belatedly, for once in his life, the strongest and strangest passion;

he suffered tremendously through it and yet was uplifted, in some way renewed and richer.[36]

Siddhartha's love of his son, however, is the smallest kind of human connection, a union of two. To experience the cosmic self, Siddhartha has to become one with the universe. His concluding integration begins with Vasudeva. "He told him now what he had never mentioned before, . . . he could tell him everything, even the most painful things."[37] Vasudeva leads Siddhartha to the river. There, the

> picture of his father, his own picture, and the picture of his son all flowed into each other. Kamala's picture also appeared and flowed on, and the picture of Govinda and others emerged and passed on. They all became part of the river . . . Siddhartha listened. . . . He could no longer distinguish the different voices. . . . They all belonged to each other . . . when he did not bind his soul to any one particular voice and absorb it in his Self, but heard them all, the whole, the unity; then the great song of a thousand voices consisted of one word: Om — perfection. . . . His wound was healing, his pain was dispersing; his Self had merged into unity.
>
> From that hour Siddhartha ceased to fight against his destiny. There shone in his face the serenity of knowledge, of one who is no longer confronted with conflict of desires, who has found salvation, who is in harmony with the stream of events, with the stream of life, full of sympathy and compassion, surrendering himself to the stream, belonging to the unity of all things.[38]

Siddhartha has reached a cosmic fulfillment. His smile is the smile of the Buddha, which reminds Govinda, who rejoins him at the end, "of everything that he had ever loved in his life, of everything that had ever been of value and holy in his life."[39]

Characteristics of the Cosmic Self

At the end of his pilgrimage, Siddhartha has become the apotheosis of a modern cosmic self. In the pages that follow, I shall use his character to explore several characteristics of the cosmic self. The first is a sense that the self is in a perpetual inward search for itself. This inward exploration finds an outward fulfillment in a oneness with the universe. Second, unlike ascetic versions of the cosmic self, which treat the physical world and especially the body as debased, Hesse's version, following the Romantic turn, glorifies nature and the body. The third characteristic of this cosmic self, however, seems to contradict this glorification of the body, for all things physical are bounded and the cosmic self escapes boundaries. At the end of its journey, the self flows into a dimension free of demarcation. Past, present, and future have no meaning. There are boundaries neither in space, nor in time, nor even in identity. Fourth, this liberation from boundaries evokes an equality unlike the equality of the market. There individuals have equal chances to succeed, free from the rankings of the obligated orientation. But cosmic equality comes from a universal melding that leaves no separate individual, no me, no you, no groups, no nations, no cultures, no societies. The final point is the goal of all quests of the cosmic self. What the cosmic self wants above all is an emotion, an ecstatic feeling of love that binds all, whose expression is the Buddha's smile. Sometimes this search leads to an intense self-absorption, as happened among the youth of the 1960s who adored Hesse, and among the flower children who took a shortcut to nirvana with drugs.

Inward and Upward

Siddhartha is divided between an outward search in book 1 and an inward search in book 2. At the start, Siddhartha knew that his search had to be inward. He pronounced "Om silently," sounding it "inwardly with the intake of breath, . . . he knew how to recognize Atman within the depth of his being, indestructible, at one with the universe." Just as Emerson said, "I find [God] in the bottom of my heart,/I hear continually his voice therein," Hesse writes that Atman dwelled "within the Self, in the innermost, in the eternal which each person carried within him." The holy books Siddhartha read, especially the Upanishads of Sama-Veda, "spoke of this innermost thing."[40]

Siddhartha, however, traveled outward to find the innermost—initially toward appearances and practices of renunciation, and later toward riches and other appearances of the successful exchanger. Hesse keeps him living at the surface in the first book. In the second, Siddhartha begins his inward journey. Now he determines to "only strive after whatever the inward voice commanded him . . . to obey no other external command, only the voice."[41]

Hesse was following a venerable Western tradition with this division between inward and outward journeys. Taylor locates its emergence with St. Augustine. More than a millennium before the Romantic movement,

Augustine introduced a "radical reflexivity" that in many ways parallels Siddhartha's discoveries as he searches for Atman. Knowing for Augustine became "particularized," in an "inner light" that cannot come "from the domain of exterior, public and common objects of knowledge and reason." What makes this view cosmic, rather than simply more of the same individualism, isolation, and aloneness that exchanger views of the self exemplified, is its goal: reflecting inward, one finds "something higher," something to revere. The "I" explodes into an ever expanding "we." "By going inward," Taylor explains, "I am drawn upward." For, "at the end of its search for itself, if it goes to the very end, the soul finds God."[42] Or, in Eastern terms, the answer to "Who am I?" is "Thou art That." The true self (Atman) is the ultimate reality. Truth is in each person waiting to be realized at the moment that selfhood is merged into the oceanic experience of That.

As nature replaced God in the modern West, this self acquired characteristics once considered properties of the soul. The self became a divine holding, something that we treat as a sacred object.[43] Emerson drew from Augustine.[44] He saw proof of a soul in the unique expression available to anyone who completed the inward search and found the voice that simultaneously expressed the self's originality and soared toward universality. This self, with its unique and sacred innermost thing, became a subject for new artistic and literary forms—portraits and biographies. Formerly, when history was told in kings' lists and when a person lived only through his function in an organismically conceived society, there was no way and no reason for an individual to think that his life or the life of anyone like him could be interesting enough to write about. As John Lyons notes, "an inner life did not exist, or if it did it followed patterns that were so universal as to be tedious."[45] But when Romantics invented a self that glowed with an inner light, character became interesting, and its unique nature became worth exploring.

That adoration of the self could have dangerous consequences. Durkheim recognized that the self that turned in on itself for holy light was subject to "egoistic suicide":

In societies and environments where the dignity of the person is the supreme end of conduct, where man is a God to mankind, the individual is readily inclined to consider the man in himself as a God and to regard himself as the object of his own cult. When morality consists primarily in giving one a very high idea of one's self, certain combinations of circumstances readily suffice to make man unable to perceive anything above himself. Individualism is of course not necessarily egoism, but it comes close to it; the one cannot be simulated without the other being enlarged.[46]

The paradox of the Romantic cosmic self is that by treating itself as a god, it may be driven by despair to destroy itself.

The Body, the Soul, and the Self

In some rough ways the three primary images of the self that I have been delineating reflect modern differentiations of the self into three parts —mind, body, and soul. The exchanger emphasizes mind, the obligated self emphasizes the body as a biological organism following its natural or God-given destiny toward genetic and generational survival, and the cosmic self emphasizes the soul, which can be found through exalted feelings.

Many cosmic orientations struggle with body-soul dualisms—tension between the material and the ethereal, between the isolation and separateness of the body and the soul's union with the universe. The body is mortal, the soul deathless; the body is time-bound, the soul is timeless; the body has height and weight, the soul is ethereal; the body is bounded by its skin, the soul is the all-one, without boundaries or dimensions. To achieve unity, renunciators negate the body, control it, and deny it its pleasures. Romantics, by contrast, treat the body as an avenue to the self.

When Siddhartha joined the Samanas, he took the renunciatory path. He "gave his clothes to a poor Brahmin . . . fasted fourteen days . . . twenty-eight days. The flesh disappeared from his legs and cheeks . . . the nails grew long on his thin fingers. . . . He lost his Self a thousand times and for days on end he dwelt in nonbeing."[47] At this point, "Siddhartha had one single goal—to become empty. . . . No longer to be Self, to experience the peace of an emptied heart, to experience the pure thought— that was his goal. When all the Self was conquered and dead, when all passions and desires were silent, then the last must awaken, the innermost of Being that is no longer self—the great secret!"[48]

His efforts, however, were not successful; no modern Western writer would imagine that they would be. Renunciation does not mesh with exchanger views of the self and therefore could not be a strong vision in the modern West. The market, after all, is about material things; in a world of renunciators there would be no market. The Romantic solution was to deny not the body but the body-soul dualism. By substituting the self for the soul, the body that had been "the lodestone of the soul" became "the altar of the self."[49]

Hesse catches that difference in one of the concluding scenes of his book. Siddhartha, having found the peace he sought, tries to explain this peace to Govinda. He picks up a stone from the ground and uses it to exemplify the natural world, whereupon it becomes a temple for the self: "This stone is stone; it is also animal, God and Buddha. I do not respect and love it because it was one thing and will become something else, but because it has already long been everything and always is everything. . . . I just love the stone and the river and all these things that we see and from which we can learn. I can love a stone, Govinda, and a tree or a piece of bark. . . . every wind, every cloud, every bird, every beetle is equally divine."[50]

The Romantic movement connected the quest for the soul within us to the Enlightenment's shift toward the secular, replacing God with nature. For Romantics ranging from the English Lake Poets, who sought inspiration in nature, to contemporary ecologists, goodness and nature have gone together. By becoming one with nature, either by accepting our responsibility toward the natural world or by locating ourselves in some bucolic idyll, the Romantic could achieve sublime elevation. The Marquis de Langle, for example, on a visit to the Lake of Thun, was carried away in typical Romantic ecstasy: "The day when I first saw this beautiful lake was almost my last: my existence was slipping from me; I was dying with *feeling*, with *delight*; I was falling into nothingness."[51] The Romantic period introduced the great "I." It was a time for italics and exclamation points. The aim was to dissolve, to leave the body just as Eckhart had earlier recommended, but now the self lost consciousness of itself as it gazed in awe and wonder at the vastness, the beauty, and the sublimity of a waterfall, a storm, or a lake.[52]

The Romantic cosmic orientation is full of exquisite moments when a nerve is touched that makes pleasure and pain one, when inwardness explodes into outward unity, and when intense immersion in the physical turns the corporeal into the spiritual. As the Romantic tradition reveled in contradiction and flouted logic, it more effectively escaped and counteracted the reason and rationality of the exchanger orientation.

Universal Oneness

We can better understand the shifts in conceptualizations of the self if we bear in mind that all ways of looking at the self are moral responses to constant human needs in the face of changing social and physical environments. In *Civilization and its Discontents*, Freud wrote of a feeling he said he never had but that his friend Romain Rolland told him about: "a sensation of 'eternity,' a feeling as of something limitless, unbounded—as it were, 'oceanic.' " This feeling, he added, "is a purely subjective fact, not an article of faith; it brings with it no assurance of personal immortality, but it is the source of the religious energy which is seized upon by the various Churches and religious systems, directed by them into particular channels, and doubtless also exhausted by them." The feeling, Freud speculated, comes from being attached to the mother and not being able at first to differentiate between oneself and her.[53]

Most developmental psychologists agree: the capacity to differentiate ourselves from others is not present at birth and must be developed. But if that is true, then, contrary to most contemporary wisdom, a sense of oneness is "natural" or at least preexisting, and the self-interested, competitive individuality of the exchanger self must be learned. This chicken-and-egg conundrum has moral consequences. If we think in exchange terms and consider self-interest the most basic human feeling, as most sociobiologists and most social scientists do, then actions that put the community first seem unnatural and can even be considered morally reprehensible. If, by contrast, we think in cosmic terms and believe that the soul is attached to some higher essence and authority, then narrow, self-interested behavior can be considered reprehensible. The current debate between "communitarians," on the one side, and those who emphasize individual rights, on the other, rests on these contrasting perceptions of the self.[54]

One indication that Romain Rolland's oceanic feelings may be ubiquitous is the sense of oneness with the universe that appears in virtually every culture. Often the feeling is expressed in organismic images that differ dramatically from the organismic images used to legitimate hierarchical systems of obligation. The latter emphasize rank and different social functions. The former see the universe as a single body, undifferentiated and cohesive.[55] Many religious ceremonies are designed to bring forth this sense of oneness. An example is the Christian ceremony of communion, in which believers become one with the body of Christ. Poetic images of this sense of oneness abound. Alexander Pope, for example, writes of a "vast chain of Being" in his "Essay on Man" and claims, "All are but parts of one stupendous whole,/Whose body Nature is, and God the soul."[56] Similarly, Emerson says in his essay "On Compensation," "The heart and soul of all men being one . . . His is mine. I am my brother and my brother is me."[57]

Oneness is a central image in *Siddhartha.* In his diary, Hesse says that wisdom "was nothing but a preparation of the soul, a capacity, a secret art of thinking, feeling and breathing thoughts of unity at every moment of life." Furthermore, he states, "Nirvana, as I understand it, is . . . the return of the individual soul to the All-soul." Like Siddhartha, Hesse went on a pilgrimage seeking "that source of life where everything had begun and which signifies the Oneness of all phenomena." His voyage to India convinced him that oneness, whatever it was and wherever it existed, would produce a harmonious condition in which every contrast and all opposing forces were finally resolved—there would be no boundaries; time would have no demarcation.[58]

Often, Western writers use time to exemplify the way different cultures and different moral orientations socially construct the objects they treat as material or spiritual. Hesse does that. In the discussion that follows, I shall do the same, using the cosmic construction of time to stand for the cosmic construction of all objects. In the exchanger orientation, time is linear; it can be spent and lost. Therefore it must be conquered, scheduled, and caged. In social orders structured by obligation, time is circular. Each day, each season, each year, or each generation repeats a round. These differences have been noted often by social scientists, who interpret them as differences between the time frame of industrialized societies and the time frame of peasant societies. Pierre Bourdieu, for example, reports that the Kabyle, a group of Algerian peasants, think of themselves as being "part of nature, immersed within it. . . . Submission to nature is inseparable from submission to the passage of time scanned in the rhythms of nature." They experience "profound feelings of dependence and solidarity toward" nature and are "indifferent to the passage of time which no one dreams of mastering, using up, or saving."[59]

Less frequently noted is the contrast between time, whether linear or circular, and timelessness that Annette B. Weiner considers in her study of women in the Trobriand Islands.[60] When Malinowski wrote about the Trobriand Islanders, he only briefly mentioned their mortuary ceremonies; he did not notice the women and the power they derived from the mortuary ceremonies.[61] In her research on the Trobriand Islanders in the 1970s, Weiner focused on the women. She found that Trobriand society is divided into two separate but articulating female and male domains. The "male domain is delimited by men's inability to control the ahistorical cosmic dimensions of time and space," which is a female domain. Males control the temporal world, while the women have a power that "extends beyond the social to concepts concerning articulation with cosmic and transcendental phenomena."[62]

The Trobriands are matrilineal and believe that the Baloma, the pure ancestral essence, is carried through women. Infants enter their individual lives imbued with the Baloma of their mother's Dala, or family line. Through the Kula (ceremonial gift-exchanging partnerships between men on different islands) and other exchanges, men manage the current relationships that guide individual passage through life. And through the So'i Sagali, the mortuary ceremony with its production and distribution of food and grass skirts, women manage the cosmic relationships that guide the spirit through birth and death. Thus, for the Trobriands, historical time, which is bounded by our own experience and what we can be told of the recent past, is controlled by men, but cosmic time, unbounded and told in timeless myths, is controlled by women. Men bring order to this life; women attach this life to the undifferentiated pool of all life.

Hesse is sensitive to all three conceptualizations of time: the cyclical generational time of the obligated self, the linear time of the exchanger, and the timelessness of the cosmic vision. His book begins with the regular patterns of time that respond to cyclical regenerative obligations: "When the customary time for the practice of meditation had passed, Govinda rose. It was now evening. It was time to perform the evening ablutions." Siddhartha leaves his father's house to escape "the cycle of time." And, later, when he is about to leave the world of the exchanger's clock, Siddhartha "reads a frightened script underneath [Kamala's] eyes and near the corners of her mouth, a script which reminded him of autumn and death." That night "he leaves the world of the exploited moment forever."[63]

In the last scene of Hesse's book, when Siddhartha is explaining his newfound peace to Govinda, he says: "The world itself, being in and around us, is never one-sided. Never is a man or a deed wholly Samsara or wholly Nirvana; never is a man wholly a saint or a sinner. This only seems so because we suffer the illusion that time is something real. Time is not real, Govinda. I have realized this repeatedly. And if time is not real, then the dividing line that seems to lie between this world and eternity, between suffering and bliss, between good and evil, is also an illusion."[64]

The river conveys timelessness for Hesse, and again he draws this metaphor from traditional Western river images. Authors as diverse as Heraclitus, Thomas Wolfe, Marcel Proust, T. S. Eliot, Thomas Mann, and William Faulkner all felt the tyranny of time and all used rivers as symbols of timelessness.[65] The river, says Siddhartha, "is everywhere at the same time—at its source and at its mouth, at the waterfall, at the ferry, at the rapids, in the sea, in the mountains—everywhere, at the same time . . . for the river there is only the present, without the shadow of a future. . . . Nothing was, nothing will be, everything has reality and presence."[66] Whether it is time, or rivers, or lives, or bodies, or stones, everything that the Romantic cosmic orientation constructs becomes everything else; all divisions and distinctions are illusions.

Equality

If selves, like rivers, are everywhere at the same time, there can be no differentiation, and thus no inequality. Taylor contends that a critical issue for contemporary societies is our "respect for the life, integrity, and well-being, even flourishing, of others." What "separates contemporary societies from others," he says, "is that most [other] societies have set boundaries around those to whom these demands apply . . . for most contemporaries this class is coterminous with the human race (and for believers in animal rights it may go wider)."[67]

Markets dismantled many feudal boundaries; consequently, market societies are more open than the ones they superseded. But the market created new differentiations—differentiations of merit. These Hesse wants to dismantle. In his final chapter, he has Siddhartha idealize "the ordinary people" and wish to become like them. At the book's opening, Siddhartha had been as fine a specimen of young manhood as anyone could be. He was a Brahmin—beautiful, obedient, and bright. Among the Samana he gained total control over his body, and with Kamala and Kamaswami he became a perfect player in games of love and exchange. He excelled at everything. But his excellence was a separation; it prevented him from finding oneness: "too many holy verses, too many sacrificial rites, too much mortification of the flesh, too much doing and striving" had filled him with arrogance. He "had always been the cleverest, the most eager—always a step ahead of the others, always the learned

and intellectual one, always the priest or the sage." Through love of his
son he becomes like the "ordinary people" and they become

> his brothers. Their vanities, . . . desires and trivialities no longer seemed
> absurd to him; they had become understandable, lovable and even worthy
> of respect. There was the blind love of a mother for her child, the blind
> foolish pride of a fond father for his only son. . . . All these little simple,
> foolish, but tremendously strong, vital, passionate urges and desires no
> longer seemed trivial to Siddhartha. For their sake he saw people live and
> do great things, travel, conduct wars, suffer and endure immensely and
> he loved them for it. He saw life, vitality, the indestructible and Brahman
> in all their desires and needs.[68]

Only when he is without hierarchy can the love and peace of the cosmic
self begin to invade Siddhartha's being. Freed from the pride of perfection by his failure as a father, Siddhartha approaches the last lap of his
pilgrimage. In Hesse's coda, all boundaries will fall, and all will be one.

Love and Ecstasy

If oneness with the universe is the goal, then love is the way. This love
is different from the generative love invented to replace duty when the
ancient system of obligation was reconstructed to guarantee new generations for market society. When Hesse says "my Siddhartha puts not cognition, but love in first place," he did not have daisy petals in mind. The
oceanic feeling that Freud wrote about—a feeling that, in Hesse's words,
"makes the experience of unity the central point"[69]—is the love found in
cosmic visions of the self. In Siddhartha's final liminal period, as Govinda
left, "Siddhartha watched him go. He still loved him, this faithful anxious friend. And at that moment, in that splendid hour, after his wonderful sleep, permeated with Om, how could he help but love someone and
something. That was just the magic that had happened to him during his
sleep and the Om in him—he loved everything, he was full of joyous love
towards everything that he saw. And it seemed to him that was just why
he was previously so ill—because he could love nothing and nobody."[70]
Siddhartha's love is more peaceful than the Marquis de Langle's ecstatic ascent into nothingness at the sight of the Lake of Thun, but their
emotions spring from the same Romantic soil.[71] Goethe's *The Sorrows of
Young Werther,* published in 1774 and immediately translated into French
and English, helped bring on Romanticism's fevered pitch. Werther pro-

vided an archetype for an age that rejected the Enlightenment's faith in reason and replaced it with belief in sensitivity as the noblest human endowment. Werther was a man of exceptional sensitivity. He soared to extravagant ecstasies and sank to the depths of fatal melancholy, destroying himself in the despair of unrequited love. His sighs, passion, and gloom ushered in a period of intemperate emotion. Displays of feeling became badges of value. Such excess embarrasses us these days, when stress is the condition about which we simultaneously complain and feel pride. But scenes of teenagers at a concert, or of cult members literally giving their all to a leader, suggest that every culture, even one bathed in reverence for rationality, offers avenues for ecstatic loss of self.

Of the three primary Western images of the self, perhaps the obligated self and the cosmic self are universal archetypes, appearing in all or almost all cultures. That would not be surprising, for every society has to invent a way to make sure that one generation will be generous toward the next, and we humans seem to need some spiritual idea of what life is all about. Sometimes we honor the priests and artists who construct these ideas, for their visions of the self and of morality enable human societies to adapt to the very changes in the social and physical that life in social and physical environments engenders.

These three primary constructs of the self and morality—the obligated self, the exchanger, and the cosmic self—combine in ideas of the gift to develop three compound ideas of self and morality. Each of these constructs would have us imagine the different kinds of boundaries around the self that I shall explore in the next chapter.

CHAPTER FOUR

Gifts, Boundaries, and the Blended Images

DURKHEIM SAYS THAT SOCIETIES BUILD "imaginary walls" and "contrived boundaries" to regulate social life.[1] In modern societies, each orientation to the self constructs a different boundary within which a moral system operates. Within each boundary there are rules people accept as legitimate—rules that stipulate how different kinds of people are to act and to be treated and also who may or must be included within a boundary and who may or must be excluded.

When people view humans as exchangers and little else, they usually try to make a simple thing of the boundaries of the selves: in time, I begin at birth and end at death; in space, my skin marks my perimeter. But other boundaries of the self are not as simple as that. All the other orientations to the self trace wider boundaries and give greater attention to our incorporation in and dependence on the biological and social fabrics that precede us and continue beyond our individual lives.

At the extremes are the exchanger orientation, which would have us erect a boundary just around ourselves, and the cosmic orientation, which would have us break down all boundaries. Between the most narrowly drawn boundaries of the exchanger self and the boundlessness of the cosmic self are the ever more inclusively drawn boundaries of the reciprocating self, the obligated self, the called self, and the civic self. All these images, with their more and less inclusive boundaries, are part of our repertoire of selves, our palette of possible moral attitudes from which we paint our ever changing social landscapes. This chapter is about the blended images—the reciprocating self, the called self, and the civic self. The literature on the gift will help to delineate these images because gifts are often used to mark boundaries of the self. That is, they mark off the social locations where I end and you begin.

Lewis Hyde's *The Gift: Imagination and the Erotic Life of Property* contrasts art as a gift with art as a commodity. In it, Hyde distinguishes between trade in gifts, which he calls eros trade, and trade in commodities, which he calls logos trade. He argues that eros trade erases boundaries while logos trade erects boundaries. Hyde wants us to imagine that as objects change hands they move between two territories. If the object is a gift, it abolishes any existing boundary. If the object does not remove a boundary, then it is not a gift. A commodity, by contrast, "will often establish a boundary where none previously existed (as, for example, in the sale of a necessity to a friend)." He adds that "commodity exchange will either be missing or frowned upon to the degree that a group thinks of itself as one body, as 'of a piece.' " And he points to the "double law" in the Old Testament, which "prohibits the charging of interest on loans to members of the tribe while allowing that it may be charged to strangers. . . . Such a law asks that gift exchange predominate within the group (particularly in the case of needy members), while allowing that strangers may deal in commodities (money let out at interest being commodity-money or stranger-money)."[2]

If we think of gifts and commodities as indicators of the orientation that prevails, then Hyde is telling us what happens to our orientations when we engage in commodity exchange or gift exchange. When we buy or sell an object, when we act as exchangers, we erect a boundary around the self, defining what is me and what is you through what is mine and what is yours. But when we give gifts, we break down those boundaries and create, instead of me and you or mine and yours, us and ours.

Sometimes people think of the different boundaries of the self in terms of concentric circles, like the circles a stone makes when thrown into a pond. Hyde writes that he finds it useful to think of the ego "as a thing that keeps expanding": "An ego has formed and hardened by the time most of us reach adolescence, but it is small, an ego-of-one. Then, if we fall in love, for example, the constellation of identity expands and the ego-of-one becomes an ego-of-two. The young lover, often to his own amazement, finds himself saying 'we' instead of 'me.' Each of us identifies with a wider and wider community as we mature, coming eventually to think and act with a group-ego which speaks with the 'we' of kings and wise old people."[3]

Heilbroner writes in similar terms, but his point is that even the "we" of kings and wise old people has limits. He believes that "the capacity to empathize widens and becomes ever more discriminatingly applied as the child grows older," but that there is a limit at the edge of every culture

> beyond which this general identificatory impulse is blocked. This limit divides those within a society from those beyond it, and demarcates the members of a group among whom a shared concern exists, even though the members may be unknown to one another, from those for whom no such concern is felt. . . . The child divides the world into two—one comprised of its original family and its subsequent extension of that family; the other of non-familial beings who may exist as human objects but not as human beings with whom an identificatory bond is possible. These same attitudes persist in the political phenomenon of "peoplehood," a phenomenon we find in every culture, ancient and modern.[4]

In the terms I am developing, Hyde and Heilbroner are describing the shifting boundary of the ego as it expands from the exchanger orientation of one to the obligated orientations, first of two and finally of a nation.

Heilbroner notwithstanding, people have imagined the boundary expanding even further as the sense of the self shifts toward the cosmic. It was from such a cosmic orientation that the biblical prophets created the Hebrew idea of a universal God. And it is with just such an amorphous cosmic sense of self that some scholars think we begin our lives. Contrary to Hyde's analysis, maturation from this point of view may be a process of contracting boundaries. This is Freud's view. According to Freud, a spiritual, oceanic sense of oneness emanates from infants' initial connection to their mothers. We begin life with no sense of an individual self or existence. Through maturation humans achieve separation.

Durkheim had a similar belief: that the collective conscience, a cosmic feeling of oneness with a group, is primary and that individualism is built on the trust engendered by the incorporation of the self into a collective identity. He was projecting a oneness not with a single other—parent or lover—but with society itself. Durkheim was probably a better historian than Hyde or Heilbroner, and Freud may have been following the principle that ontogeny repeats phylogeny, for Taylor tells us that before the seventeenth century, when the idea of a social contract was introduced, the question of how the community came to be was simply not an issue. The existence of the community was taken for granted. The big innovation of contract theorists from Grotius on, he says, is that they do wonder how the community began: "Previously that people were members of a community went without saying. It didn't need to be justified relative to a more basic situation. But now the theory starts from the individual on his own. Membership of a community with common power of decision is now something which needs to be explained by the individual's prior consent. . . . People start off as political atoms."[5]

From these different assumptions about what comes first flow different approaches to such moral issues as altruism and selfishness. Theories of the social order that emanate from an exchanger perspective assume that people begin as political monads. They argue that societies are generated by the willingness of individuals to give up some autonomy in order to satisfy basic needs—for security (Hobbes) or prosperity (Locke). As in any contract, the individual gives in order to get. Most other theories of the self assume the opposite—the separating out of individuals from a common center.

John Hewitt divides social theorists into two types, the optimists and the "pessimists." He imagines that they stand at either end of an axis of variation in American culture. At one pole are the pessimists, who tend to be historians, sociologists, and social critics. Hewitt lists Christopher Lasch, David Riesman, and Robert Bellah among them. They assume a more cosmic self at first and a society that forces contraction. For them, society is an essential source of support and nurture for the individual. They believe that society is in decline and that in the past, "a more stable social order produced individuals whose lives were bounded by tradition and community, who were not keenly self-conscious, whose identities were secure, and whose perceptions of self were shaped by institutional involvements and commitments." In the terms I am developing, these pessimists favor the orientations of the cosmic self and obligated self, but they believe that these orientations have given way to the exchanger self. At the other pole are the optimists. They tend to embrace exchanger orientations, believing that the more collectivist orientations constrain the individual. Among this group Hewitt lists nineteenth-century advocates of the "mind cure" and more recent "humanistic psychologies." He includes promoters of "positive thinking" and followers of Carl Rogers's psychology of self-actualization. These theorists are convinced that "rugged individualism" and a "new form of human consciousness will lead to the 'greening' of America." The self is "celebrated as having the potential not only to achieve whatever it seeks but also to triumph over society's attempted domination of it."[6]

Among early sociologists, Comte would be Hewitt's optimist, Durkheim his pessimist. Their differences can be demonstrated in their views on altruism. Comte, who coined the term *altruism* in addition to the term *sociology*, used a variant of *autrui* from the French, or *alter* from the Latin, to counterpose ideas of the self and the other. Even if the individual acts in another's interests, these roots emphasize that two distinct actors, the self and the other, are involved.[7] Accordingly, for Comte altruism is "the feeling which prompts the sincere and habitual desire of doing good . . . the benevolent impulse . . . universal love . . . social sympathy [and] . . . living for others." Progress and social evolution "must consist above all in the development of altruism."[8]

For Durkheim, however, "altruism" denotes a melding of the self in the commonality so that there is no distinction between self and other.[9] Unlike Comte and the optimists, who take off from an individualistic, exchanger model of social interaction, Durkheim took the collective as his starting point and found "false . . . the theory which makes egotism the point of departure for humanity and altruism only a recent conquest." In his view, altruism is the fundamental basis of society: "Because the individual is not sufficient unto himself, [and] it is from society that he receives everything necessary to him, . . . [h]e becomes accustomed . . . to regarding himself as part of a whole, the organ of an organism."[10]

According to Durkheim, man is a moral being only because he lives in society. Thus morality for Durkheim, as for Comte, involves solidarity within the group, but for Comte it is something that must be developed from an individualistic base, whereas for Durkheim it is something that must be protected from the attacks of a too-individualistic, highly differentiated society that is in danger of losing a solidarity grounded in mutual dependency.

Taylor makes an interesting point concerning these differences. Selfhood and morality, he says, are "inextricably intertwined themes." Every society has the idea that "human beings command our respect." However, the "boundary around those beings worthy of respect may be drawn parochially," as he claims they were in earlier cultures, but "among what we recognize as higher civilizations, this always includes the whole human species."[11] He goes on to say: "What is peculiar to the modern West among such higher civilizations is that its favoured formulation for this principle of respect has come to be in terms of rights. . . . [T]hese are rights *under* law, . . . [our] concurrence is now necessary, . . . [now it is possible to] waive a right, thus defeating the immunity. This is why Locke, in order to close off this possibility in the case of his three basic rights, had to introduce the notion of 'inalienability.' "[12] Here I would disagree with Taylor and join Hewitt's pessimists. They emphasize that the modern West draws the boundary not least parochially but most parochially. That is why it must invent the idea of contracts to create community and also the laws of rights to protect individuals from the group with which they have no sense of oneness.

Boundaries and Gifts

A rich literature compares gifts with commodities and gift-based relationships with exchange-based relationships. One weakness in that tradition, a fault I have been trying to avoid throughout this book, is that it contrasts the exchanger (and his commodities) with all other conceptualizations of the self (and their gifts). The exchanger has center stage, while the wide variety of images considered as gift relationships hover in the background. They are discussed primarily in terms of the one similarity among them, namely, that goods and services change hands in ways unlike commodity exchanges.

Although the exchange of goods and services plays a central role in exchanger views of the self, the exchange of goods and services is a minor feature in most of the world's moral systems. Polanyi, who tried to explain the two massive world wars of the twentieth century, was struck by the centrality of markets in modern society. He observed that until the modern period, social relations were marked by an "absence of the motive of gain; . . . absence of the principle of laboring for remuneration; . . . absence of the principle of least effort; and especially, the absence of any separate and distinct . . . economic motives."[13] The point he was making applies to all current views of the self aside from the exchanger view: in them economic life is enmeshed in social relations; economic advantage alone can never justify social action. Other views do not perceive the world as an environment focused on exchange economics, nor are their moral systems designed to accommodate market relationships.

In order to see the variety of other orientations to the self that still hold sway in the modern world, I have tried throughout this book to de-center the exchanger view. In this chapter I continue that effort with a discussion of the three most commonly discussed gift relationships and their correspondence to three orientations to the self that blend characteristics of the primary orientations. The texts I shall use in the following discussion of combined types are Bronislaw Malinowski's *Argonauts of the Western Pacific,* Marcel Mauss's *The Gift: Forms and Functions of Exchange in Archaic Societies,* Richard Titmuss's *The Gift Relationship: From Human Blood to Social Policy,* and Lewis Hyde's *The Gift: Imagination and the Erotic Life of Property.* Malinowski and Mauss describe what I call the "reciprocator" or "reciprocating self," Hyde describes the "called self," and Titmuss describes the "civic self."

The reciprocating self combines features of the exchanger and the obligated-self orientations. In the United States at this time, the reciprocating self comes to the fore most notably in friendship relationships. The called self combines features of the cosmic self and the obligated self. Its characteristics are usually invoked when we think of artists and religious devotees. The civic self combines features of the cosmic self and the exchanger and is the orientation to the self that was invented in ancient Greece and adapted to modern democracies over the past few centuries to allow and demand behaviors we call good citizenship.

The Reciprocating Self

Contemporary Western images of the gift relationship begin with the work of two anthropologists, Marcel Mauss and Bronislaw Malinowski. It is to them that almost everybody turns for a point of departure when they want to write or think about the gift. Mauss used many ethnographies in his influential analysis of gift exchange. One was Bronislaw Malinowski's description of the Kula Ring on the South Sea Islands near the eastern tip of New Guinea. There, trading partners exchange two types of ceremonial gifts—large white shells that can be worn like bracelets around the upper arm and necklaces made of small flat red shells. These articles, of great symbolic but no practical value, circulate in opposite directions around a wide ring of islands. The bracelets travel counterclockwise, and the necklaces travel clockwise. This exchange signifies a great deal about the trading partners' social standing. It also permits them to trade in commodities.[14]

Malinowski, and others since him, were drawn to examine the Kula Ring trade because it was so different from commodity exchanges. The most important difference, one that is mentioned in virtually every analysis of the gift, is the "deep tendency to create social ties through exchange of gifts."[15] These are not the foreordained ties of systems of obligation nor the loose, superficial, ad hoc connections of exchange. Gifts are needed in most societies because exchange leaves people too much alone, and because systems of obligation bind people with ties too permanent to permit exchange relationships. Reciprocity offers something between the ad hoc isolation of exchange and the narrow confines of obligated-self relationships. It draws features sometimes from the exchanger view, sometimes from the obligated-self orientation, and sometimes from both, creating a new concept in its combination of characteristics.

To illuminate friendship and reciprocity, I shall draw on a remarkable correspondence conducted for a little more than a year between two poets, Leslie Marmon Silko and James Wright. They met twice, once at a writer's conference three years before the correspondence began, and again when Silko visited Wright as he lay dying of cancer. Except for these two meetings, their entire friendship is on paper. Thus their correspondence, published in a book called *The Delicacy and Strength of Lace*, provides a rare window into the process through which a friendship builds. The first letter was from Wright to Silko:

Misquamicut
Rhode Island
August 28, 1978

Dear Mrs. Silko,

I trust you won't mind hearing from a stranger. Not entirely a stranger though. About three summers ago I heard you read some stories and poems at that national poetry conference in Michigan. At that time I realized, like everybody else who was present, that your reading brought us all into the presence of something truly remarkable. Since then, I've read your work in some anthologies, always with the same feeling. . . . I could call *Ceremony* one of the four or five best books I have ever read about America. . . . my very life means more to me than it would have meant if you hadn't written *Ceremony*. . . . I am very happy that you are alive and writing books.

Sincerely,
James Wright [16]

"Your letter came," Silko responded, "at a time when I needed it most. So many sad things have happened with my marriage and my children—it is good to know that my work means something." [17]

Wright's note was a precious gift. At a time when some of her family ties had unraveled, another poet wrote to initiate new ties and to offer her *a place* in the world of poets. From systems of obligation, reciprocity takes the idea of statuses, or places in society. Reciprocity locates people socially. The power of reciprocal relationships to locate the self, however, has an ingredient of individual creativity that is taken from the exchanger self. Whereas systems of obligation work from a preset organismic society-wide model of statuses into which people fit themselves or are placed by others, friends construct social space for each other. Friendship, and to some extent all forms of reciprocity, creates the places it fills.

But friends walk on eggs. Friendships, like exchange relationships, are voluntary, so we must always try to please our friends. Unlike positions in hierarchical systems of obligation, where persons are placed by birthright more often than by any other criteria, the places in reciprocal relationships are earned. We cannot relax or be as "at home" in a friendship as we often are in obligated-self relationships. An obligated self, if he is a couch potato, can drink beer and watch the tube, or, if it is her pleasure, she can pad around in scuffs and curlers. At-home folk are obliged to put up with whatever we are—we are all that they have to fill the slot we occupy.

Silko and Wright were very careful of each other. Each letter gave thanks for the one it answered; often the writer apologized for not writing sooner or better, and they always let each other know how important the letters were. Characteristically, even after almost a year of letters, Silko says: "The poems you sent were so filled with your special wonder and the sound of peace you find in evening light, I wanted surely to have a letter waiting for you when you reached New York, but like the lizard, I didn't. If I couldn't have the time I needed for a letter to you, then I wouldn't write. I think I trust your understanding in this. . . . I promise you an altogether better letter next time, Jim." [18]

Emerson said that friendship "treats its object as a god, that it may deify both." [19] The Silko-Wright correspondence exemplifies this. In his third letter, written after Silko had sent him some poems, Wright wrote of finding the "proper ceremony" for his life: "I hope you'll forgive me for appropriating that word [the title of her novel] . . . but . . . I need it." The ceremony, he tells her, is one of rising early and pondering for a few hours. Since receiving her poems he says he has been spending those morning hours reading her work and her letter. With words like *ceremony* and with the early morning ritual he established, Wright created a sacred place for their friendship. Their letters resound with reverential praise:

Wright to Silko
October 12, 1978

As you wrote with something like absolute finality in "Storyteller," it is essential that the story be told, and that someone go on telling it. I don't think it's mere flattery to tell you that no living writer known to me so deeply grasps that truth, and its significance, as you do. I know I need that truth, and your clarification of it, and I am very far from being the only one.[20]

Praise lets the spirit grow. Praise from someone you admire, someone already located where you would like to be, someone who can bring you into his territory, is a special treasure. "I have to guard against my tendency to feel like I am an outsider, that I don't belong to the current American writing scene," writes Silko. "But I trust your voice, just as I trust a few others."[21] Even when we fit the place, we may feel unworthy of the haven that a friend builds. But friendship takes care of that; it makes both partners equal to the places offered. Wright praises Silko, and the very praise inspires her: "I never know what will happen when I write a letter," says Silko. "Certain persons bring out certain things in me."[22]

Systems of obligation have a place for everyone and the means to keep people in their places. They are neat that way. Reciprocity, like exchange, is messy. Not only do people have to construct the places they will fill, but usually achievement rather than ascription decides who will enter a position. Like exchangers, reciprocators are fluid characters who can voluntarily change their alliances. Americans often praise people who, exhibiting the steadiness that systems of obligation require, maintain their old friendships in spite of rising fortunes. The underlying belief is that only snobs drop old friends as they climb social ladders. Research indicates, however, that friends tend to be on a par. The nature of friendship and reciprocity, which demand equality, usually forces climbers to drop friends who don't keep up.

Probably the most important feature in reciprocity is the balance that friends work hard to maintain. If they fail to preserve balance, the relationship may slip into one of the two primary constructions of the self whose features reciprocity combines — the exchanger or the obligated self. From the exchanger orientation, the idea of the reciprocator takes notions of equality, merit, and fluidity. As exchangers, we talk of "level playing fields" and "equality of opportunity." The equality of exchange is a faceless thing — people are equal the way currency is equal and, like coins and bills, persons may have different denominations or specialties, but one teacher or bricklayer is exchangeable for any other. When we come to the equality of reciprocity, we see that it draws a leveling quality from the exchanger view of the self, but combines this quality with the particularity of the obligated self. One friend cannot be easily replaced with another.

Silko and Wright made subtle but constant efforts to establish equality. They were, however, not equal. She was young, he middle-aged; she a woman, he a man; she early in her career, he established; she at the close of a marriage, he in a good marriage. Sometimes he advised her, almost as a teacher advises a student. Sometimes they grappled with their age difference of twenty or so years. She said that he reminded her of her grandfather. He pointed out that a fellow poet, Larry Woiwode, was "roughly your age, perhaps a couple of years older."

In many ways they were better suited to be mentor and student than friends. Perhaps because of that, Wright especially strove for equality. When Silko wrote about her divorce, Wright wrote about his and about a son who saddened him; when Silko wrote about difficulties with students, Wright commiserated; and always, Wright praised her work, not from the standpoint of a teacher but from the standpoint of an admiring colleague. Her response to his first letter begins and ends with appreciations of his poetry, just as his first letter began with appreciation for hers. But though he calls her "abundant," her appreciation of his work is not as effusive as his appreciation of hers. G. H. Mead has said that the meaning of any interaction is a three-part affair consisting of a gesture by one party, the response of the other party, and the response of the first party. We can see something of that happening as Wright creates a balance of praise by extravagantly thanking Silko for her brief words on his book *To a Blossoming Pear Tree,* thereby making her praise for his work seem as lavish as his praise for hers: "You make me happy with your words about *To A Blossoming Pear Tree.* I think, at bottom, the most one hopes for in writing a book is to find a true response from someone who one cares about and genuinely respects."[23]

Social scientists have not had as much to say about friendship as about relationships embedded in such structured institutions as the family or the state, but when they have analyzed friendship, they often point to its equality. S. N. Eisenstadt, for instance, says that in friendship "mutual trust is consistently based on the relative equality of the participants in their relationship."[24] Similarly, when Paul Lazarsfeld and Robert Merton studied friendship patterns in two housing projects, they found that "like attracts like," not only in status but in values as well. Those with similar values will become friends. Those with dissimilar values will not become friends, or if they do become friends, one person will deemphasize the contrast of values in order to avoid a confrontation on that issue, "for the friends, by virtue of their attachment, are strongly motivated to modify their values in the service of easing strains on the relationship. In the cumulative give-and-take of the friendship, initial divergences of value tend to be reduced."[25]

The use of gifts to create and maintain reciprocal relationships is a prominent focus of anthropologists' accounts. One practice often noted is the exchange of identical gifts to foster equality. Herbert Hogbin, for example, reports that among the Polynesians, "a ball of sennit ceremonially presented may be returned by a similar ball of exactly the same size, presented with exactly the same ceremony. Or again, a parcel of food may be returned by another parcel of the same kind of food cooked according to the same recipe."[26] As part of the Yukaghir marriage ceremony, "relatives who have received a reindeer give a reindeer."[27] And in the Kula Ring, where bracelets are exchanged for necklaces, Malinowski noted several ceremonies in which "A gives to B an object, and B on the same day returns the very same object to A."[28]

The custom is not limited to preliterate societies. Although Lévi-Strauss joins his fellow anthropologists in assuming that gift reciprocity is a thing of the past—"Reciprocal gifts," he declares, "are . . . a type of phenomenon which today is abnormal and exceptional and of purely anecdotal interest,"—he describes two modern Western examples. In cheap restaurants in the south of France, strangers seated at the same table pour equal amounts of wine from identical bottles into each other's glass; in German beer halls strangers do the same with beer. Clearly, there is no material profit in these interchanges of equivalent things, identical things, or sometimes even the same thing passed back and forth. As Lévi-Strauss notes: "The two bottles are identical in volume, and their contents similar in quality. Each person in this revealing scene has, in the final analysis, received no more than if he had consumed his own wine. From an economic viewpoint, no one has gained and no one has lost. But the point is that there is much more in the exchange itself than in the things exchanged."[29]

The "more" is relationship. Once the wine or beer has been poured into the other's glass, the two strangers will be able to converse as equals. It is an offer of friendship. Identical gifts mark places on social maps that are made equal through the exchange of such gifts. Far from being abnormal or exceptional today, such gifts are commonplace—that is, if we consider gestures of notice as the gifts they are.

Gestures are markers or displays that align or rank interacting individuals, says Erving Goffman.[30] We give and take identity and social existence from each other through such subtle gestures as tone of voice, smiles and frowns, attention paid and notice not taken, the averted eye and the glance that pierces, open arms and turned backs, kisses, handshakes, slaps and bows. Many of the gestures that regulate social intercourse in Western societies are performed by two or more persons identically and simultaneously. Such gestures are the functional equivalents of the exchange of identical gifts that anthropologists report in simple societies. They mark equivalent places in reciprocal relationships.

Actions that mark positions of equal value use identical markers. Among the Trobriand Islanders, for instance, identical gifts are "characteristic of the relationship between friends."[31] Such relationships are, in their equality, like relationships between exchangers. But where reciprocal gift exchanges come closer to obligation, where the gifts mark positions that are unequal, the gifts will be unequal. Then gestures may be decidedly one-sided, such as the "hate stare" described by Goffman:

> It is possible for one person to stare openly and fixedly at others, gleaning what he can about them while frankly expressing on his face his response to what he sees—for example, the "hate stare" that a Southern white sometimes gratuitously gives to Negroes walking past him. It is also possible for one person to treat others as if they were not there at all, as objects not worthy of a glance, let alone close scrutiny. . . . Here we have "nonperson" treatment; it may be seen in our society in the way we sometimes treat children, servants, Negroes, and mental patients.[32]

Staring at and looking through someone can be accomplished unilaterally. Therefore these gestures mark not only difference but inequality. Like a bow, they can be performed by a single person. Like one hand clapping, producing silence rather than sound, a gesture may become its opposite if it is not equally and simultaneously reciprocated. Rejection, not acceptance, is the meaning of such a gesture, and a hierarchical system of obligation rather than a system of reciprocity is denoted. In societies and situations where obligation rather than friendship is emphasized, there is likely to be more of unilateral gesturing, more staring and bowing, and less of coupled gesturing, less kissing and handshaking.

Reciprocal gifts generate the equality of sameness. In all that has been written about friendship, a common idea is the concept of friends mirroring each other. For instance, Ecclesiasticus advises us to "have no fellowship with one that is mightier and richer than thyself: for how agree the kettle and the earthen pot together? For if the one be smitten against the other, it shall be broken. . . . A man will cleave to his like. . . . What fellowship hath the wolf with the lamb? So the sinner with the godly. What agreement is there between the hyena and a dog? And what peace between the rich and the poor?"[33] Aristotle corroborates: "There is a saying 'amity is equality' and this is most fully realized in the friendships between good men. . . . a friend is another self. Friendship is essentially a partnership. Also a friend is a second self, so that our consciousness of a friend's existence, when given reality by intercourse with him, makes us more fully conscious of our own existence."[34] Bacon went even further by calling a friend more than a second self: "It was a sparing speech of the Ancients to say that a friend is another himself; For that a friend is far more than himself; Men have their Time, and die many times in desire of some things, which they principally take to heart: the bestowing of a child, the finishing of a work, or the like. If a man have a true friend, he may rest almost secure, that the care of those things will continue after him; so that a man hath, as it were, two lives in his desires."[35] Bringing the same theme to the United States, Emerson said, "In loving a friend men are loving their own good, as a good man benefits a person whose affection he wins. Each party to a friendship therefore both promotes his own good and makes an equal return in goodwill and in the pleasure that he gives."[36]

Emerson also said about friendship that it "must not surmise or provide for infirmity." In its voluntary nature, in its demand that we be our best, friendship seems to make us hide our warts. But then how can friends relax and be themselves? That is, how can a friendship be anything but shallow? The question may have to do with a distinction Talcott Parsons makes between expressive, or emotional, and instrumental, or useful, relationships. Friends may expose their infirmities, they may even be helpful to one another, but friends may not *expect* help from each other; whatever help they give must be incidental to their affection.

There is one infirmity, however, that friendship is designed to assuage: loneliness. In response to a letter in which Silko told of her loneliness and sadness, Wright told Silko about someone whom he hadn't yet met who sent a note saying "I'm so lonely I can't stand it. I don't mean solitude. I need solitude. But loneliness rots the soul." Wright worries that his "response will sound improbable and 'literary'" but, he says, he wrote back to the stranger that he would "find him in Chicago. . . . and . . . bring . . . two pretty girls and a bunch of bananas." And he did. Now Wright says he knows Silko's loneliness and pain over her broken marriage and lost custody battle: "I once endured a divorce. I mention this, not to tell you the story of my life, which is commonplace and boring, but only to suggest that I can understand how bruised, even shattered you have felt."[37]

Friends acknowledge each other, their happiness and their pain; infirmities can be one more link bonding friends. The social place that friends make for each other is for emotional interchange and mutual enjoyment rather than the rational, competitive, and economic interchange of the exchanger self or the functional complementarity of the obligated self. Ideally, people in reciprocal relationships give and receive roughly equal amounts of the same things—affection, mutual regard, companionship. In these relationships, gifts represent correspondence—a phone call is answered by a phone call, an invitation by an acceptance and a return invitation, and an object by a return object of roughly equal value. Reciprocators who do not maintain the balance can be sanctioned emotionally through punishments that arouse feelings of remorse, shame, or guilt. Often, especially in modern reciprocal relationships, failure to maintain the balance in a relationship leads to expulsion from the social position. Friends who don't return invitations or answer letters and phone calls are usually dropped, and the boundary that they had built around the social space they constructed will dissolve.

The Called Self: Artists and Saints

Infirmities evoke an entirely different response in the world of the called person. In this orientation, they may provide opportunity. Mother Teresa, who has become an icon, exemplifies one type of called person, the devotee. Almost every telling of her story includes the moment in 1946 when she heard the voice of God commanding her "to leave the comfort of her convent, to go and live among the poorest of the poor in the vast city beyond." Following the call, she "obtained permission from the Pope, . . . changed into a plain white cotton sari and founded a new religious order whose vocation was to relieve the misery of the most neglected of men."[38] Mother Teresa, unlike exchangers, felt that she had no choice. Hers was not to reason why, but to ease men's suffering as they die.

On the same field between the cosmic self and the obligated self stands the artist. Lewis Hyde's book *The Gift* is about artists and their gifts. Although he establishes a simple dualism between commodities and gifts that is typical of analyses of the gift relationship, Hyde emphasizes characteristics that are different from reciprocity, and he frequently has to rely on his own considerable gifts as a poet to hide the discrepancies between gift reciprocity and his particular use of gift terminology. What Mother Teresa exemplifies and Hyde describes is the orientation that I label the "called person" view of the self.

The called self combines characteristics of the cosmic self and the obligated self. Like the cosmic self, the called self is spiritual. Called persons are said to receive their gifts not from other humans but from a cosmic or spiritual source. The devotee receives a call from God; the artist from the muse or some cosmic or spiritual source. Like the obligated self but unlike the pure cosmic self, the idea of the called self emphasizes the life-giving, generative qualities of the obligated self. Hyde says the gift is like food. It "must always be used up, consumed, eaten; it is property that perishes." [39]

Gifts require devotion. Gifted artists speak of losing themselves much as Siddhartha loses himself, but artists lose themselves in active pursuit of their work while Siddhartha sits gazing in the river, a beatific smile on his lips, producing nothing. Artists, by contrast, do not float into a misty nothingness; they stick to their canvases, tap words into their typewriters or computers, and create a common culture for real communities. Like the cosmic self, the called person seeks selflessness. Unlike cosmic images of selflessness, which involve an escape from the body, images of the called self are intensely physical. Whether the belief is that God calls the devout to love and succor the agonized body or that the muse calls on the artist to create a coherent shape out of words or clay or paint, the called self expresses its spirit in a physical medium, transforming physical material that may be ugly or chaotic into something ordered and lovely. Like Siddhartha's stone, a work of art is fluid, always becoming something else with each new interpretation.

Hyde chose Walt Whitman to be his exemplar of the gift-creating artist. He had good reason to do so. Whitman embodies both types of calling—that of the devout and that of the artist. During the Civil War he tended sick soldiers much as Mother Teresa tends the dying people of Calcutta. His poetry, also a calling, refers frankly to bodies and physical nature. Hyde speaks of Whitman as "Emerson's enthusiast, Emerson with a body." He tells how Emerson, who was moved by *Leaves of Grass*, nonetheless "walked Whitman around Boston trying to persuade him not to speak so frankly about the body in his poems."[40] Emerson would probably not have minded Whitman's references to the body if they were in the Romantic vein, exalting the beauties of nature. But Whitman's talent was to find beauty where most of us would find ugliness, in nature's horrifying and putrid parts. This artist opens our eyes to beauty we dare not see.

Hyde makes a connection between gifts and disease. He notes that the missionary serving lepers completes her gift when she has contracted the disease; he points out that Whitman's comrade, Peter Doyle, suffered from a skin eruption called "barber's itch," which Whitman may have associated with syphilis, the "love disease." "My darling," Whitman wrote to Doyle, "if you are not well when I come back . . . we will live together, & devote ourselves altogether to the job of curing you." Hyde, writing in the days before AIDS, says that the association between love and disease needed less imagination before penicillin made cures easier: "As vegetable life has the chemistry of compost, so, for Whitman, we humans may clean our animal blood through the chemistry of love."[41]

There are, however, differences between the artist who makes the chaotic coherent and the nun who establishes "The Place of the Pure Heart—Home for Dying Destitutes." The nun collapses boundaries between the healthy and the deathly, between the accepted and the rejected, between the living and the dying. Artists collapse boundaries within groups that share a culture. We say that artists are "gifted." But theirs is an odd sort of gift. It belongs, in some sense, not to themselves but to their communities. Their gift travels not from one individual to another but from the artist to a common culture. To make this point, Hyde cites Joseph Conrad: "The artist appeals . . . to that in us which is a gift. . . . He speaks to our capacity for delight and wonder, to the sense of mystery surrounding our lives; to our sense of duty, and beauty, and pain; to the latent feeling of fellowship with all creation—to the subtle but invincible conviction of solidarity that knits together the loneliness of innumerable hearts, to the solidarity . . . which binds together all humanity—the dead to the living and the living to the unborn."[42] Innumerable hearts, all humanity, the dead, the living, and the unborn—these are impersonal bonds and cosmic connections. But they are not as ethereal as the cosmic sense of oneness. Through their work, artists create a common culture and a boundary surrounding that culture and the people who share it.

Hyde stresses that an artist's work is a gift, not a commodity, and that artists risk losing their creative powers if they watch too closely as their productions go to market. Whether Hyde's argument would stand an empirical test is not the point. Clearly, much work produced with no market in mind and called "art" by its maker is pedestrian, whereas some work produced for a market, such as Shakespeare's plays, are inspired. The point is that Hyde expresses a familiar moral view—the idea of art as a special kind of production and of artists as special kinds of people. Works produced as gifts, says Hyde, enable us to "enter gracefully into nature . . . to receive, contribute toward, and pass along the collective treasures we refer to as culture and tradition."[43]

In a secular age, many people, uncomfortable with the idea of religious callings, find the idea of artistic callings easier to accept. "There is a set of ideas and intuitions," says Taylor, "still inadequately understood, which makes us admire the artist and the creator more than any other civilization ever has; which convinces us that a life spent in artistic creation or performance is eminently worthwhile." This image rooted in "a semi-suppressed side of Plato's thought which emerges . . . in the *Phaedrus* where he seems to think of the poet inspired by mania as capable of seeing what sober people are not."[44] Our respect for the special vision of artists induces us to take their opinions about politics seriously even though they may have no more special expertise in public affairs than the next person.

Taylor traces the idea of a calling to a synthesis of the Platonic order of ideas and the "Jewish-Christian-Islamic religious tradition that God as creator himself affirms life and being." In Catholic cultures, the term *vocation* is usually limited to votaries, to life in priestly or monastic settings, but the Puritans extended the idea of a godly life to everyone. Every employment, even the meanest, "was a calling for the Puritans, provided it was useful to mankind and imputed to use by God." In that spirit, one might try, as James Wright did, to make a ceremony of life, rising early and contemplating quietly before others wake. Puritans did something of the sort, turning all kinds of work and daily life itself into a calling.[45]

Paradoxically, the discipline, the steadiness, and the ceremony of an everyday life approached as a calling often produces large profits in the market. Puritans were troubled by this turn. To ward off the threat that godly practices might lead to earthly profits, John Cotton advised "diligence in worldly business and yet deadnesse to the world."[46] He warned against those who "profane their lives and callings" by using them "to get honours, pleasures, profits, worldly commodities etc." (which is just what Hobbes says humans naturally quest after). Cotton's shoemaker, like Hyde's artist, has to guard against the chance that if the products of his calling are marketed, their exchange value will predominate and the self will slip from called person to exchanger.

Cotton and Hyde were bothered by the different kinds of boundaries and senses of equality in exchanger and called-person orientations. The exchanger wants competitions to be free of the feudal hierarchies and privilege of the obligated self, but inequality will (and should) result from the competition. Called persons, by contrast, struggle for a cosmic equality that breaks down boundaries. Mother Teresa was in constant war against the forces of exchange. Her work often attracted philanthropists who wanted to introduce a note of luxury or inequality into her order. She was quick to root it out. Just as almost every telling of her story recounts the day she received the call, almost every telling also recounts one of the many times she turned down a contribution that would introduce ostentation or inequality into her mission. The example that Dominique Lapierre gives in her *City of Joy* is of a grant, from the Calcutta city government, of thirty-three rupees a day to care for some of the children in Mother Teresa's mission. After six months "a meeting was held in the government building. A dozen bureaucrats in *dhotis* examined the nun's account books. They asked questions, quibbled over details, and criticized. Exasperated, Mother Teresa stood up. 'You think you can demand that I spend thirty-three rupees on the children you sponsor,' she exclaimed indignantly, 'when I can spend only seventeen on our other children who are by far the more numerous. How can I spend thirty-three rupees on some and seventeen on others? Who could do a thing like that? Thank you gentlemen, but I will do without your money.' " [47]

Even as Mother Teresa knocked down the boundaries the Calcutta bureaucrats tried to erect within her mission, she struggled with other boundaries that kept insinuating themselves between herself, her followers, and the people they served. A camel may pass through the eye of a needle more easily than a rich man may pass through the gates of heaven, but what about a saint? Rank-reversal ceremonies, such as kissing the feet of the beggar, and the begging bowl of the Buddha are ritual attempts to create equality. But such displays of humility are paradoxical. A begging Buddha, or a nun kissing the beggar's foot, brandishes the difference between a called person who chooses poverty and the truly poor, the exchanged, who are forced to beg and kiss feet.

A sense of gratitude may do more to chase hubris and level inequalities. Georg Simmel calls gratitude "the moral memory of mankind. . . . one of the most powerful means of social cohesion." [48] Gratitude evens the ground between givers and receivers as it travels among them. Hyde imagines the gift flowing like water seeking its level: "The gift moves toward the empty place. As it turns in its circle it turns toward him who has been empty-handed the longest, and if someone appears elsewhere whose need is greater it leaves its old channel and moves toward him. Our generosity may leave us empty, but our emptiness then pulls gently at the whole until the thing in motion returns."[49] After receiving a gift and before passing it on, we suffer gratitude. We were below the level of the gift when it came to us. As we enjoy the gift, as we use it, the gift works in us until we become equal to it; then we can give it away. "Passing the gift along is the act of gratitude that finishes the labor . . . the end of the labor of gratitude is similarity with the gift or with its donor." Once this equality has been achieved, once we and those from whom we received gifts are at the same level, we may feel a lingering and generalized gratitude, but we won't feel it with the urgency of indebtedness.[50]

The Civic Self

Mother Teresa may seem saintly to some, but others voice strong objections. I once asked students and friends what they thought of her. Most thought she was saintly. But I was stunned by the number of those who responded in vehemently angry tones. To some, the nun had lost the struggle to level difference; her holiness seemed a holier-than-thou attitude; they saw arrogance and hubris. Others, of a more activist bent, opposed her acceptance of the poverty she served. Rather than easing the poor to their death, they thought that goodness meant raising the poor from their penury.

This group drew from a different tradition. For them, the proper response to misery was the citizen's response: correction. The citizen, or civic self, combines traits of the exchanger—rationality and practicality—with traits of the cosmic self—a yearning for unity. The citizen wants results and would turn the world into one sane, rational, healthy union. The citizen would eradicate poverty, not assuage it; would make peace on earth a reality, not a prayer.

In his classic study of the British Blood Transfusion Service, titled, like Hyde's book, *The Gift*, Richard Titmuss describes a relationship and a sense of the self that is fundamentally different from both the reciprocal exchange of gifts that Malinowski and Mauss describe and the gifts of called persons. Titmuss called the Transfusion Service a "gift relationship" because, like Hyde, he was following a tradition that called almost all relationships a gift relationship if they diverged from market exchange. But he was aware of how far the Transfusion Service departed from Kula Ring partnerships, and he listed the "unique attributes" that distinguish the gift of blood "from other forms of gift." He points out that gift reciprocity establishes a feeling-bond between two people, while bonding and thickening ties between identifiable individuals are totally lacking in the British Blood Transfusion Service: "The gift of blood takes place in impersonal situations . . . the recipient is in almost all cases not personally known to the donor." Largely because givers and receivers are unknown to each other, most of the positive and negative social controls governing reciprocity are absent from the Blood Transfusion Service:

> There can be no personal expressions of gratitude or of other sentiments. There is no obligation imposed on the recipient himself to make a corresponding gift in return . . . there are no personal, predictable penalties for not giving; no socially enforced sanctions of remorse, shame or guilt; for the giver there is no certainty of a corresponding gift in return; . . . [and for the recipient] there is no obligation . . . to make a corresponding gift in return. [Indeed, givers] . . . do not expect and would not wish to have a blood transfusion.[51]

This is not, as is sometimes assumed, a difference between gift relationships in complex, technologically advanced societies and those in small, simple societies. All three types of "gift" relationship—the one described by Malinowski and Mauss, the one described by Hyde, and the one described by Titmuss—can be found in both types of society.

Distinguishing between the reciprocating type and the civic type in simple societies, Marshall Sahlins calls the first type exchanges of "two parties known familiarly as 'reciprocity'" and the second type "pooling" or "redistribution"—"centralized movements: collection from members of a group, often under one hand, and redivision within this group." Reciprocity, says Sahlins, emphasizes vice-versa, between-relations, where "the action and reaction of two parties [and the] social fact of sides is inescapable." Pooling, by contrast, "is socially a *within* relation, the collective action of a group": "Thus pooling is the complement of social unity and . . . 'centricity'; whereas, reciprocity is social duality and 'symmetry.' Pooling stipulates a social center where goods meet and thence flow outwards, and a social boundary too within which persons (or subgroups) are cooperatively related."[52] Citizens pool their resources. Hobbes's citizen was a self that could be partitioned, one part being given over to the collectivity to create that fictitious individual, the Leviathan, or the state. Centuries later the state would gather and redistribute a variety of goods that would have astounded Hobbes—blood, for instance.

In the British Blood Transfusion Service, as in most pooling or welfare systems, a resource flows from those who are able to contribute toward those who are in need. Contributors and users are usually anonymous members of a collective. Usually some collective system maintains the pool even as it is used, and often, as in the case of taxation, contributions are not voluntary. Rather than a balance or reciprocity between what is taken and what is given, pooling achieves a leveling of resources and a floor below which the least member of a collective is kept from falling (a safety net). The goal of pooling is to produce a shared civic environment (a nation, for example) without internal boundaries.

The civic self emerged as a by-product of the market and foreshadowed the Romantic Revival. Markets released individuals from systems of obligation and brought together people without ties or responsibilities to each other. The market dismantled boundaries that had ordered a society in which the obligated self was dominant, so the challenge was to create moral ground for common ventures. The state was invented to govern strangers. The citizen was invented to people the state.

Creators of the modern state drank from ancient troughs, but the contemporary idea of state and citizen, drafted to complement the exchanger, is quite modern. Here was an isolated individual, free to act independently, but able to create a shared environment on rational grounds. The sharing has been expanding over the last two centuries in ways described by T. H. Marshall. First came political rights, limited to the minority of society's members who would have full citizenship—males, whites, and property owners. Then as boundaries fell from feudal estates, social rights were added. Last came economic rights and the welfare state.[53]

The modern idea of the citizen combines characteristics of the cosmic self and the exchanger. Its egalitarian spirit derives, on the one hand, from cosmic leanings toward universal oneness—"one nation indivisible" —and, on the other, from the exchanger's predilections for contractual fairness—"with liberty and justice for all." Plato gave us the idea of rational equality. Hyde shows us how Whitman struggled with differences between rational equality and the oneness of cosmic equality. Whitman leaned toward the cosmic equality, distrusting reason: learned astronomers had nothing to tell him about the stars. But he also declares in the logos vein, which the citizen takes from the exchanger, that it is "indispensable to my own rights that others possess the same." Whitman's democracy, like Plato's, would rid the land of all the special privileges that order systems of obligation, especially those vestiges of "European chivalry" that ordered "the feudal, ecclesiastical, dynastic world," and which still, Whitman felt, held sway in the New World: "Of all dangers to a nation as things exist in our day, there can be no greater one than having certain portions of the people set off from the rest by a line drawn—they not privileged as others, but degraded, humiliated, made of no account." He affirmed, "I will not have a single person slighted or left away." According to Hyde, Whitman's lists—"Kanuck, Tuckahoe, Congressman, Cuff, I give them the same, I receive them the same"—"put hierarchy to sleep." They did that in a cosmic way, by encompassing "such a wide range of creation that our sense of discrimination soon withdraws for lack of use, and that part of us which can sense the underlying coherence comes forward." The mind then "refuses commerce with what we might call 'the brain that divides' or with any spirit which might divorce him from his newly wedded soul." The self loses its boundaries as all life fuses into a cosmic oneness:

> Through me the afflatus surging and surging—through me the
> current and the index
> I speak the pass-word primeval—I give the sign of democracy.

With his lists, Whitman breaks down barriers, but in so doing he dims the contours of the idiosyncrasies he treasures. Even as he heralds the equal worth of all, he wants to combine that with the intense individualism of the Romantic self.[54]

In ideal images of the citizen, there is nothing of the obligated self, although characteristics of the obligated self linger in ideas and feelings of ethnicity and nationalism. If the citizen and the nationalist were not so different, Plato might not have insisted that the philosopher-king be free from family connections. The wide boundaries surrounding the modern state, embracing strangers, do not sit well with hierarchical systems of obligation. Citizen's projects are social programs and political practices that level differences, not the flag-waving, I-love-my-country-better-than-you-do of the chauvinist. One coin or citizen is the same as another; everything that can be obtained by one should be available to all; everything required of one must be required of all. No discrimination here, except of a denominational or categorical kind—the elderly do not have to perform military service and the very young do not have to serve on juries.

In the next chapter we shall explore the emotions, the means through which we keep track of changing boundaries. Each orientation to the self erects a different boundary, an imaginary wall. Within each wall lies a sense of the self, isolated as an exchanger, paired as a reciprocator, placed in an organismic functional system as an obligated self, encompassing whole cultures as the called self, oozing out to the universe as the cosmic self, and contracting again with internal partitions around the citizen. Clearly these are not all of the orientations that guide the lives of contemporary Americans. But they are some of the most salient ones. They were invented at different times; they are moral systems and boundary systems. They tell us what kinds of relationships we may establish with each other, what kinds we should avoid, and what, ideally, ought to be happening within those relationships. With so many different boundaries, so many different orientations to the self and others, we need to be always sensitive to what is happening at the many boundaries to the self. Our emotions are like a sensory organ letting us know what is happening at these boundaries.

CHAPTER FIVE

A Theory of Culture and Emotions

USUALLY, WE THINK OF GIFTS as physical objects. That is because the exchanger view of the self prevails. In the exchanger scheme of things, physical objects matter very much. They are palpable: they can be counted, sorted, added, and subtracted. The rational mind does not have to guess about physical objects. But the physical part of a gift is not what matters: a gift is a marker of social position. This is especially true of the sort of gifts that are gestures of everyday life. Such gestures as smiles, glances, handshakes, and tone of voice show that persons know and accept their place, or as Naylor showed in *The Women of Brewster Place*, they may indicate rejection of social place. Etta, the black girl who looked white people in the eye, was chased out of town.[1] With simple gestures she had upset the social order and forced the underlying social structure out into the open.

What is at stake in the slightest gestures that surround all social encounters is a reinforcement of or attack on the social structure. Such reinforcement or attack has little to do with the physical qualities of objects used as gifts. Gifts, gestures, words, and other social signals let us know when a social interaction is proceeding in ways that will allow us to enter a new and valued social place and when it is proceeding in ways that indicate that we are in danger of being forced into a degraded identity. They let us know when we are being expelled from an old association that we treasured and when we are escaping an association we hated. What matters are our places in the social environment. That is why we construct images of who we might be. And that is where emotions come into play. As Guy E. Swanson says, "People are aroused as selves when they see their position in social relations as open to change whether from threats or opportunities. Arousal ends when there is no prospect of change."[2]

The constant construction, repair, and destruction of boundaries around each image of the self are what emotions are all about. Like an insect's feelers, and like our own eyes, skin, and ears, our emotional capacity allows us to analyze expression instantly. It lets us immediately sense and evaluate the social world around us. Whereas our skin responds to such physical phenomena as temperature, shape, and texture, our emotions respond to such social phenomena as gestures of rejection and acceptance.[3] Emotions let us know when we are engaged in an interaction that is not changing the boundaries around our many selves and when we are engaged in an interaction that does involve shifting boundaries; they also allow us to juggle many moral systems simultaneously and to know which are in use, just as the cones in our eyes allow us to see many colors simultaneously and to distinguish among them.

Gifts, including emotional expression, are signals that tell us about social boundaries. We respond emotionally. Emotions are place markers, says Candace Clark, who adds that emotions may be classified in two groups: "introjected" emotions give us information about where we stand in the social world, and "extrojected" emotions are those that we display.[4]

Emotions have only recently been added to the subject matter of philosophy, anthropology, and sociology, disciplines that once drew a sharp line between their subject matter—what was considered rational, cognitive, and intentional in human behavior—and matters outside their purview—what was considered irrational, nonrational, and emotional.[5] According to the traditional model, emotions are biologically innate, involuntary, affective states that are capable of influencing intelligence, language, and culture, but which are not directed by them.[6] Now, although some researchers still draw a firm line between innate emotion and cognition,[7] a growing number look for the connections between emotion and thought.[8] Among them, there is much variation. Some think of emotions as feelings, others see emotions as the names we attach to feelings, others think of emotions as the response we make to feelings—the "force" that "moves"—and still others think of emotions as a combination of all of these.[9] For some, emotions are things in themselves, like ribs or fevers. Others see them as social constructs.[10] Some use such terms as *feelings, affect, emotion, sentiment,* and *mood* interchangeably, and others differentiate among them, using *affect* as the most inclusive term, *emotion* to refer to arousal, *sentiment* to refer to a state more enduring than momentary arousal, and *quala* to refer to sensation, that irreducible feeling not expressed through verbalization.[11] Some divide emotions into two groups, the ones they characterize as primary or basic, which they say are innate and universal, and others that they say are culturally derived from the basic emotions. An early example of this dichotomy in sociology was Charles Horton Cooley's distinction between "basic" emotions and "sentiments." He defined sentiments as "socialized feeling, feeling which has been raised by thought and intercourse out of its merely instinctive state and become properly human." "Love," he said, "is a sentiment, while lust is not; resentment is, but not rage."[12]

Thinking of emotions as innate or basic has intuitive appeal. When we reflect on our feelings, they seem to have arisen spontaneously. Moreover, emotions seem largely out of our control—even after Hochschild has shown quite convincingly that in many occupations their display is purchased and that job training often includes emotion training: we learn to feel what we are paid to express.[13]

Once again, in the case of emotions, as with any other human characteristic that seems innate, cultural and historical variation is the litmus test. If the phenomena does not vary, then it may be innate. If it does, then it cannot be innate. Research that traces particular human feelings over time and across cultures strongly suggests that no matter how "natural" feelings seem, they are specific to a particular time and culture.[14] Surely, people have the capacity to feel in all cultures. People in other times and cultures, however, probably did not feel what we feel in situations that rouse our emotions. Following a review of historical and cross-cultural research, Richard A. Shweder concluded that "there is no empirical reason to believe that feelings are interpreted as emotions in all cultures, much less as the *same* emotion." He therefore advises us not to trust anyone who says they really know whether basic, universal emotions exist.[15]

Sociobiologists, steeped in the individualism of our age, speculate on the genetic basis of much human behavior, especially such emotions as the urge to compete. Some go so far as to invent and glorify the "selfish gene," an imaginary configuration of RNA and DNA that uses our bodies as vessels to travel from one generation to another.[16] Considering the variation in the historical and cross-cultural records, along with our difficulty in understanding cultures with emotional orientations different from our own, we would be better off to think of our bodies as providing humans with *capacities* rather than *programs* for behavior. Then we might postulate that as we evolved into creatures who could conceive of themselves as separate, we also developed a long period of infant dependency, a rich and varied emotional capacity, and, most important, the capacity for language, so that we might teach emotions to new generations and thereby maintain the social connections that make human life possible.

However emotions evolved, they seem to be the capacity that allows humans to build, maintain, or dissolve boundaries around the self. They provide us with the ability to feel a kind of glue binding us to some people and a kind of wall separating us from others. The great strength of those bonds and walls can be gleaned from antagonisms that persist from generation to generation—vide Northern Ireland and Bosnia.

I think that the most fruitful way to look at emotions is to use G. H. Mead's work on self, cognition, and emotions as a point of departure. Mead is often faulted for lacking a theory of emotions, but recently published work reveals this criticism to be incorrect: he did have a theory of emotions developed in concert with John Dewey.[17] It focused on the consummation of "social acts" that have value. A social act is one whose achievement depends on actions of another party. Our culture gives us ideas of goodness, or value; our feelings are aroused as we anticipate success or inhibition of our attempts to achieve a good. Connecting Mead's theory to my analysis of images of selves, we can say that images of selves are among the ideas of what is good that cultures consist of. They are part of what Mead called the generalized other, a culture's vocabulary of motives, emotions, and role relationships.

For Mead, the self is a process that constantly alternates between action and reflection: in an "I" phase we act, in a "Me" phase we reflect. We can also say that in the I phase we *feel* and make instantaneous responses to social interactions based on the emotions we feel. The I can thus be thought of as the feeling phase of the self as well as the acting phase.

One point Mead made is that we can know the I only in retrospect—that is, in the Me phase, when we reflect on our actions and interpret them. Then we also reflect on our feelings and interpret them—especially in these times of intense psychological introspection.[18] Reflection is internal conversation during which the generalized other that contains our culture's vocabulary of motives and emotions provides us with tools we use to articulate what we feel.

C. Wright Mills added that the generalized other provides a socially constituted viewpoint from which we approve or disapprove of arguments as logical or illogical. To that I shall now add that just as the generalized other is the seat of an intellectual apparatus from which we judge the form and logic of an argument, it is also the seat of an emotional apparatus from which we approve or disapprove of feelings as "appropriate" or "sick." Concepts of sanity and appropriate emotional response, like concepts of logic, depend on agreement among the members of a community. What we call mental illness is similar to immorality in that both are deviations from norms.[19]

Mead had a broad view of the contents of the generalized other: "Every feeling has its relation to some idea," he said. "Feelings develop in relation to the forms of knowledge that govern a whole class or period, its age's universe of discourse."[20] Mills refined that idea, arguing that the generalized other contains not an entire universe of discourse but only selected social experiences.[21] The generalized other is specific to the behaviors of economic classes. Thus, while it is true that what we call mental illness is similar to immorality in that both are deviations from norms, those norms vary by class, region, ethnicity, gender, and other social structural divisions.[22]

So far, I have adopted Mead's theory of emotion and extended Mills's refinement of the generalized other to include emotions, treating emotions much as Mills treated cognition. I do not, however, intend to equate cognitive and emotional processes. A major difference, one that I think can account in large measure for the apparently inborn quality of emotional responses, lies in the socialization process: most of the content of the generalized other that influences cognitive processes is internalized during secondary socialization, whereas most of the content of the generalized other that influences emotional processes is internalized during primary socialization. Here I am building on Cooley's idea of primary and secondary groups and Berger and Luckmann's extension of that idea into concepts of primary and secondary socialization.[23]

Primary socialization is a process that begins at birth and continues until the child has internalized most of the essential aspects of her culture—its language, its values, and its ways of doing most things that have to do with daily life. Secondary socialization is a process through which we learn the more technical and specialized knowledge of our culture. The lessons of primary socialization occur imperceptibly as a part of living; the lessons of secondary socialization are intentional and are set off from daily life in such special places as schools. Most important from the point of view of learning a culture of emotion, the internalization of primary socialization is mediated by significant others, people about whom we have intense feelings, whereas the internalization of secondary socialization is mediated by specialists in education—teachers, supervisors, and others—people about whom we need not feel deeply.

Thus, primary socialization—a process of subtle, indirect, emotionally intense internalization—develops the emotional capacity and suits it to the society at an early age, while secondary socialization—a process of formal, direct, sometimes intellectually intense internalization—develops the cognitive capacity and suits it to the society at a later age. Because emotional socialization occurs imperceptibly, mediated by significant others, we cannot remember when we learned the culture of emotions, we cannot remember a time when we did not know it, and we cannot imagine feeling differently. That is why our emotions seem natural or innate even though variations in emotional culture over time and social space tell us that they cannot be.[24] Thus, just as we are taught to speak a mother tongue, we are taught to love, hate, feel awe, anger, disdain, respect, and all the other emotions that seem so natural. The emotional culture needs to be taught to each new generation. Without such instruction, or socialization, we wouldn't know when our folk thought it right to laugh or cry, or whom to love, trust, or fear.

Now I wish to make three points that will connect the foregoing theory of emotions to a culture's images of selves. First, just as our linguistic and cognitive capacities allow us to invent and construct an infinite variety of words, ideas, and meanings, so too our emotional capacity allows us to invent an infinite variety of identities, human connections, and social structures. Cultures narrow the choices to a manageable few, each culture generating different ideas about feelings and about the social connections and walls that need to be reconstructed in each new psyche. Second, societies can be and are organized differently. They can have, and some do have, not just one but several social structures, each with a distinctive orientation to the self and a distinctive morality, all operating simultaneously. The culture of the United States at the end of the twentieth century is marked by an unusually large repertoire of competing images to which its members' responses are often interpreted as ambivalence.[25] Finally, our emotional capacity allows us to keep track simultaneously of several boundaries to the self.

Our ability to feel good and feel bad—and to make each other feel good and feel bad—is the brush we use to paint boundaries around our different selves. At the inside of any boundary are feelings of attraction, connection, and similarity. At the outside are feelings of aversion and difference. Many sociologists make a connection between what we feel and where we stand in a social hierarchy. Theodore Kemper and Randall Collins, for example, argue that social relationships have only two basic dimensions—power and status—and that two kinds of social behavior are related to them. Power is "oriented toward control, dominance, coercion, threat, punishment and assertion of self over others." "Status accord" includes behaviors that are supportive, friendly, congenial, affectionate, and rewarding. Kemper and Collins believe that labels indicating emotion can be categorized according to the relational dimension that elicits them.[26]

Like Kemper and Collins, I think it may be possible to sort behaviors and the emotions they elicit into two broad categories; unlike Kemper and Collins, I do not think that the categories would be power and status, at least not in the way we generally use those terms.[27] Like magnets, emotions may have a side that attracts and a side that repels. Then, thinking of emotions as the capacity with which we sense social action at the boundaries of our images of the self, we could think of two basic emotional orientations, one attaching, the other repelling.

Some of the attaching emotions, the pleasurable ones, may be similar to Kemper and Collins's idea of status. These emotions tell us that you and I are one and that that is good. But in the attaching category we also find the punishing emotions of guilt and shame, through which we are kept from leaving the groups that want to hold us. We may feel either pride or shame toward groups to which we belong. Systems of obligation, however, often require us to bear an identity that we must preserve even if this bond and identity are often costly to individuals, as in the case of a pariah people such as African-Americans or Jews. The repelling emotions may be somewhat similar to Kemper and Collins's idea of power. These are the wall-building emotions, which tell us that differences and separation exist between us.

The boundaries we draw around the self, the lines of inclusion and exclusion, are social. They define social entities into which we are or are not incorporated. These bounded groups are arranged according to different ideas about what the good is. We feel good when we leave an association that we would like to think is beneath us, or when we are allowed into a group that represents a step up. We feel bad when we are expelled from an association we value, or when we are forced into an association that we consider degrading. Where groups are hierarchically ordered by some scheme of goodness, and where social mobility is possible, gatekeepers in high positions are likely to enjoy the positive feelings that come from being courted by those who would like to move up.

Most researchers who study emotions generally observe that most emotional arousal is a response to social encounters. Feelings are aroused because emotions are our means of monitoring the social world. Whatever else its subject, all human interaction includes signs, usually very subtle ones, by which we tell each other what is happening at the wide spectrum of boundaries that surround the various images we hold of who we might be and of where in a variety of social orders we might belong.[28]

Images of Selves, Their Boundaries, and Our Emotions

In Chapter 2, I drew a connection between the expansion of market economies and the introduction of literatures, such as the novel, that let us focus on emotions of attachment, especially romantic love—a necessary emotion in an orientation that was promoting voluntary contracts in every relationship, including marriage. Now I wish to resume that line of thought. I wish to look once more at the boundaries each orientation draws around the self, this time focusing on the approach to emotions that is part of the content of each image of the self. Again, I shall start with the exchanger self because it is the predominant view of the self in the contemporary United States. And once more these images will be separated for heuristic purposes, but just as most paintings use many colors, so does most social action draw on many images.

The Cool Exchanger

The exchanger-self image brought new feelings of shame and disgust into the universe of discourse that was internalized within the generalized other. The exchanger is a solitary person. His interest and emotions are aroused when his self-interest is at stake, and as Durkheim noted, "if interest relates men, it is never for more than some few moments. It can create only an external link between them. In the fact of exchange, the various agents remain outside of each other, and when the business has been completed, each one retires and is left entirely on his own. Consciences are only superficially in contact; they neither penetrate each other, nor do they adhere."[29]

This narrow boundary around the self and the emotions that maintain it developed over several centuries. Norbert Elias's study of Miss Manners's medieval and Renaissance predecessors teaches us that what disgusts us would not have fazed our ancestors. Even as adults, they had to be told "one ought not to spit across the table or blow one's nose on the tablecloth" and "it is impolite to greet someone who is urinating or defecating." It took centuries of gradually rising thresholds of repugnance and embarrassment for Western cultures to develop the training in mood and manners that makes our skin crawl at the touch of some others and makes our throats catch and regurgitate at the sight of someone else's spittle in our plate.[30]

The difference between our feelings and our ancestors', Elias assures us, is a matter not of health and hygiene but of new relationships brought on by the market. The invention of "civilized" manners and the feelings that go with them preceded germ theory. Whether we are talking of disgust, shame, or embarrassment, the emotions we now feel are "feelings which have been socially nurtured under quite specific conditions and . . . are constantly reproduced" to maintain a new structure of social relations. From about the Renaissance onward, "in the notion of the individual 'ego' in its locked case, the 'self' [is] divided by an invisible wall from what happens 'outside.' . . . Civilizational self-controls, functioning in part automatically, . . . are now experienced in individual self-perception as a wall, either between 'subject' and 'object' or between one's own 'self' and other people ('society')."[31] This invisible wall is a central feature of the exchanger morality and orientation.

"Moderation, control, order, and discipline," writes R. S. Perinbanayagam, "became the standards of the Protestant culture that grew out of the Renaissance and the Reformation. . . . Such a philosophy of emotions was a natural corollary of the view that the individual was sufficient unto himself and should not project his self into that of others." Following the Reformation, people were expected to control their emotions because they were not supposed to depend on others for support and approval and "hence did not have to allow [their] emotions to enter, more than was absolutely necessary, into social actions and social relationships."[32] Rationality, objectivity, calculation, and self-interest were elevated to the rank of truly human quality, while emotion became their opposite—a characteristic of lower orders, a dangerous influence, and a weakness that preys on the unwary.

When the exchanger image of the self predominates, we strive for self-mastery, which we interpret as reason's control and the self's liberation from the chaos of desire.[33] Rational exchangers hold emotions in check. The favored method in these post-Freudian days is psychological and intellectual: emotions, we believe, can be tamed if brought out into the open and understood.

An outstanding feature of the exchanger orientation is its transformation of almost everything into commodities, emotions included. Emotional services are sold by people in a long line of occupations, including not only the flight attendants and insurance peddlers that Hochschild writes about but also cadres of mental health workers paid to help the exchanger keep his feelings in order. In another of those paradoxes of the market-dominated society, we have built such high and stable boundaries around ourselves and our feelings that, to a large degree, the purpose of all activities, all buying and selling, is to bring us pleasant emotions and help us avoid unpleasant emotions. Young adults of the Pepsi generation are told that a sip of soda will lift their spirits as they play on the beach; wives are told that they can escape shame if they buy the right detergent to prevent dirty rings on their husband's shirt collars. Positive emotions become the promise of advertisers, who try like cupids to inveigle unwary customers to fall in love with a car or a box of soap.

The Fervent Cosmic Self

Distrust of emotions and championing of reason do not capture our entire ideological stage. In addition to fearing the capriciousness and power of emotions, we also believe that they can give life its energy, its meaning, and even its virtue—if it feels good, it must be good, and if it feels bad, it must be bad. This more positive attitude toward emotions is an element of the cosmic image of the self.

Taylor notes recurrent revolts against the glorification of reason. He points to Christian thinkers who argued that reason could as easily be the devil's servant as God's, and to Luther, who denounced reason as "that whore." In part because of this tradition, Romantics and others argued that rational control may "stifle, desiccate, repress us; that rational self-mastery may be self-domination or enslavement."[34]

Cosmic and exchanger orientations toward emotions are often contrasted. The authors of *Habits of the Heart* call the exchanger orientation "utilitarian individualism" and the cosmic orientation "expressive individualism." Utilitarian individualism stresses the satisfaction one feels in accomplishments and the importance of individual energy and initiative directed toward success. Expressive individualism stresses the happiness that follows the development of individual talents. A similar contrast is Turner's "institutional" and "impulsive" emotion culture. We may experience institutional meanings of emotion when we are in full control of our feelings and expression. Then we focus our efforts on achieving and maintaining widely shared standards for feeling and expression, thereby upholding institutionalized values. The "impulsive" pattern is a perspective that emphasizes spontaneous, uninhibited emotion, unregulated by institutions. Thus one feels and expresses emotion simply because of awareness of situational stimuli and sensations. Idiosyncratic emotions are thought to reveal a hidden self that is not directly visible in institutionally prescribed emotional displays. One's "real" or "true" self is experienced when one is free of conventions and facades and when one abandons or disregards institutional norms regulating emotions.[35]

What I call the Romantic cosmic image is comparable to expressive individualism or the impulsive orientation. In it, the self is bounded by an interior wall. When reflecting on themselves from this perspective, people feel that their "true identity" is something locked away inside them, separate from the crass world outside. And yet, while closing in on the smallest gem of the self, this orientation imagines an ecstatic explosion in which all boundaries are dissolved and the self is rendered one with all being in timeless boundlessness.

Sometimes the contrast between the exchanger orientation and the Romantic cosmic orientation, in their approach to emotions, is taken to be a difference between cultures. E. M. Forster, for example, once compared his own feelings with those of his Indian friend as they were parting after a week's holiday. He noted the difference between a citizen of a "prudent middle-class nation, always anxious to meet my liabilities," and an Oriental who "has behind him a tradition, not of middle-class prudence, but of kingly munificence and splendour." The friend, Forster reported, "was plunged in despair. He felt that because the holiday was over all happiness was over until the world ended." In typical exchanger fashion, Forster admonished his friend to "buck up." Later, he told the friend that he thought it "inappropriate" to "display so much emotion upon so slight an occasion." The friend, speaking in a Romantic vein, said: "Your whole attitude toward emotion is wrong. Emotion has nothing to do with appropriateness. It matters only that it shall be sincere. I happened to feel deeply. I showed it. It doesn't matter whether I ought to have felt deeply or not." Forster replied that he valued emotion as much as his friend, but that if he "poured it out on small occasions" he might have "none left for the great ones" and might be "bankrupt at the crises of life." Noting his own use of the word *bankrupt*, Foster reflected again that he was speaking as a member of a middle-class nation while his friend spoke as an Oriental: "He feels his resources are endless, just as John Bull feels his are finite. As regards material resources, the Oriental is clearly unwise. Money isn't endless. If we spend or give away all the money we have, we haven't any more, and must take the consequences, which are frequently unpleasant. But as regards the resources of the spirit, he may be right. The emotions may be endless. The more we express them, the more we may have to express." [36]

Forster had come to a view of emotions similar to Hyde's view of gifts: they grow through use. But he had begun with the view that prevails in such nations as England and the United States, where the exchanger self rules more often than not. And that self teaches us to control and dole out our emotions as if, like money, they were scarce.

The Image of the Obligated Self

Different emotions help monitor social action at the different boundaries that encircle the obligated self. One boundary lies around the married couple, another around the family, another around the ethnic group, and so on. Within each of these boundaries, the obligated self has a relatively stable place where boundaries seldom change. When they do, the change is usually marked by rites of passage—weddings, funerals, graduations, and the like. As long as boundaries are not shifting and everybody acts according to the rules of social position, emotions simmer quietly. When boundaries shift, or when someone breaks the rules by neglecting the care they are required to give another or by failing to show the respect or love that is due, then feelings of betrayal, anger, and guilt boil over.

These emotions, which children learn early from their families, are said to be both what one ought to feel and what a healthy person would "naturally" feel. Arguments supporting such "naturalness" often appear in the context of otherwise "rational," "objective," and "scientific" explanations of the world. Thus an article on the pain of childbirth, which appeared in the Science section of the *New York Times* in 1996, concluded with the speculation that the human fetus remains in the womb for a final month of fattening so that the mother will not be able to resist her cute, chubby infant in spite of the difficulty of bringing the baby into the world. [37]

Emotions that the obligated self should feel "naturally" are embedded in the subtle instruction of most contemporary narratives—sitcoms, novels, and feature articles in newspapers. One example is a story by Delores Kong, a reporter for the *Boston Globe*. It is about her mother, Hong Fong, who was raised in China in the 1940s and 1950s. Hong Fong's father used her birth certificate to bring a friend's son to the United States. When Kong asked her mother to talk about it, she was surprised that there was no "crying, no quaver in her [mother's] voice, no bitterness in telling what her father did." Instead, her mother explained matter-of-factly that "parents would put down a baby girl as a baby boy, so the papers could be used to bring someone else's son over." That was just what was done; no strong feelings were involved.

By contrast, Kong reports another parental slight that "drove a stake through my mother's heart." Soon after her mother was born, the Japanese invaded their town and her grandmother fled with her baby girl and other children to the mountains. Unable to care for her infant daughter, she wrote to her husband in America, "I can't raise Hong Fong anymore." Fong's mother died shortly after writing those words. When Fong heard of that letter, she was hurt "more than anything." Kong explains that Fong's "mother's early death and her culture's preference for sons over daughters, both of these [Fong] can understand and live with. But to know that her mother did not want her—even if only for one instant and under the most difficult of circumstances—was a hurt that would never go away. Being rejected by her mother, when the mother-daughter should be the one lasting bond in a society where daughters have little else, was unbearable."[38]

What this story, and others like it, tell us is that we feel intense emotion when we are excluded where we should be included—that is, when people or groups whose obligation it is to consider us part of themselves expel us. To be justly excluded, even if it is an exclusion that causes great physical pain, and perhaps death, does not rouse emotional pain. (And to be included or cared for when one does not hold a claim on another's attentions rouses gratitude.) In the world of obligation, emotions rise and fall as the walls around groups or people rise and fall, those walls being manifested by the way people meet or neglect their obligations to include and exclude, to love or hate, and to respect or dishonor each other.

A Final Word on Love in the Six Images

I shall round off this discussion of emotions and boundaries to the self by exploring the meaning of love in the six orientations. In this discussion, as in any that asks the meaning of a particular emotion, say love, or hate, or shame, or pride, we cannot be asking about human nature or about any particular emotion in general. The answer to the question "What is this thing called love?" has got to be "It depends." It depends on the meaning of love in a particular culture at a particular time. All that can be said about love in general is that it is an attaching emotion, something that people who share a boundary may feel for each other. It is a kind of social glue.

A single name may be attached to many different emotions, with the emotion varying according to the orientation. A good example is love. In all orientations, love is an attaching emotion, an inside emotion, a feeling of oneness. But it has as many different meanings as a culture has orientations to the self. That is because the kind of attachment is different within each boundary around the self. The exchanger thinks of love as a commodity and expects a good return for his investment in love. Friends exchange the gift of love. The obligated self thinks of love as something that is required between children and parents, and between spouses. The called and cosmic orientations take love into the cosmic realm and toward that oceanic feeling of oneness Freud wrote about. Finally, there are the citizen's love of order and country and the possibility of heaven on earth that moves the civic self.

There are many words for love. *Love* itself is derived from the German *Laub*, from which we get *lovely*, meaning pleasing to the sight, and *lovable*, meaning attractive on account of beauty. *Erotic*, from the Greek *Eros*, is closest to our idea of romantic love, evoking desire and sexuality. Nearby is *libido*, derived from the Sanskrit *lubhyati*, meaning desire. *Philo* is a combination form found in *philanthropy* (benevolence to mankind) and *philosophy* (love of knowledge). *Agape*, a Greek word for the love feast of the early Christians, is now the word for God's love.

Let us imagine the six images of the self in a circle. As we go around the circle starting with the cosmic orientation and ending with the civic orientation, we will be starting with the orientation that imagines the self without boundaries and with feelings of oneness with the universe. Next comes the called person. It too has a sense of universal oneness, but with a difference. There is a boundary surrounding the called person, which must be crossed to achieve a desired universal oneness. Within the boundary is a gift—good health, riches, youth, talent, genius. That gift is like a hot potato: it must be given. By helping people with less money or health, or by producing a work of art, the gifted person crosses the boundary and finds the path to universal love.

When we leave the region of the called person, we enter the territory of permanently bounded images. Firm boundaries stand around the family, the nation, and the ethnic group in the obligated-self orientation, around the pair or group of friends in reciprocal images, and around the individual in the exchanger image. Coming full circle, we arrive at the citizen with her partitioned self. The citizen remains as whole and isolated as the exchanger and at the same time partitions off a portion of the self for the state or the world. This is a particularly modern form of boundlessness and national or universal oneness.

Siddhartha represented the cosmic love of boundlessness, a melting into the all-one. Agape is a Western version of cosmic boundlessness. Taylor says that the "original Christian notion of agape is the love that God has for humans which is connected with their goodness as creatures (though we don't have to decide whether they are loved because good or good because loved). Human beings participate through grace in this love."[39] Agape emphasizes the boundless love that God feels for all people, the afflicted and the beautiful.

The difference between a cosmic bonding with the whole of creation and the similar bonding of the called person is that the cosmic orientation demands nothing more of us: along with Siddhartha, we can gaze into the river, see the all-one, and be connected to eternity. In contrast, the called person's bond is earthy. It requires us to do something in this world—to ease a stranger's pain, to create art. In his book *The City of Joy*, Dominique Lapierre writes of Westerners who feel called to God's service in Calcutta, that city where poverty oozes like an abscess through the streets. One day a missionary went to meet Mother Teresa. As he entered the mission, he was struck by the absence of horror there: "no longer were the wretched people who had come together in this place tormented with anguish, solitude, destitution, or neglect. They had found love and peace." When Lapierre visited, Mother Teresa was "bathing the wounds of a man who was still young but who was so thin that he looked like one of the living dead discovered by the Allies in the Nazi concentration camps." She was speaking softly to him in Bengali. As she stopped tending the man to speak with her visitor, she noticed a young American in jeans and called him over: " 'Love him,' she ordered. 'Love him with all your might.' She handed the young man her tweezers and cloth. . . . Her gaze strayed over the room full of prostrate bodies and she added, 'They give us so much more than we give them.' " [40]

Mother Teresa spoke in the language of the gift, which is almost a sure sign that she is speaking from one of the blended images. And, although there is a sense of balance or reciprocity in her words, there is huge inequality between the healthy youth and the ailing man that he tended. That difference screams for balance: the healthy, those who are better off, are receiving not a gift of equal value, as in friendship, but a gift of greater value: "They give us so much more than we give them," says Mother Teresa. "I get so much more than I give," says a volunteer in New Haven's schools. [41]

Mother Teresa (and perhaps the school volunteer and all those who repeat this calculus of charity) is speaking of the love of God, of the pathway to God's love that the destitute and dying build for the young and healthy. She is instructing the young man in agape. By loving and caring for the man, the youth will himself become godlike. He will see the cadaverous man that Mother Teresa has commanded him to love as God would see him—that is, as good because he is loved.

The devotion that creative artists feel toward their work can be similar. The work cannot in itself return love, but it can be the avenue through which we sense a universe without boundaries. In her second letter to James Wright, Leslie Silko introduced the character who would bring their correspondence to the subject of love. It was a rooster: "I just fed the rooster a blackened banana," she wrote. "He has been losing his yellowish collar feathers lately, and I'm afraid it might be that he isn't getting enough to eat. But I suppose it could be his meanness too." [42] Half a year later she told Wright that coyotes killed the rooster and his three white hens. "He was a mean and dirty bird," she writes:

> But we loved him in a strange sort of way. . . . We are told we should love only the good and the beautiful, and these are defined for us so narrowly. Monday I will be 31. Maybe it has taken me this long to discover that we are liable to love anything—like characters in old Greek stories who set eyes on an oak tree or a bucket and fall in love hopelessly, there are no limits to our love. [43]

Wright responds:

I received your beautiful—and very sad—letter. Of course I never saw your rooster, and he never had a chance to jump me, but I can share your feelings for him, and for the small white hens. What you wrote about the improbability of loving this fierce little creature struck me very deep, because your words are so close to a passage in Spinoza's *Ethics*. The passage has given me some pain, but finally it is heartening and bracing, because it is, in my own view, the clearest statement of the plain truth that I know. Spinoza says that the human being is a miraculous creature, and his miracle consists in his capacity for love. He can love anything, from an atom all the way to God. But it is just here, says Spinoza, that the tragic difficulty arises. For man must realize that his capacity for love gives him no right to demand that anyone love him in return. Not anyone. Not even God. I have found that a hard thing to face, but, there is something in it that goes beyond pain.[44]

Spinoza and Wright were writing about a cosmic love, in which the feeling of universal oneness is its own response. This is a spiritual love, not a relationship among persons, or, if persons are included, then all persons are included, living, dead, and yet to come.

Although it is true that our capacity for a cosmic sort of love gives us no right to demand love in return, especially not from God, we can and do expect love in return for the love we bestow on others within the boundaries drawn by obligated, reciprocal, and exchanger relationships. All draw a boundary around the self that includes some persons and excludes others. Sometimes hate and love are spoken of as opposites; other times as having many similarities. If we look at what is happening at the boundaries to the self in these images, the similarities between these two apparently opposite emotions become evident.

Always at stake when emotions are aroused is social interaction that changes, or threatens to change, the location around a boundary of a self. We do not hate strangers who stay on their side of a boundary and do not bother us. But if a stranger whom we wish to exclude invades our boundary, he becomes our enemy, and we hate him. For example, a married couple are supposed to love each other, but they do not hate the people on the other side of the boundary that surrounds them, only the ones who might try to cross the boundary and invade the privacy of the pair, or try to entice a member of the pair out of the relationship. We expect nothing from persons on the other side of a boundary beyond respect for the boundary. But from persons within a boundary, persons who are included in an image we hold of ourselves, we may expect very much indeed.

Obligated-self identities are coterminous with a group's boundary—the group can range in size from a couple to a nation. When Soames's father, James, asked Irene why she didn't show more wifely affection, she replied from a Romantic cosmic orientation, which holds that feelings are outside one's control: "I can't show what I haven't got." Soames, the exchanger, couldn't understand. Like the flight attendants that Hochschild wrote about, who were trained to manage their emotions and appear pleasant, and even to feel pleasantly disposed, toward disagreeable passengers, Soames and his father James saw it as a failure of will and willingness when Irene did not take herself in hand and act the proper wife.[45] "That she did not love him, had tried to love him and could not love him, was obviously no reason. He that could imagine so outlandish a cause for his wife's not getting on with him was certainly no Forsyte."[46] And she was certainly no exchanger, either. The exchanger orientation would have us think of love as something to be bargained over, contracted for, and traded.

Contemporary Western cultures have turned romantic love into a motor well suited to market-dominated societies. It drives us down a road that serves as a bridge between the worlds of exchange and obligation. With romantic love these cultures have invented an emotion that joins individuals while maintaining their independence and rationality. Because true love is considered enjoyable, it is something we might rationally pursue. If it is obsessive, as it sometimes seems to be, love makes us lose the control so critical to exchangers. Even then, the trade is deemed worthwhile because control gives way to great pleasure. Moreover, although love is sparked by another and connects one to another, it is intrinsically individual because it seems to come from within. Others merely provide the enzyme that activates an innate power.

Thus, even a rational person might experience love. Modern beliefs about love also bridge the obligated and exchanger views of the self with explanations of why the individual may at times depart from rationality. Some descriptions portray love as an irresistible force so powerful it can override rationality. For example, we entertain the notions that romantic love subjects helpless victims to cupid's capricious arrows and that parents, especially mothers, are so naturally bonded to their offspring that they cannot avoid sacrificing themselves. Thus the myths about women—

that mothers bond to their offspring and that females are irrational — combine to produce an explanation for female caregiving: it is as natural and effortless as breathing and, as females are not rational, you can't expect them to be self-interested.[47]

Turning now to the civic orientation, the blend of exchanger and cosmic orientations, we come to an interesting distinction: the difference between a citizen's and a nationalist's love of country. Sometimes nationalism and citizenship are treated as synonymous because their objects, the state and nation, overlap. That makes it seem as though the boundary of the nationalist self and the boundary of the citizen self are the same. They are not. The nationalist self draws an obligated-self boundary that includes all those sharing a particular nationality. By contrast, along with the concept of citizenship came the idea that the self could be partitioned, only one part being given to the state. Citizenship arouses a sense of oneness with others engaged in the modern experiment of building goodness on earth.

Nationalism arouses a set of emotions similar to the obligations of fealty developed in the family, which is why the nation is often thought of as a family writ large. We speak, for instance, of our mother country or our fatherland. The emotional and structural similarity between families and nations is one reason nationalism lends itself so well to the Freudian analysis many commentators have applied to it.[48] Such analyses focus on infancy as an "extended period of helplessness and development through which all human beings must pass and in which the elements of their adult personalities are first molded."[49] Features of this crucial period include a sense of omnipotence in which the infant feels that the world is an extension of herself, responding to its cries with food, warmth, and tactile support. Most infants experience sufficient response from the world to survive this period, but no matter how well the world responds, infants are not in fact omnipotent and the world inevitably disappoints. Now the infant is forced to recognize the independent existence of an outer world. With that recognition comes the frightening awareness that far from being omnipotent, the baby is virtually powerless, dependent for life itself on the ministrations of adults over whom he has little control. The child then learns to identify with those adults and to please them in order to survive.

When theorists of nationalism translate this developmental narrative to nationalism, the nation (or political authority) takes the place of the parent. Then the nation is said to provide "a sense of psychological security by re-creating the accustomed relationships of sub- and super-ordination to which our long period of helpless dependency has accustomed us."[50] Like the family, the nation confers an identity and is associated with positive feelings such as love of country (or family) and pride in the achievements of one's group. In other words, just as a family engenders the sense of a single identity, with one boundary surrounding all its members, a nation engenders a sense of a single identity, with one boundary surrounding all the members of a nation.

The love, or sense of oneness, that citizenship invokes is a very different sort of emotion. It combines the practicality and ability to partition the self of the exchanger type with the boundlessness of the cosmic type. It engenders feelings that Taylor identifies as "civic humanism," the belief that humans properly motivated can build a heaven on earth. During the creative or nation-building phase, citizenship is charismatic. But as Max Weber warned, the charismatic moment passes. Then citizenship is marked by rationality and a quiet passion for order, security, and peace. The modern state depends on laws—on what Lewis Hyde calls logis power. Logis power is tepid; it draws from the exchanger's rationality and fear of emotion.

Laurel Langman, a sociologist who analyzes nationalism in Freudian terms, asks, "How does the fanatic differ from the patriot?" Patriots, or citizens, gain self-esteem "from knowing that their action is a human good in and of itself." Fanatics, by contrast, want recognition. Perceived injustice to a patriot's group raises righteous indignation. Narcissistic rage from the personal humiliations of childhood rouses a fanatic's anger. "This is the difference between the little Hitler beaten by his father and the little Nelson Mandela, loved by his parents."[51] Langman connects Durkheim's suggestion that the belief in immortality of the soul was based on the perception of society enduring beyond the life span of any particular member with Ernest Becker's suggestion that the most powerful of human emotions is the fear of death. He concludes that "the desire for the persistence of one's group is a normal condition of life, a basis for self esteem and articulation of the heroic as a defense against the inevitability of death."[52]

All kinds of things happen to humans—birth, growth, sickness, hunger, satiety, death—but how a people will identify them, make meaning of them, and feel about them will depend on culture. Our own culture has devised many sets of feelings and ideas about the nature of things and ourselves. Its high degree of variety and complexity may be unique. Perhaps that is why we have arrived at what has been called the postmodern moment of recognizing the fluidity of all cultural beliefs. Some people despair at the lack of an anchor, the lack of what Taylor calls hypergoods. If all beliefs, all moral systems, are viewed as humanly created, then how can any of them have supreme authority? But recognizing their human origins (and the human origins to claims of supernatural origins for one set of morals or another) does not reduce the force of moral systems. They gain their power over us when we are very young; they seem inevitable.

What seems as much of a "fact" as a tornado or hunger is the human need to create and maintain boundaries around the self and to invent moral orientations that tell us what we may and may not do and be. For that we have language and feelings. They give us flexibility, but they give us solidity too. Languages change, but they change slowly, and so too do moral systems change, and with them emotions. We invent them all, but we do not invent them in a day.

Epilogue

THROUGHOUT THIS BOOK, I have adopted a social constructionist orientation. That view sees our beliefs, norms, morals, ways of thinking, and ways of feeling as cultural constructs that are constantly being reinforced and reformed as people in a society adapt to changes in their environment. Social constructionism originated in the critical positivist tradition of post-Enlightenment social philosophy. Most recently it added emotions to the phenomena it explains.[1] What this book adds to that tradition is the insight that a culture can simultaneously employ many moral systems, that each moral system sets a different boundary around the self, and that emotions allow us to sense what is happening at the boundaries to the many selves we have internalized.

The idea of different images of the self moving us to feel and act differently is akin to role theory. But role theory imagines a single moral order organized into social statuses and roles. It does not imagine several systems operating simultaneously, each with a different sense of the self and different ideas of what is right and what is wrong. When we reflect on ourselves or others and when we enter into relationships, we recognize that we sense ourselves differently, feel differently, think differently, and act differently from time to time and from place to place, and we expect others to do the same. When people are being mothers, for example, we expect them to put their children's interests before their own —to engage in what Sara Ruddick calls "maternal thinking" rather than "rational" thought.[2] To use another example, we demand that public servants act in the public interest rather than their own. Finally, some of us are moved to empathize with and send relief supplies to disaster victims on the other side of the globe—even if months earlier those victims were our mortal enemies.

Such variations do not occur simply because people are actors playing roles, or because they are taking positions in social structures associated with particular behavior patterns and feelings that are deemed appropriate. The idea of a person as a role-player does have a particularly modern, market-inspired meaning, especially for the exchanger, who can weigh the different roles available and choose rationally among them. But roles are different from selves. Role theory imagines one self playing a variety of roles, some of which have greater importance to the person. It does not recognize that the same role, for instance, a member of a Town Committee, can demand a variety of behaviors, emotional displays, and feelings, depending on the image that participants have of the self that has entered the role. Women and men enacted the role of Town Committee Member differently because different moral orientations were expected of women and men.

Perhaps in order to have these insights one had to be a woman who was becoming an adult at the moment when the world of exchange was opening to women while the system of obligations was changing only slightly. I did not know when I began this study that my experience of life had ingrained in me a moral order quite different from the moral system that lay behind my initial question: Why were the women on the Town Committees working so hard even though they were not reaping rewards the men would have expected to receive for similar services? The question arose from a moral system and a vision of who I could be to which neither I nor any woman I knew could wholly subscribe. Although it was a system I had been taught in school, it was not the one women were raised for, nor was it the one men expected from women. It was a system designed for markets and for men. That moral system assumed that all people were free to choose where and how they would labor, that they would make that choice on rational grounds, and that their decision would be based on the rewards they would receive for their energies and talents. In that system, goodness and wealth are equated. The good society is a place of liberty and freedom where individuals take care of themselves and the state maintains just enough order to make sure that people compete for the goods they desire in a peaceful, nonviolent way.

That world has an image of toughness and fairness. Its moral system has been developing over centuries to provide for markets and international trade, to smooth the intercourse of strangers, and to encourage the highest economic use of resources, natural and human. It encouraged invention. It allowed and even inspired a wide variety of social relationships that had formerly been unimaginable or forbidden. Those once forbidden activities ranged from money lending and money borrowing at whatever rate the market would bear to the sale of labor, also at whatever rate the market would bear. It permitted and even encouraged the once forbidden practices of human geographical mobility, and the exploration and development of new corners of the geographical, intellectual, and productive world. Its view of man is the one that I have been calling the exchanger. He has his own interests at heart, he is competitive, he is independent, he develops his marketable resources whatever they are, and he values hard work for the rewards it will bring him. All these familiar values made the work women did on the Town Committees, work that was as often attacked as rewarded, so hard to understand.

As we come to the close of the twentieth century, we can look back on almost a half-century of social change during which the exchanger orientation became the one an increasingly large percentage of the population was allowed to adopt—at least in some measure. Through the civil rights and women's movements, women and ethnic and racial minority groups made demands and entertained aspirations once considered legitimate only for white males. Daily newspapers record the ebb and flow of social change. On November 17, 1996, for example, the *Boston Sunday Globe*'s front page carried two articles with the following headlines: "National Battle Brewing on Rights" and "Army Scandal Fallout." The first article was about several skirmishes in the continuing battle over civil rights: the passage of California's Proposition 209, banning affirmative action programs; the civil case brought against Texaco by black employees claiming discrimination in promotions and raises, supported by a tape recording in which high-ranking executives complain about Chanukah and Kwanzaa and agree to destroy evidence that the "black jelly beans are sticking to the bottom of the bag"; and the claim that an Avis Rent-A-Car franchise in North Carolina systematically denied automobiles to black customers. The second article reported on sexual harassment in the armed forces. The story begins with Kathleen Lee, a twenty-five-year-old army trainee, proud of her ability to repair tanks, who says she would rather work for a man. " 'You just automatically think of men as leaders,' she said. 'It's hard to find females to be leaders.' "

Here is a woman who can picture herself doing work that few women would have been allowed to attempt half a century ago, a woman who clearly has adopted an exchanger image of herself and other women when it comes to technical capabilities, or to the objects that women may work with. But when it comes to social relationships, to the way people can work together, the traditional obligatory self is still deeply ingrained. Kathleen Lee, like a large proportion of contemporary women and men, automatically pictures men, not women, nor people in general, as leaders.

Books claiming that women are very different from men currently enjoy great popularity in the United States.[3] They ring true. Why wouldn't they, if the obligated-self orientation of our culture is still deeply patriarchal and ethnically discriminatory? Books claiming gender difference (few these days claim ethnic or racial difference) usually presume that differences between women and men in feeling, understanding, and behavior are biological. (Some don't address questions of etiology, which amounts to the same thing.) Thereby readers enjoy the comforting notion that we live in a culture with only one moral system, the system of exchange.

Physiology, however, does not explain why women and men in the United States sometimes seem to speak in different tongues and act as though they came from different planets. If it could, the gender differences we see in the United States would be constant across cultures. We know that they aren't. One culture assigns characteristics to women that another culture assigns to men. Moreover, every study tells us that there is more diversity among men and among women than there is between the sexes.

I knew all that before I tried to answer the question of why the women on the Town Committees were working so hard with so little reward. But before embarking on this book, I thought (as most people still do) that there was only one moral system and that it guided women as well as men. That is why I wondered first what the women did—it was so well hidden. Later, when my research uncovered their many hours of work, I wondered why they did so much for such scant rewards.

I was not asking why men didn't do what the women did—that work had so little manifest moral grounding that I could not even articulate what it was (although I was doing it myself most of my waking hours). It was so invisible that I often wondered what would happen if women stopped doing what they were doing, not just in the political parties but in society in general. The answer was not near at hand.

As long as everybody stayed in the sphere of his or her gender, those two moral systems seemed complementary, and their different orientations could remain hidden behind such catchy concepts as "women's intuition" or "boys will be boys." But when women started wondering why few, if any, women were in the highest ranks of the business and political hierarchies of the United States (and when African-Americans and others wondered why they could not be as successful as some English- and European-Americans), the accommodations in the obligated-self orientation that had developed alongside the exchanger orientation began to unravel.

The unraveling has had some unexpected consequences. Work that was once performed out of sight is getting even less attention than it was when I began this study. Those who depend most on that work, children especially, have suffered.[4] One of the most powerful responses has been attempts to restore the old order. Accurately calling the problem a moral one, people are joining together to plead for "moral recovery." They use words such as "family," "morals," and "values" in their slogans and labels for their organizations. Sometimes they say we have to go back to a time when "men were men and women women." One example of that kind of thinking is the book by poet Robert Bly called *Iron John: A Book about Men.* Unlike his Victorian forebears whose claims rested on pseudoscience, Bly bases his presumption of sexual difference on myth. The book begins with the assumption that our culture fails to take its young men through adolescence to adulthood. The problem, he thinks, is that we have lost our myths. His book is meant to fill the gap. It tells the tale of a young man traveling through initiation rites under the guidance of a mythic, fatherly male spirit—Iron John.

Bly hit a vital nerve in our culture, or else his book would not enjoy its cult following. And Bly is right, up to a point: with patriarchies under attack, contemporary men are confused about themselves. They do need new myths. But what Bly offers is an old myth for a new age. His is an attempt to resurrect myths developed for patriarchies, societies that needed to separate the men from the women, that depended on a gendered division of labor, that needed to believe there was a male spirit and a female spirit, that needed to supply with myths the differentiation that was not supplied by nature.

Today myths that exaggerate sexual differentiation are retrograde. There is far less labor that only women can provide: we live longer, we have fewer children, and almost all of them reach maturity. Therefore very little time needs to be spent by one generation in pregnancy and suckling in order to produce another generation. On the male side, machines have replaced the need for upper-body strength. As less and less time is spent doing the reproductive labor that only women can do, as women and men increasingly do the same productive work, we need poets and story-tellers who will fill our minds with new images of who we might become. The new myths will bring the sexes together. The new images will make women and men seem as similar as they are becoming, not as different as people just escaping feudalism thought they had to be.

The new myths will create new images of the obligated self. A strong possibility, if we are to give the young the care they need, is a new concept of adulthood. The exchanger orientation that made so much of money and the market used paid employment as a measure of adulthood and worth: if you are able to support yourself, then you are as grown up as you need to be. This orientation turned marriage into an exchange and the economic support of a household into virtually the only obligation a father had. When the exchanger orientation prevails, boundaries around the individual remain high, emotional ties are discouraged, and commitments have no moral grounding. A new image of the obligated self might do what most societies have always done: it might connect adulthood with responsibility for others and might measure moral worth by the constancy and quality of the care one gives to others.

This has been a sociologist's book. Its purpose was to examine many of the moral orientations that guide contemporary Americans, both to recognize their continuing influence on contemporary morality and to organize them so they could be easily understood and compared. One goal was to explain the wide range of human behavior that is inexplicable within a vision of human nature limited to the exchanger. But the more important goal was to recognize that many current political issues are being fought among people who fail both to clarify the orientation they wish to apply to particular situations and to recognize the contradictions among orientations.

The exchanger orientation, for example, values a "level playing field," "equality of opportunity," "inequality of results," and the rights of individuals to spend their money however they wish. When that money is spent to support political candidates and zoning regulations that prevent economically integrated communities and school districts, the level playing field quickly erupts into steep mountains and deep valleys. Soon schools create castes, with children falling into almost the same ranks their parents had filled. In order to create the educated workforce that a market system requires, the state counters with court orders for busing, magnet schools, and other education-equalizing mechanisms. These are not likely to work as long as the exchanger's values of free use of unequal resources can be used to create inequalities in civic arenas. Exchange is an inherently unstable social environment: today's winners are tomorrow's losers—unless the winners can find a way to turn the resources they win into a private world that masquerades as a civic world (suburban school systems, for example) or into positions in a social world of exclusive clubs that mimic the divisions of a feudal society. Only the application of the exchanger's values in arenas where they are appropriate and the applications of the values of other orientations where they are appropriate can maintain a social environment in which the balance between the orientations can outweigh the disadvantages of each.

What we need, now that we can recognize several orientations operating simultaneously, is to look at the strengths and weaknesses of each so that its application can be most appropriate. From artists we need images of people who do what people in complex modern cultures actually do: we need images of people who are able to adopt a range of moral orientations depending on the situation.

Notes

The following abbreviations have been used:

DASOL   Silko and Wright, *The Delicacy and Strength of Lace*
FS   Galsworthy, *The Forsyte Saga*
L   Hobbes, *Leviathan*
S   Hesse, *Siddhartha*
WOBP   Naylor, *The Women of Brewster Place*

INTRODUCTION

1. Margolis, "The Invisible Hands." See also my "Redefining the Situation" and "Bargaining, Negotiating and Their Social Contexts."

2. Federal Glass Ceiling Commission, "Good for Business."

3. Tocqueville, *Democracy in America.* Tocqueville discusses mores, or habits of the heart, in vol. 1, pt. 2, chap. 9. He considers the tyranny of the majority in vol. 1, pt. 2, chap. 7, and individualism in vol. 2, pt. 2, chaps. 2 and 3.

4. Kelman, *Making Public Policy,* p. 10.

5. People have been warning against excessive individualism and mass society ever since Tocqueville. Relatively recent examples by scholars in various fields can be found. In economics, these include Boulding, *The Economy of Love and Fear;* Phelps, *Altruism, Morality and Economic Theory;* Sen, "Rational Fools"; Collard, *Altruism and Economy;* Margolis, *Selfishness, Altruism, and Rationality;* and Schelling, *Choice and Consequence.* For the background to this work in the writings of Bentham, Tawney, and Polanyi, see Kaun, "The Economists' Theory of Ideology." For examples in the field of sociology, see Bellah et al., *Habits of the Heart;* and Hewitt, *Dilemmas of the American Self.* For examples in psychology, see Hunt, *The Compassionate Beast;* and Kohn, *No Contest* and *The Brighter Side of Human Nature.* For a philosophical example, see Taylor, *Sources of the Self.*

6. See Averill, "The Structural Bases of Emotional Behavior"; Averill and Nunley, "Grief as an Emotion and as a Disease"; Crawford et al., *Emotion and Gender,* pp. 1-54, 92-109, and 151-166; Demo, "The Self-Concept over Time"; Denzin,

On Understanding Emotions; Ellis, "Sociological Introspection and Emotional Experience"; Franks and Gecas, *Social Perspectives on Emotion;* Giddens, *Modernity and Self-Identity;* Harré, *The Social Construction of Emotion;* Heiss, "Interactionist Theory and Emotions"; Hochschild, "Emotion Work, Feeling Rules and Social Structure" and *The Managed Heart;* Kemper, "Toward a Sociology of Emotions"; Lofland, "The Social Shaping of Emotion"; Rorty, *Explaining Emotions;* Scheff, *Microsociology;* Scherer, Wallbott, and Summerfield, *Experiencing Emotion;* Shaver, Wu, and Schwartz, "Cross-Cultural Similarities and Differences in Emotion and Its Representation"; Shott, "Emotions and Social Life"; Shweder and LeVine, *Culture Theory;* and Thoits, "The Sociology of Emotions."

7. Taylor, *Sources of the Self,* p. 105.

8. On the need to develop taxonomies, see Kemper, "Social Relations and Emotions," p. 209.

9. I am limiting this analysis to contemporary culture in the United States along with its (mostly) Western European antecedents. Whether the typology of moral orientations and images of the self developed here could be used effectively to organize moral orientations and images of the self in other cultures is a question for future research. I suspect that the "obligated self" may be universal, that some version of the "cosmic self" can be found in any culture that draws a boundary between itself and other peoples, and that the "exchanger self" appears in cultures that develop a market economy.

10. On the distinctions among concepts of "self," "person," and "agent" see Mauss, "A Category of the Human Mind"; Taylor, *Sources of the Self,* p. 12; and Swanson, "The Powers and Capabilities of Selves."

11. See Agnew, *Worlds Apart;* Hirschman, *Rival Views of Market Society;* and Taylor, *Sources of the Self.*

12. The quotation is from Gagnon, "The Self, Its Voices and Their Discord," p. 4. On the idea that our sense of self is a historically limited mode of self-interpretation see also Taylor, *Sources of the Self,* p. 111, and Carrithers, Collins, and Lukes, *The Category of the Person.*

13. For a general analysis of the way images and meanings change within a culture and, in particular, the way the women's movement is reshaping the image of woman, see Margolis, "Redefining the Situation."

14. Elias, *The Civilizing Process,* pp. 248-249.

15. See Berger and Luckmann, *The Social Construction of Reality.*

16. Most notably, rational choice theory cannot explain why people should risk their own health and well-being to rear their children. One effect of the prevalence of the rationalistic view is that children in the United States are increasingly subjected to inadequate food, shelter, and health care, poor education, and violent environments. See Hamburg, *Today's Children.*

17. See Taylor, *Sources of the Self,* and Calhoun, "Morality, Identity, and Historical Explanation."

18. See Taylor, *Sources of the Self,* pp. 103-107.

19. Miller, *Toward a New Psychology of Women,* pp. 22-23.

20. Koestler, "The Yogi and the Commissar."

21. See Martin, *Reclaiming a Conversation.*

22. Koestler, "The Yogi and the Commissar," p. 3.

23. Gould, "Triumph of a Materialist." For other critiques of dualism, especially from a feminist perspective, see Starhawk, *Truth or Dare*, and Sjoo and Mor, *The Great Cosmic Mother.*

24. Koestler, "The Yogi and the Commissar," p. 4.

25. The quotation is from Nussbaum, *Love's Knowledge*, p. 3.

26. Mills, "Situated Actions and Vocabularies of Motive."

27. Galeano, *The Book of Embraces.* See also Montaigne, *Complete Works,* p. 196, and James, *The Principles of Psychology,* pp. 281–282.

CHAPTER ONE: The Exchanger

1. Agnew, *Worlds Apart,* x–xi.

2. On the seminal role that Hobbes played in modern thought, especially in the politics, psychology, and morality of market society, see Strauss, "On the Spirit of Hobbes's Political Philosophy," and MacPherson, *The Political Theory of Possessive Individualism.*

3. The use of *man* rather than a generic term, such as *person* or *human,* does not in these labels represent an unintentional or unthinking misuse of gender-specific terms. These views of the self were gender specific. They were not meant to apply to women. A different sphere of life's activity and a different sense of the self were invented for women (see Chapter 2).

4. See MacPherson, "Hobbes's Bourgeois Man."

5. See Aldrich, *Old Money.*

6. *L,* p. 20 (chap. 3).

7. *L,* p. 59 (chap. 8).

8. *L,* p. 69 (chap. 10).

9. For a discussion of equality in Hobbes, see MacPherson, *The Political Theory of Possessive Individualism,* pp. 74–75.

10. *L,* pp. 103–104 (chap. 13).

11. *L,* p. 79 (chap. 11).

12. Agnew, *Worlds Apart,* p. 13.

13. *L,* p. 70–71 (chap. 10).

14. MacPherson, *The Political Theory of Possessive Individualism,* p. 39.

15. Ibid., p. 9.

16. Ibid., pp. 18–19. For a strong argument against interpreting Hobbes as the theorist of bourgeois society, see Thomas, "The Social Origins of Hobbes's Political Thought."

17. Examples include Karenin in Tolstoy's *Anna Karenina* and Lopahin in Tchekov's *Cherry Orchard.*

18. Harrison, "The Woman Lit by Fireflies," pp. 40–41.

19. *L,* p. 69 (chap. 10).

20. The quotation is from Sanford Sternlicht's biography of Galsworthy. I chose Soames Forsyte from a stock of such characters in contemporary literature. Although Galsworthy's writing has been judged less than first-rate because his characters are one-sided and because he suggests so little and reveals so much, his exaggerations and explicitness work well for my purpose: to provide a portrait of the exchanger. For a review of the critical appraisals of Galsworthy see Fréchet, *John Galsworthy.* Nega-

tive views include: Woolf, "Modern Fiction" and "Mr. Bennett and Mrs. Brown"; Lawrence, *Phoenix*, pp. 539–556, and *Selected Essays*, pp. 217–230; and Ford, *The Pelican Guide to English Literature*, vol. 7, pp. 212, 216, 284, and 372. As Galsworthy achieved fame and fortune during his last decade of life, "his reputation in intellectual and literary circles was moving in the opposite direction" (Fréchet, *John Galsworthy*, p. 3). Some critics, however, treated Galsworthy favorably. See Church, *Growth of the English Novel;* Collins, *English Literature of the Twentieth Century;* and Scott-James, *Fifty Years of English Literature.*

21. Fréchet, *John Galsworthy*, p. 49. For other biographies and critiques of Galsworthy and his works see the selected bibliography in Sternlicht's *John Galsworthy*, pp. 135–139, and Stevens and Stevens, *John Galsworthy.*

22. *L*, pp. 74–75 (chap. 10). On the importance of vanity in Hobbes's analysis see MacPherson, *The Political Theory of Possessive Individualism*, p. 172, and Strauss, "On the Spirit of Hobbes's Political Philosophy."

23. *FS*, p. 32.

24. *FS*, p. 41.

25. *FS*, pp. 171–173.

26. MacPherson, *The Political Theory of Possessive Individualism*, p. 48.

27. MacPherson faults Hobbes's political theory for its failure to recognize that possessive markets generate class cohesions. See *The Political Theory of Possessive Individualism*, p. 265.

28. *FS*, p. 385. Compare this scene with the final scene of Anton Tchekov's *Cherry Orchard*, wherein the ancient and failing valet, Firs, is forgotten and left behind by the family he has attended all his life. The doors are locked; he tries the handles; when they don't give, he sits down on a sofa and murmurs, "They have forgotten me. . . . Never mind. . . . Life has slipped by as though I hadn't lived. . . . Ech! I'm good for nothing." These scenes bring to mind Hegel's insight in *The Phenomenology of Mind* that servants' view of the world is more complete than their masters'. The servant knows all about the master and knows how things work, whereas the master is oblivious to the work and the workers that make life possible.

29. On this point see Hyde, *The Gift*, and also the discussions based on Hyde's work in Chapter 4 of this book.

30. This issue arose when a mail order company altered the cover of a catalogue that an artist had drawn. The artist claimed that the catalogue company had purchased the right to use the painting on their cover but not the right to alter the painting. Hyde deals with similar questions in *The Gift.*

31. *FS*, pp. 11 and 46.

32. *FS*, p. 74.

33. *FS*, p. 16.

34. *FS*, p. 18.

35. Hyde's *Gift* offers an extensive contrast between these two types. See also Chapter 4 of this book.

36. *FS*, pp. 171–173.

37. *FS*, p. 48.

38. *FS*, pp. 52–53.

39. *FS*, p. 124.

40. *FS*, p. 133.

41. *FS*, p. 134.

42. *FS*, pp. 236–237.

43. *FS*, p. 124.

44. *FS*, p. 262.

45. Collier, *Indians of the Americas*, p. 57.

46. See Margolis, *The Managers*.

47. Theory itself silences phenomena outside its purview—a point feminists often make. See, for example, Flax, "PostModernism and Gender Relations in Feminist Theory."

48. *FS*, p. 720.

49. *FS*, p. 479.

50. *FS*, p. 116.

51. See Rogow, *Thomas Hobbes*, and Merchant, *The Death of Nature*.

52. Merchant, *The Death of Nature*, pp. 193–194. See also Taylor, *Sources of the Self*. Taylor sees this movement emerging from a "mode of thinking roughly designated 'neo-Stoic' in the late sixteenth and early seventeenth centuries, associated with Justus Lipsius, and in France with Guillaun de Vair." According to Taylor, neo-Stoicism foreshadowed the idea of disengagement with "an increasing emphasis on a model of self-mastery which prepares the Cartesian transposition to the model of instrumental control . . . neo-Stoicism was bound up with a broad movement among political and military elites towards a wider and more rigorous application of new forms of discipline in a host of fields: . . . the military . . . civil administration . . ." (p. 159). See also Foucault, *Discipline and Punish*.

53. For a discussion of the intellectual circles in which Hobbes traveled see Rogow, *Thomas Hobbes*, pp. 10, 102, 106–109, and 133, and Merchant, *The Death of Nature*, pp. 194, 206–207, and 321.

54. Rogow, *Thomas Hobbes*, p. 103. Agnew (*Worlds Apart*, p. 91) suggests the English physician and protopsychologist John Bulwer as another influence. Hobbes may have been familiar with Bulwer's work, whose governing idea was that "perfection was attainable only through motion, the soul was known only in motion, passions were nothing but motions." Taylor (*Sources of the Self*, p. 148) shows that Hobbes was almost certainly influenced by Descartes.

55. Hobbes's attempt to follow Galileo's method has been frequently remarked upon: for examples, see Hirschman, *The Passions and the Interests*, p. 13; MacPherson, *The Political Theory of Possessive Individualism*, pp. 30 and 77; Peters, introduction to *Body, Man, Citizen;* and Watkins, "Philosophy and Politics in Hobbes."

56. Merchant, *The Death of Nature*, pp. 209, 192–193; MacPherson, *The Political Theory of Possessive Individualism*, p. 31; *L*, p. 3 (introduction). Rogow suggests that it was not only the general disorder of his times but also "the insecurities and uncertainties of his childhood" that may account for Hobbes's "personal quest for order and security." These personal insecurities may have been "fused, as it were, in his determination to make a science of his own political principles" (*Thomas Hobbes*, p. 102).

57. Coleman, *Foundations of Social Theory*, p. 504; Merchant, *The Death of Nature*, p. 31.

58. Agnew, *Worlds Apart*, p. 14; *L*, pp. 133–134 (chap. 16). Note that although Hobbes contended that "the use of Metaphors, Tropes, and other Rhetoricall figures, instead of words proper," led to "absurd assertions," he was not above using them.

59. Strathern, *The Gender of the Gift,* p. 135.

60. Taylor, *Sources of the Self,* p. 158.

61. Ibid., p. 159.

62. *FS,* pp. 190, 45.

63. *FS,* p. 190.

64. Wikse, *About Possession,* pp. 16, 20, and 18–19.

65. Ibid., p. 26.

66. Ibid., pp. 27–28.

67. *FS,* pp. 8 and 55–56.

68. Galt, "Our Mother Tongue"; Erikson, *Everything in Its Path,* pp. 81–82.

69. *FS,* pp. 74 and 239.

70. *FS,* p. 42.

71. *FS,* pp. 45 and 90.

72. Engels, *The Origin of the Family,* p. 134.

73. *FS,* p. 171.

74. Agnew, *Worlds Apart,* pp. 59–60.

75. Ibid., pp. 96–97, 98, and 112–113.

76. *As You Like It,* act 2, scene 7; *Richard II,* act 5, scene 5. See Agnew, *Worlds Apart,* p. 14.

77. The worth of humans does not always rise and fall with markets. As the twentieth century draws to a close, we find market values, as measured by stock markets, rising, but human values, as measured by the condition of children, falling.

78. See Hartsock, *Money, Sex and Power,* p. 215.

79. Corporation managers, for example, are notably affable and go out of their way to live in standard tract houses. Because both their selves and their houses are so frequently on the market, both must have a wide appeal, and neither their manners nor their houses should be too particular. See Margolis, *The Managers.* See also Coldwell Banker Residential Real Estate, "Everything You Need to Know to Prepare Your Property for Sale." This pamphlet, written in 1989, advises sellers to "make a buyer 'feel at home' " by creating "an environment similar to that found in a model home."

80. Agnew, *Worlds Apart,* p. 122.

81. Hirschman, *Rival Views of Market Society,* pp. 35 and 37–39.

82. *L,* p. 32 (chap. 5); Taylor, *Sources of the Self,* pp. 119–121; Coleman, *Foundations of Social Theory,* p. 503.

83. Fichte, *The Science of Rights,* pp. 424–426.

84. See Margolis, *The Managers,* and Sennett and Cobb, *The Hidden Injuries of Class.*

85. Wikse, *About Possession,* pp. 10–15 and 1.

86. Nietzsche, *Thus Spake Zarathustra,* p. 189; *FS,* pp. 4 and 359.

87. *FS,* p. 61.

88. See Taylor, *Sources of the Self,* p. 20; Collins, *Sociological Insight,* p. 4; Weber, *The Protestant Ethic and the Spirit of Capitalism,* p. 182.

CHAPTER TWO: The Obligated Self

1. Frost, "Education by Poetry," p. 718.

2. See Moore and Johnson, "A Re-Examination of Teacher Discrimination";

Felice, "Black Student Dropout Behavior." But see also Williams, "Teacher Prophecies and the Inheritance of Inequality."

3. Linton, *The Study of Man*, p. 115.

4. Sorokin, *Social Mobility*, pp. 136-139.

5. Bernard, *The Female World*, p. 27.

6. Ibid., p. 27.

7. Taylor, *Sources of the Self*, p. 65.

8. See Inman and Baron, "Influence of Prototypes on Perceptions of Prejudice"; Bledsoe et al., "Trends in Racial Attitudes in Detroit"; and Kaplowitz, Broman, and Chen, "Perceptions of Social Facts about Blacks and Whites."

9. Baumeister, *Identity*, pp. 5-6.

10. Taylor, *Sources of the Self*, p. 35.

11. Washington, *Up from Slavery*, p. 91. See also Lyons, *The Invention of the Self*, p. 29.

12. *WOBP*, p. 4.

13. British philosopher David Hume (1711-1766) questioned the assumption that the whole is more than the sum of its parts. Previously, the holistic assumption had made it hard to perceive the individual. When that tradition was challenged, it was easier for the individual to become the unit of attention, of action, and of existence. That is a basic premise of exchanging-self views. All other views of the self adhere, in one way or another, to the holistic notion.

14. Strauss, *Mirrors and Masks*, p. 20. See also Lyons, *The Invention of the Self*, p. 29.

15. See Strathern, *The Gender of the Gift*, and Carrithers, Collins, and Lukes, *The Category of the Person*.

16. See Strathern, *The Gender of the Gift*, p. 1.

17. Radcliffe-Brown, *Structure and Function in Primitive Society*, pp. 193-194.

18. Maine, *Ancient Law*, pp. 121, 122, 133, and 140.

19. Matthew 5:29-30.

20. See Gierke, "The Idea of Organization"; Ullmann, *The Individual and Society in the Middle Ages*, pp. 24-25; and Tuan, who writes, "In traditional China, . . . under the influence of Confucianism, the biological model of the family was extended to the neighborhood, the village, the province, and ultimately the empire of the civilized world" (*Segmented Worlds and Self*, p. 30).

21. Sociological functionalist theory and systems theory are in this tradition. See Parsons, *The Social System;* Merton, *Social Theory and Social Structure;* and Alexander, "The Parsons Revival in German Sociology."

22. Manu, *Institutes of Hindu Law*, verse 87.

23. For example, in the preface to Manu, *Institutes of Hindu Law*, translator William Jones writes: "Whatever opinion . . . may be formed of MENU and his laws, in a country happily enlightened by sound philosophy and the only true revelation, it must be remembered, that those laws are actually revered, as the word of the Most High, by nations of great importance to the political and commercial interests of *Europe*, and particularly by many millions of *Hindu* subjects, whose well directed industry would add largely to the wealth of *Britain*, and who ask no more in return than protection for their persons and places of abode, justice in their temporal concerns, indulgence to the prejudices of their old religion, and the benefit of those

laws, which they have been taught to believe sacred, and which alone they can possibly comprehend." Jones's supercilious tone, and the presumption that his England was "happily enlightened" by a sounder philosophy than that of the many millions of Hindu subjects, helped to legitimize the new system of obligation that kept subject peoples subordinate and added so much to the wealth of Britain.

24. John of Salisbury, *The Statesman's Book,* p. 65. (Salisbury claimed that he was taking his text from Plutarch, but no other record ascribing these words to Plutarch remains. See the preface of his translation.) Relevant discussions of organic theories of society include Gierke, "The Idea of Organization"; Barnes, "Representative Biological Theories of Society"; Coker, "Organismic Theories of the State"; McCloskey, "The State as an Organism, as a Person, and as an End in Itself"; and Weldon, *States and Morals.*

25. Merchant, *The Death of Nature,* pp. 1 and 102–111.

26. According to John of Salisbury, in *The Statesman's Book,* p. 247.

27. *Henry V,* act 1, scene 2 (first produced in 1598).

28. See Martindale, *The Nature and Types of Sociological Theory,* pt. 2. The organismic metaphor has played a central role in sociological theorizing from August Comte to Talcott Parsons and in the work of such contemporary systems theorists as Jürgen Habermas.

29. Martindale, *The Nature and Types of Sociological Theory,* p. 68.

30. Tuan, *Segmented Worlds and Self,* p. 30.

31. Aristotle, *Politics,* bk. 1, sec. 2, p. 26.

32. Reiss, *Family Systems in America.*

33. See, for example, Olson, *The Logic of Collective Action.*

34. Lévi-Strauss, *The Elementary Structures of Kinship,* p. 39.

35. The image of the independent male is clearly contradicted by statistics showing that single males suffer more ill health and lower life expectancies than married males, whereas the opposite is true for females. Moreover, most working-class families have always depended on female earnings. See Bernard, *The Future of Marriage;* Lowe and Smith, "Gender, Marital Status, and Mental Well Being"; Mookherjee, "Mental Well-Being, Gender and Marital Status"; and Porter and Kessler-Harris, *Out to Work.*

36. Turnbull, *The Mountain People.*

37. Ibid., pp. 134–135.

38. Ibid., pp. 135–136.

39. See Eyer, *Mother-Infant Bonding.*

40. Turnbull, *The Mountain People,* p. 134.

41. Actually, Ik children do not become isolates at three. Instead, they leave their mothers to become members of children's groups. Studies of urban street children suggest that by three or four children may have imbibed enough of the ways of their culture to be able to find their way into street gangs and thereby survive. See Le Roux, "Street Children in South Africa"; Aptekar, "How Ethnic Differences within a Culture Influence Child Rearing"; and Alexandrescu, "Street Children in Bucharest."

42. deMause, "Our Forebears Made Childhood a Nightmare."

43. For a more detailed discussion of emotions, especially love, in the six orientations, see Chapter 5 of this book.

44. For a contemporary example of this argument, see Angier, "Why Babies Are Born Facing Backward, Helpless and Chubby." Note that this view is similar to, but

not the same as, Fichte's explanation of a wife's subjugation to her husband. He did not draw on nature. He argued that women are subservient to their husbands because their reputations are at stake. Both constructions focus on self-interest and are within the exchanger mode.

45. Hirschman, *Rival Views of Market Society*, p. 41.

46. Neal, "Commitment to Altruism in Sociological Analysis"; see, for example, Hardin, "The Tragedy of the Commons," "Living on a Lifeboat," and *The Limits of Altruism.*

47. Wilson, *Sociobiology*, p. 3.

48. Ibid., pp. 106–112.

49. Axelrod, *The Evolution of Cooperation.*

50. See Tec, *When Light Pierced the Darkness* (p. 150), chapter 10 of which is an interesting discussion of altruism during the Holocaust. Tec explains the altruistic behaviors of righteous Christians as stemming from their independence and individually shaped moral standards and values. Based on the interview evidence she presents, I think that these Christians were strongly guided by a cosmic orientation that led them to act in ways that departed from the obligated values of their local community.

51. See Taylor, *Sources of the Self*, pp. 286–287. Epic themes appear to be returning in the work of such major contemporary writers as Toni Morrison, Salman Rushdie, and Isabel Allende.

52. *WOBP*, p. 40.

53. Brooks, *Reading for the Plot*, pp. 5–7; see also Watt, *Rise of the Novel.* But see Doody, who in *The True Story of the Novel* argues that the novel's origins were probably Egyptian and perhaps even as old as the Cro-Magnons.

54. *FS*, p. 70; *WOBP*, p. 20.

55. *WOBP*, p. 19.

56. *WOBP*, p. 9.

57. Lyons, *The Invention of the Self*, p. 87.

58. *FS*, p. 766.

59. *WOBP*, p. 25.

60. Durkheim, *The Division of Labor*, pp. 203–204. Note that the popular contemporary counsel to live in the present indicates that the exchanger, who does just that, is not the only view of the self that guides our lives. If it were, such counsel would be unnecessary.

61. In the variations of the prisoner's choice dilemmas that Axelrod studied, he found that time increases cooperation. See also Homans, *The Human Group*, pp. 135 and 243, and *Social Behavior*, pp. 316–320.

62. P. 21. O'Connor plays on the etymology of *guest*, *host*, and *hostage* (all derived from *ghosti*, represented as *hosti*, meaning stranger, and also enemy).

63. Much has been written about differences between the linear sense of time in Western industrialized cultures and the circularity of time in peasant cultures. The point I am making is that the difference is not simply between industrialized and peasant cultures but continues to exist in the different orientations within industrialized cultures. Ekeh, for example, differentiates between French collectivistic sociology and American individualistic sociology (what I would call the sociology of obligatory culture and the sociology of exchange culture): "The time frame in collectivistic sociology tends to be much broader than that in individualistic sociology; while the

former has usually concerned itself with social processes that span an individual's life, individualistic sociology is more likely to focus on processes that form only part of the individual's life experience" (*Social Exchange Theory*, p. 17; see also p. 70, on time in functionalist sociology).

64. In an earlier draft, I had written "*sic*" after "full bloodied." Sam Kaplan pointed out that some people make the mistake of saying "full bloodied" when they mean "full blooded," and my "*sic*" may have appeared to criticize Naylor's keen ear for speech.

65. *WOBP*, p. 86.

66. Hyde, *The Gift*, p. 195.

67. *WOBP*, p. 20.

68. See Eliot Jacques, in Hassard, *The Sociology of Time*; Boorstin, *The Discoverers*, pp. 1-78; Rosenberg and Birdzell, *How the West Grew Rich*; Landes, *Revolution in Time*; Zerubavel, "Private Time and Public Time"; Rudolph von Ihering, *The Evolution of the Aryan*, p. 117; and Weber, who on p. 151 of *Ancient Judaism* says: "The fact that in contrast to Babylonia, the day of rest in Israel became or remained a regularly recurrent day is simply to be explained by the greater prevalence in Palestine of peasant economic interests and customs oriented around the local urban market as over against the predominance of astronomical knowledge of genteel priests among the Babylonians. . . . In Israel . . . the interest of peasants and small town burghers in the regular recurrence of the market day was decisive."

69. Landes, review of *How the West Grew Rich*.

70. See Hochschild, *The Second Shift*.

71. Hyde, *The Gift*, p. 22; Sahlins, *Stone Age Economics*, p. 4.

72. Hassard, *The Sociology of Time*, p. 12.

73. See, for example, Stewart, *The Partners*. Stewart reports that an associate at Cravath, Swaine & Moore was able to bill IBM for twenty-seven hours in a single day because of time zone changes in a flight to California.

74. Lakoff and Johnson, *Metaphors We Live By*, p. 8.

75. See Coser, *Greedy Institutions*; Hartsock, *Money, Sex and Power*, pp. 43 and 215; Haravin, *Family Time and Industrial Time*; and Moore, *Time and Society*.

76. Bolles, *What Color Is Your Parachute?*

77. See Lopata, "Review Essay: Sociology," pp. 172-175; Lopata and Thorne, "On the Term 'Sex Roles.'"

78. Redfield, "The Folk Society," p. 300.

79. Lyons, *The Invention of the Self*, pp. 40, 43, and 37. Also see Stauffer, *English Biography before 1700*, p. 5.

80. See Goffman, *Gender Advertisements*, pp. 1-9; *Stigma; Asylums;* and *Presentation of Self in Everyday Life*.

81. *WOBP*, pp. 59-60.

82. *WOBP*, p. 2.

83. *WOBP*, p. 7.

84. In *The City in History*, Mumford contrasts the walled, bounded container village that is hostile to strangers with the open magnet city that attracts strangers. See also Marcuse, *One Dimensional Man*, and Cohen, *Two-Dimensional Man*.

85. See Elshtain, *Public Man, Private Woman;* and Bensman and Lilienfeld, *Between Public and Private*.

86. U.S. Congress, *Civil Rights*, pp. 1200-1201.

87. *WOBP*, pp. 30–33.

88. Goffman, *Asylums*, p. 18.

89. Mauss, "A Category of the Human Mind," p. 8.

90. *WOBP*, p. 34.

91. *FS*, p. 117.

92. *WOBP*, pp. 27–28.

93. Maine, *Ancient Law*, pp. 152–153.

94. See Davis and Moore, "Some Principles of Stratification," and Parsons, "A Revised Analytical Approach to the Theory of Social Stratification."

95. See Ryan, *Blaming the Victim*.

96. Linton, *The Study of Man*, pp. 115, 117. For many examples, see Whyte, *The Status of Women in Preindustrial Societies*.

97. For example, see Zborowski and Herzog, *Life Is with People*.

98. See Mead, *Sex and Temperament in Three Primitive Societies*.

99. Watson, *Behaviorism*, p. 82.

100. See Baldwin, *Sumptuary Legislation and Personal Regulation in England*.

101. For discussions of investments in vestments, the way dress can be used to place the self in a more favorable light and then finally into a more favorable position, see Agnew, *Worlds Apart*, p. 85, and Wikse, *About Possession*, pp. 20 and 34, where he shows connections between *custom, costume,* and *creditum.* Men as well as women use vestments as investments. Subtle differences between the two-hundred-dollar and two-thousand-dollar suits mark men for success even when dress restrictions limit them to uniform clothing. On the related subject of the way dress marks "good" and "bad" girls in nineteenth- and twentieth-century fiction and also on the use of such images to set and maintain boundaries, see Fiedler, *Love and Death in the American Novel;* Bernard, *The Sex Game;* Martin, "Seduced and Abandoned in the New World"; and Fox, " 'Nice Girl,' " p. 807.

102. Comte, *System of Positive Polity*, p. 196.

103. Ibid.

104. Ibid., p. 188.

105. Ibid., p. 169.

106. Ibid., p. 180.

107. Ibid., p. 197.

108. See Gould, *The Mismeasure of Man;* Russett, *Sexual Science;* and Lewontin, Rose, and Kamin, *Not in Our Genes*.

109. "Recherches anatomiques et mathématiques sur les lois des variations du volume du cerveau et sur leurs relations avec l'intelligence." Translation from Gould, *The Mismeasure of Man*, pp. 104–105.

110. Russett, *Sexual Science*, p. 45.

111. Durkheim, *The Division of Labor*, pp. 56–60. For extended discussions of Durkheim's views on women see Wityak and Wallace, "Durkheim's Non-Social Facts about Primitives and Women," and Lehmann, *Durkheim and Women*.

112. Enclosures of the commons have been called a revolution of the rich against the poor because they enriched the lords and nobles at the expense of the peasants (Polanyi, *The Great Transformation*, p. 34.) Enclosure Acts began in the eleventh century, turning lands that had once been open to all the villagers into hedged sheep runs and fields. At first, some obligations were preserved—at least in law. One of the

earliest Enclosure Acts, the Statute of Merton, which became law in 1236, required the lords to leave "as much pasture as sufficeth to their tenements." But as the centuries passed (and in spite of occasional laws and commissions to stem or reverse the trend), the lords "who saw good profit in sheep farms" acted as if they were free of "considerations as to whether these enclosures left 'sufficient' waste for the tenant." By the close of the nineteenth century, the common lands from which about half the English people had once drawn their fuel and sustenance were all but gone (Geary, *Land Tenure and Unemployment,* pp. 34 and 50).

113. Marx, *Capital,* p. 168.

114. Smith, *The Theory of Moral Sentiments.*

115. As Andrew Skinner says in his introduction to Smith's *Wealth of Nations:* "The book sold well, not least because the general 'philosophy' which it contained was so thoroughly in accord with the aspirations and circumstances of the age. . . . Smith stated his famous theme of economic liberty with telling force, and in a manner which apparently caught and held the attention of his contemporaries" (p. 13).

116. Polanyi, *The Great Transformation,* p. 30.

117. For example, by Durkheim and Spencer.

118. For example, by Toennies, Mauss, Cooley, and Kropotkin.

119. But see Collins's point in *Sociological Insight* that Durkheim argued that even in societies held together by organic solidarity, trust, not contract, is the basis of cohesion.

120. Chodorow, *The Reproduction of Mothering,* p. 6; Archbold, "Impact of Parent Caring on Women"; Hess, "Aging Policies and Old Women"; Porcino, "Testimony before the New York State Governor's Task Force on Aging"; and Fowlkes, "Katie's Place." Even in business organizations devoted essentially to exchange and competition, the roles women assume tend to stress community and care rather than individuality and exchange. See Hochschild, *The Managed Heart;* Kanter, *Men and Women of the Corporation;* and, on women's work to generate community spirit and cooperation rather than competition in voluntary organizations, Daniels, "Good Times and Good Works."

121. See Cott, *The Bonds of Womanhood.*

122. Gilligan, *In a Different Voice.* Gilligan does not speculate on the source of these differences; she merely shows that boys and girls follow different moral paths to maturity.

123. Benedict, *Patterns of Culture.*

124. Friedan, *The Feminine Mystique.*

CHAPTER THREE: The Cosmic Self

1. Eckhart, *Meister Eckhart,* p. 188. Also see Hyde, *The Gift,* pp. 54–55, and Schurmann, *Meister Eckhart.*

2. This is not to say that the contemporary mind always demands empirical proof and reason. Often scientific dressing is enough (as noted in the previous chapter). Consider the similarities between Eckhart's conception of the body as a vehicle for the soul to take its God-ordained voyage and the idea entertained by some sociobiologists (Dawkins, *The Selfish Gene*) that our lives and bodies are merely vehicles to transport "selfish genes" from one generation to the next.

3. Quoted in Blau, "Emerson's Transcendentalist Individualism," p. 81, whose footnote reads: "Quoted in James Elliot Cabot, *A Memoir of Ralph Waldo Emerson, I* (Boston and New York: Houghton Mifflin Co., 1877), pp. 133–34."

4. Taylor, *Sources of the Self*, p. 19. Also see Lasch, *The Culture of Narcissism*, pp. 80–81; Malcolm, *Psycho-Analysis;* and Westen, *Self and Society*, pp. 358–359.

5. Durkheim, *Suicide*, p. 254.

6. Ibid., pp. 255–256 and 364.

7. Taylor, *Sources of the Self*, p. 62. These are the central values of the different constructions of the self: the exchanger values rational mastery; the placed person, family life and fame; and the cosmic self, expressive fulfillment.

8. Ibid., p. 63 and p. 4.

9. Ibid., p. 4; see also Agnew, *Worlds Apart*, on the private self.

10. Lyons, *The Invention of the Self*, p. 16. Emerson says, "Every man is a new creation, can do something best, has some intellectual modes and forms, or a character the general result of all, such as no other agent in the universe has" (Cabot, *Memoir*, p. 133). For discussions of the contrast between the exchanger orientation and the Romantic cosmic orientation, see Hewitt, *Dilemmas of the American Self*, pp. 7–8, and Bellah et al., in *Habits of the Heart*, who see the contrast as a difference between two types of individualism, "utilitarian individualism" and "expressive individualism." See also Taylor, *Sources of the Self*, p. 101.

11. See Margolis, "Women's Work."

12. Gagnon, "The Self, Its Voices and Their Discord," p. 1.

13. Note, for example, Robert Persig's *Zen and the Art of Motorcycle Maintenance.*

14. In 1919, according to Thomas Mann, Hesse's *Damian* "struck the nerve of the times and called forth grateful rapture from a whole youthful generation who believed that an interpreter of their innermost life had risen from their own midst" ("Introduction," p. ix). Again in Germany in the late 1940s and 1950s and in the United States in the 1960s, Hesse was the "adored favorite" of entire generations of youth (Otten, *Hesse Companion*). Those waves have subsided; still, many among the younger generation and those who are no longer young continue Eastern practices of Yoga and meditation.

15. For two opposing views of *Siddhartha* see Ziolkowski, "Siddhartha," and Shaw, "Time and the Structure of Hermann Hesse's *Siddhartha*." Shaw believes that *Siddhartha* is structured after the Buddha's life, and his teaching about the Four Truths (chaps. 1–4) and about the Eight-Fold Noble Path (chaps. 5–12). Ziolkowski counters that Shaw's analysis "does violence to the natural structure of the book" and is "structurally fallacious." He believes that, rather than following the Buddha, *Siddhartha* "is Hesse's attempt . . . to reject the Buddhist way" (pp. 154–155). A text open to diverse interpretations seems to be what Hesse intended. When young correspondents sought his guidance, Hesse abstained, saying that he did not wish to be a counselor, physician, or leader. The "Hesse whom they read, love, or blame, is an image of their own Self. They recognize in him only what is akin to their own thinking and ask him for confirmation of these thoughts, and guidance. This I cannot do. They have to find their Way themselves. I am only their mirror!" The following analysis is in that spirit; my interpretation of Hesse's *Siddhartha* reflects my thoughts.

16. *S*, p. 4.

17. *S*, p. 1.

18. *S*, p. 2.

19. *S*, pp. 3 and 5.

20. *S*, pp. 7 and 9.

21. *S*, pp. 10–12.

22. *S*, p. 28. Hesse chooses names carefully: the Buddha, whose proper name is Gautama, was also called Siddhartha, "the one who has reached the goal." Govinda means "follower" or "companion." See Ziolkowski, "Siddhartha," p. 168.

23. *S*, pp. 31–32.

24. *S*, pp. 33–34.

25. See Turner, *From Ritual to Theatre*, pp. 20–60.

26. See Ziolkowski, "Siddhartha," pp. 157–160; Otten, *Hesse Companion*, p. 76; and Meyerhoff, *Time in Literature*, pp. 14–18.

27. See Ziolkowski, "Siddhartha," p. 168 n. 89.

28. *S*, p. 47.

29. *S*, pp. 61–62.

30. Ziolkowski, "Siddhartha," pp. 160–166.

31. *S*, pp. 61 and 63.

32. *S*, pp. 71, 73, 77, and 78.

33. *S*, pp. 81 and 88.

34. *S*, p. 39.

35. *S*, p. 62. On page 59 Kamala says, "You are the best lover that I have had. . . . And yet, my dear, you have remained a Samana. You do not really love me—you love nobody."

36. *S*, p. 99.

37. *S*, p. 108.

38. *S*, pp. 110–111.

39. *S*, p. 122.

40. Blau, "Emerson's Transcendentalist Individualism," p. 82, and *S*, pp. 1 and 4.

41. *S*, p. 39.

42. Taylor, *Sources of the Self*, pp. 130–131.

43. See Durkheim, *The Elementary Forms of the Religious Life*, pp. 240–272; Goffman, "The Nature of Deference and Demeanor"; and Lyons, who notes in *The Invention of the Self* that " 'I' is grammatically a slippery sign and a slipperier concept. It appears only as inflection attached to a verb in many languages. Or it is reserved for God or God's priestly or royal emissary like the royal we. But the Romantic movement brings a new I into usage. Somewhere between the grammatically functional and the imperial first person there is that I which is the feeling, tenderly loved, secularized soul, which we have come to think of as the self" (pp. 55–56).

44. Taylor, *Sources of the Self*, pp. 39, 111, and 129.

45. Lyons, *The Invention of the Self*, p. 44.

46. Durkheim, *Suicide*, p. 364.

47. *S*, pp. 10–12.

48. *S*, p. 11.

49. Lyons, *The Invention of the Self*, p. 14; see also Bedient, *Architects of the Self*, and any issue of *Self* magazine, which makes a cult of the body.

50. *S*, p. 117.

51. Taylor, *Sources of the Self*, p. 298.

52. In the aesthetic movement of the sublime, one seeks a deeper, spiritual, tran-

scendent self in nature (God's handiwork) and in travel to places that inspire terror (such as the Alps or Niagara Falls). Their danger induces awe and fear. After 1750 these ideas spread throughout the Western world, in an exchange of ideas furthered by travel, cheap paper, and translations. See Ferguson, *Solitude and the Sublime;* Hipple, *The Beautiful, the Sublime, and the Picturesque in Eighteenth-Century British Aesthetic Theory;* McKinsey, *Niagara Falls;* Monk, *The Sublime;* and Weiskel, *The Romantic Sublime.* My thanks to Louise Scott for bringing these books to my attention.

53. Freud, *Civilization and Its Discontents,* p. 11.

54. On the side of individual rights, we find Ronald Dworkin and the ACLU. Communitarians include Robert Bellah, Amitai Etzioni, Philip Selznick, and Mary Ann Glendon.

55. See Merchant, *The Death of Nature.*

56. Pope, *An Essay on Man,* ll. 237–241 and 267–268.

57. Emerson, "On Compensation," p. 124.

58. Ziolkowski, *Hermann Hesse,* p. 83; and Hesse, *Aus einem Tagebuch des Jahres,* p. 206, quoted in Ziolkowski, "Siddhartha," p. 158.

59. Bourdieu, "Time Perspectives of the Kabyle," pp. 220–221.

60. Weiner, *Women of Value, Men of Renown.*

61. Malinowski, *Argonauts of the Western Pacific.*

62. Weiner, *Women of Value, Men of Renown,* pp. 23 and 12.

63. *S,* p. 6.

64. *S,* p. 115.

65. Ziolkowski, "Siddhartha," p. 157.

66. *S,* p. 87; for similar passages see pp. 69 and 72.

67. Taylor, *Sources of the Self,* p. 4. See also pp. 214–215, where Taylor turns to Hirschman's idea that glory was rejected in favor of political stability and adds: "This 'bourgeois' ethic has obvious levelling consequences, and no one can be blind to the tremendous role it has played in constituting modern liberal society, through the founding revolutions of the eighteenth century and beyond, with their ideals of equality, their sense of universal right, their work ethic, and their exaltation of sexual love in the family." Taylor, however, overstates the respect that contemporaries have for each other and for life, and the leveling effects of modern liberal society. The civil rights and women's movements have advanced modern processes of leveling, but their success is far from complete.

68. *S,* p. 106.

69. From Hesse, *My Belief,* p. 179.

70. *S,* p. 76.

71. See Taylor, *Sources of the Self,* p. 475, for the intensity of cosmic visions.

CHAPTER FOUR: Gifts, Boundaries, and the Blended Images

1. Durkheim, *Moral Education,* pp. 26–27.

2. Hyde, *The Gift,* pp. 60–61.

3. Ibid., p. 17.

4. Heilbroner, *The Human Prospect,* p. 135.

5. Taylor, *Sources of the Self,* p. 193.

6. Hewitt, *Dilemmas of the American Self,* pp. 4–10.

7. See Wikse, *About Possession,* p. 304.

8. Comte, *Positive Philosophy,* pp. 11–19, 158, 4, and 253.

9. See also Kaun, "The Economists' Theory of Ideology," p. 34.

10. Durkheim, *The Division of Labor,* pp. 196 and 228.

11. Taylor, *Sources of the Self,* pp. 3 and 11.

12. Ibid., p. 12.

13. Polanyi, *The Great Transformation,* p. 47.

14. Malinowski, *Argonauts,* pp. 81–104.

15. Ibid., p. 175.

16. *DASOL,* p. 3.

17. *DASOL,* September 9, 1978, p. 4.

18. *DASOL,* September 12, 1979, p. 81.

19. Emerson, "Friendship," p. 217 (the concluding sentence of the essay).

20. *DASOL,* pp. 21–23.

21. *DASOL,* October 3, 1978, p. 8.

22. *DASOL,* October 3, 1978, p. 7.

23. Mead, *Mind, Self, and Society,* p. 76. *DASOL,* October 28, 1978, pp. 26–27.

24. Eisenstadt, *Patrons, Clients, and Friends,* p. 2.

25. Merton, *Social Policy and Social Research in Housing.*

26. Hogbin, "Polynesian Ceremonial Gift Exchange," p. 13.

27. Lévi-Strauss, *The Elementary Structures of Kinship,* p. 54.

28. Malinowski, *Argonauts,* pp. 184–185.

29. Lévi-Strauss, *The Elementary Structures of Kinship,* pp. 61 and 58.

30. Goffman, *Gender Advertisements,* pp. 1–9.

31. Malinowski, *Argonauts,* p. 184.

32. Goffman, *Stigma,* pp. 83–86.

33. Ecclesiasticus 13:2.

34. Aristotle, *Nicomachean Ethics,* books 7, 8, and 9.

35. Bacon, "Essay XXVII: Of Friendship."

36. Emerson, "Friendship." See also Oliver Goldsmith, *The Vicar of Wakefield* (1925 [London: J. M. Dent & Sons; New York: Dutton], p. 22): "disproportionate friendships ever terminate in disgust . . . let us keep to companions of our own rank."

37. *DASOL,* October 12, 1978.

38. Lapierre, *The City of Joy,* p. 228.

39. Hyde, *The Gift,* pp. 143 and 8.

40. Ibid., p. 169.

41. Ibid., p. 210.

42. Ibid., p. 153.

43. Ibid., p. 39.

44. Taylor, *Sources of the Self,* p. 22.

45. Ibid., pp. 218, 221, and 223.

46. From ibid., p. 223.

47. Lapierre, *The City of Joy,* pp. 231–232.

48. Simmel, "Faithfulness and Gratitude," pp. 388–389.

49. Hyde, *The Gift,* p. 23.

50. Ibid, p. 47.

51. Titmuss, *The Gift Relationship,* p. 74. Lévi-Strauss might call this "indirect ex-

change." See Ekeh, *Social Exchange Theory,* for a discussion of the varieties of gift exchanges.

52. Sahlins, *Stone Age Economics,* p. 188.

53. Marshall, *Class, Citizenship and Social Development.*

54. Hyde, *The Gift,* pp. 196 and 163–164. The first Whitman quotation is from "Thought," first published in 1860 as part of "Thought 4," p. 438; the list is from *Leaves of Grass,* first published in 1855, l. 101; and the last quotation is from Whitman's "Democratic Vistas," which Hyde calls a "long, rambling, postbellum meditation on art and politics."

CHAPTER FIVE: A Theory of Culture and Emotions

1. *WOBP,* p. 60.

2. Swanson, "On the Motives and Motivation of Selves," p. 17.

3. I am adopting Hochschild's extension of Freud's theory that anxiety fulfills a "signal function." See Hochschild, *The Managed Heart,* pp. x, 28–29, and 220–222; and Freud, "Inhibitions, Symptoms, and Anxiety."

4. Clark, "Emotions and Micropolitics in Everyday Life." Clark took the terms "introjected" and "extrojected" from Kemper's *Social Interactional Theory of Emotions.*

5. For the early history of the sociology of emotions, see Kemper, "Themes and Variations." For early work in other disciplines, see Rorty, *Explaining Emotions.*

6. Darwin's *Expression of Emotions in Man and Animals* laid the groundwork for this view. See Harré, "An Outline of the Social Constructionist Viewpoint."

7. See, for example, Ekman, "All Emotions Are Basic."

8. See Averill, "The Acquisition of Emotions during Adulthood"; Calhoun, "Subjectivity and Emotion"; DeSousa, *The Rationality of Emotion;* Harré, *The Social Construction of Emotion;* and Hochschild, *The Managed Heart.*

9. See Collins, "On the Microfoundations of Macrosociology," and Swanson, "On the Motives and Motivation of Selves."

10. See McCarthy, "Emotions Are Social Things"; Franks, "Mead and Dewey's Theory of Emotion"; and Shweder, "You're Not Sick, You're Just in Love."

11. For those who do not differentiate, see Shott, "Emotion and Social Life," p. 1319; for those who do, see Gordon, "The Sociology of Sentiments and Emotion"; Franks, "Mead and Dewey's Theory of Emotion"; and Armon-Jones, "The Thesis of Constructionism."

12. Cooley, *Social Organization,* p. 177. Recent work on brain structure may support Cooley's view. Studying fear in rats, whose brains he says are not different in this respect from human brains, Joseph LeDoux locates emotion in the amygdala. LeDoux distinguishes between what he calls "emotions," such as fear in rats, and "feelings," which are connected to cognition (Blakeslee, "Using Rats to Trace Anatomy of Fear," p. C1). It may be that there are two quite different human responses that appear "emotional." The first is a reflex, like pulling your hand away from a fire. The other is cognitive. Then, if I were to adopt the LeDoux terminology, I would retitle this chapter "A Theory of Culture and Feelings."

13. Hochschild, *The Managed Heart.* See also Clark, "Emotions and Micropolitics in Everyday Life."

14. For studies of shifts in European emotions over the past few centuries, see Elias, *The Civilizing Process;* De Rougement, *Love in the Western World;* Jacoby, *Wild Justice;* and Gay, *The Bourgeois Experience.*

15. Shweder, "You're Not Sick, You're Just in Love," p. 40.

16. Dawkins, *The Selfish Gene.*

17. See Ward and Throop, "The Dewey-Mead Analysis of Emotions." They say that Mead's work on emotions has been largely obscured by scholars' over-reliance on *Mind, Self and Society* and on the fragmentary and dispersed nature of his writings on emotions. See especially p. 466, and notes 3 and 4. See also Franks, "Mead and Dewey's Theory of Emotion."

18. On the contemporary near obsession with emotions, see McCarthy, "Emotions Are Social Things," and Franks, "Mead and Dewey's Theory of Emotions," p. 28.

19. Mills, "Language, Logic, and Culture."

20. Quoted in McCarthy, "Emotions Are Social Things," p. 59.

21. See Mills, "Situated Actions and Vocabularies of Motive," p. 674; and Berger and Luckmann, *The Social Construction of Reality.*

22. See Scheff, "The Labelling Theory of Mental Illness"; and Reich, "The World of Soviet Psychiatry" and "Gregorenko Gets a Second Opinion."

23. Cooley, *Social Organization,* pp. 23-31; Berger and Luckmann, *The Social Construction of Reality,* pp. 129-146.

24. The line between primary and secondary socialization is not impenetrable. Berger and Luckmann write about resocialization, a process used in brainwashing or in the intense training of musicians and athletes. For a description of a similar process in the training of middle managers see Margolis, *The Managers.* The resocialization that occurs in adulthood takes on many characteristics of primary socialization.

25. For an example, see Weigert, *Mixed Emotions.*

26. Kemper, "Toward a Sociology of Emotions," "How Many Emotions Are There?" and "Social Relations and Emotions," p. 211; Kemper and Collins, "Dimensions of Microinteraction," p. 41.

27. See Franks, "Power and Role-Taking," pp. 159-161.

28. See Ekman and Davidson, *The Nature of Emotion,* p. 138.

29. Durkheim, *The Division of Labor,* p. 100.

30. Elias, *The Civilizing Process,* pp. 106 and 130.

31. Ibid., pp. 115-116, 257, and 69-70.

32. Perinbanayagam, "Signifying Emotions," pp. 79-80.

33. Taylor, *Sources of the Self,* p. 115.

34. Ibid., p. 116.

35. Turner, "The Real Self." See also Gordon, "Institutional and Impulsive Orientations in Selectively Appropriating Emotions to Self," p. 115; and, for the culture of emotions, see Swidler, "Culture in Action."

36. Forster, "Notes on English Character."

37. Angier, "Why Babies Are Born Facing Backward, Helpless and Chubby."

38. Kong, "Daughter of China."

39. Taylor, *Sources of the Self,* p. 516.

40. Lapierre, *City of Joy,* pp. 233-234.

41. Fund-raising letter from School Volunteers for New Haven, September 1996.

42. *DASOL*, October 3, 1978, p. 6.

43. *DASOL*, March 2, 1979, pp. 40–41.

44. *DASOL*, March 14, 1979, pp. 45–46.

45. *FS*, p. 190.

46. *FS*, p. 45.

47. See, for example, Eyer, *Mother-Infant Bonding.*

48. See Langman, "The Nation and the Self," pp. 5–6: "Perhaps the earliest attempts at a depth psychological understanding of nationalism were the studies of the Frankfurt School of Critical Theory of the rise of National Socialism under Hitler."

49. Heilbroner, *The Human Prospect,* p. 127.

50. Ibid., p. 129.

51. Langman, "The Nation and the Self," p. 24.

52. Ibid., p. 23.

EPILOGUE

1. Armon-Jones, "The Thesis of Constructionism."

2. Ruddick, *Maternal Thinking.* This expectation is so strong that mothers who do not put their children's interests first are threatened with incarceration, actually incarcerated, or required to "remain on some form of birth control." See, for example, "Woman Agrees to Sentence That Requires Birth Control," *New York Times,* January 5, 1991, p. 6; and Altheide, "Gonzo Justice."

3. See, for example, Robert Bly, *Iron John;* John Gray, *Men Are from Mars, Women Are from Venus;* Camille Paglia, *Sexual Personae;* and Deborah Tannen, *You Just Don't Understand.*

4. See David A. Hamburg, *Today's Children,* and Susan Chira, "Study Confirms Worst Fears on U.S. Children."

Bibliography

Agnew, Jean-Christophe. 1986. *Worlds Apart: The Market and the Theater in Anglo-American Thought, 1550-1750.* Cambridge: Cambridge University Press.

Aldrich, Nelson. 1988. *Old Money: The Mythology of America's Upper Class.* New York: Knopf.

Alexander, Jeffrey C. 1984. "The Parsons Revival in German Sociology." *Sociological Theory* 2: 394-412.

Alexandrescu, Gabriela. 1996. "Street Children in Bucharest." *Childhood* 3, no. 2 (May): 267-270.

Altheide, David L. 1990. "Gonzo Justice." Paper presented at the Stone Symposium, St. Petersburg, Florida, January 25-28.

Angier, Natalie. 1996. "Why Babies Are Born Facing Backward, Helpless and Chubby." *New York Times,* July 23, sec. C, p. 1, col. 4.

Aptekar, Lewis. 1990. "How Ethnic Differences within a Culture Influence Child Rearing: The Case of the Colombian Street Children." *Journal of Comparative Family Studies* 21, no. 1 (Spring): 67-79.

Archbold, Patricia G. 1983. "Impact of Parent Caring on Women." *Journal of Applied Family and Child Studies* 32 (1): 39-45.

Aristotle. *The Politics.* 1981. T. A. Sinclair, trans. Harmondsworth, England: Penguin.

————. *The Nicomachean Ethics.* 1986. Martin Oswald, trans. New York: Macmillan.

Armon-Jones, Claire. 1986. "The Thesis of Constructionism." In *The Social Construction of Emotions,* ed. Rom Harré, pp. 32-56. New York: Basil Blackwell.

Averill, James R. 1986. "The Acquisition of Emotions during Adulthood." In *The Social Construction of Emotions,* ed. Rom Harré, pp. 97-118. New York: Basil Blackwell.

————. 1992. "The Structural Bases of Emotional Behavior: A Meta-Theoretical Analysis." In *Emotion: Review of Personality and Social Psychology,* ed. Margaret S. Clark, pp. 1-24. New York: Sage.

Averill, James R., and Elma P. Nunley. 1988. "Grief as an Emotion and as a Disease: A Social Constructionist Perspective." *Journal of Social Issues* 44 (3): 79-95.

Axelrod, Robert. 1984. *The Evolution of Cooperation.* New York: Basic Books.

Bacon, Francis. [1625] 1857. "Essay XXVII: Of Friendship." In *Bacon's Essays,* with annotations by Richard Whately, pp. 262–269. London: John W. Parker and Son.

Baldwin, Francis Elizabeth. 1926. *Sumptuary Legislation and Personal Regulation in England.* Baltimore: Johns Hopkins University Press.

Barnes, Harry Elmer. 1925. "Representative Biological Theories of Society." *Sociological Review* 17: 121–300.

Baumeister, Roy F. 1986. *Identity: Cultural Change and the Struggle for Self.* New York: Oxford University Press.

Bedford, Errol. 1986. Emotions and Statements about Them. In *The Social Construction of Emotions,* ed. Rom Harré, pp. 15–31. New York: Basil Blackwell.

Bedient, Calvin. 1972. *Architects of the Self: George Eliot, D. H. Lawrence, and E. M. Forster.* Berkeley: University of California Press.

Bellah, Robert N., Richard Madsen, William M. Sullivan, Ann Swidler, and Steven M. Tipton. 1985. *Habits of the Heart: Individualism and Commitment in American Life.* Berkeley: University of California Press.

Benedict, Ruth. [1934] 1961. *Patterns of Culture.* Boston: Houghton Mifflin.

Bensman, Joseph, and Robert Lilienfeld. 1979. *Between Public and Private: The Lost Boundaries of the Self.* New York: Free Press.

Berger, Peter L., and Thomas Luckmann. 1967. *The Social Construction of Reality: A Treatise in the Sociology of Knowledge.* New York: Doubleday, Anchor.

Bernard, Jessie Shirley. 1968. *The Sex Game.* Englewood Cliffs, N.J.: Prentice-Hall.

———. 1981. *The Female World.* New York: Free Press.

———. 1982. *The Future of Marriage.* New Haven: Yale University Press.

Blakeslee, Sandra. 1996. "Using Rats to Trace Anatomy of Fear, Biology of Emotion." *New York Times,* November 5, sec. C, p. 1.

Blau, Joseph L. 1977. "Emerson's Transcendentalist Individualism as a Social Philosophy." *Review of Metaphysics* 31 (1): 80–92.

Bledsoe, Timothy, Michael Combs, Lee Sigelman, and Susan Welch. 1996. "Trends in Racial Attitudes in Detroit, 1968–1992." *Urban Affairs Review* 31, no. 4 (March): 508–528.

Bly, Robert. [1990] 1992. *Iron John: A Book about Men.* New York: Vintage Books.

Bolles, Richard Nelson. 1971. *What Color Is Your Parachute?* Berkeley: Ten Speed Press.

Boorstin, Daniel J. 1991. *The Discoverers; an Illustrated History of Man's Search to Know His World and Himself.* New York: Random House.

Boulding, Kenneth. 1973. *The Economy of Love and Fear: A Preface to Grant Economics.* Belmont, Calif.: Wadsworth.

Bourdieu, Pierre. 1990. "Time Perspectives of the Kabyle." In *The Sociology of Time,* ed. John Hassard, pp. 219–337. New York: St. Martin's.

Brooks, Peter. 1984. *Reading for the Plot: Design and Intention in Narrative.* New York: Knopf.

Brown, K. C., ed. 1965. *Hobbes Studies.* Cambridge: Harvard University Press.

Cabot, James Elliot. 1877. *A Memoir of Ralph Waldo Emerson.* Boston: Houghton Mifflin.

Calhoun, Craig. 1989. "Subjectivity and Emotion." *Philosophical Forum* 20: 195–210.

———. 1991. "Morality, Identity, and Historical Explanation: Charles Taylor on the Sources of the Self." *Sociological Theory* 9 (2): 233–263.

Carrithers, Michael, Steven Collins, and Steven Lukes, eds. 1985. *The Category of the Person.* Cambridge: Cambridge University Press.

Chira, Susan. 1994. "Study Confirms Worst Fears on U.S. Children." *New York Times,* April 12, p. 1.

Chodorow, Nancy. 1978. *The Reproduction of Mothering.* Berkeley: University of California Press.

Church, Richard. 1951. *Growth of the English Novel.* London: Methuen.

Clark, Candace. 1990. "Emotions and Micropolitics in Everyday Life: Some Patterns and Paradoxes of 'Place.'" In *Research Agendas in the Sociology of Emotions,* ed. Theodore D. Kemper, pp. 305–333. Albany: State University of New York Press.

Cohen, Abner. 1974. *Two-Dimensional Man: An Essay on the Anthropology of Power and Symbolism in Complex Society.* Berkeley: University of California Press.

Coldwell Banker Residential Real Estate. 1989. "Everything You Need to Know to Prepare Your Property for Sale." Pamphlet.

Coleman, James. 1988. "Free Riders and Zealots: The Role of Social Networks." *Sociological Theory* 6 (1): 52–57.

———. 1990. *Foundations of Social Theory.* Cambridge: Harvard University Press, Belknap Press.

Coker, F. W. 1910. "Organismic Theories of the State." In *Studies in History, Economics, and Public Law.* Columbia Studies in the Social Sciences 38 (2): 1–209.

Collard, David. 1978. *Altruism and Economy: A Study in Non-Selfish Economics.* Oxford: Robertson.

Collier, John. [1947] 1948. *Indians of the Americans: The Long Hope.* New York: New American Library, Mentor Books.

Collins, Arthur Simons. 1951. *English Literature of the Twentieth Century.* London: London University Tutorial Press.

Collins, Randall. 1975. *Conflict Sociology: Toward an Explanatory Science.* New York: Academic Press.

———. 1981. "On the Microfoundations of Macrosociology." *American Journal of Sociology* 86 (March): 984–1012.

———. 1982. *Sociological Insight: An Introduction to Non-Obvious Sociology.* New York: Oxford University Press.

Comte, Auguste. [1851] 1873. *The System of Positive Polity.* John Henry Bridges, trans. New York: Burt Franklin.

Cooley, C. [1909] 1962. *Social Organization.* New York: Schocken Books.

Coser, Lewis A. 1974. *Greedy Institutions: Patterns of Undivided Commitment.* New York: Free Press.

Cott, Nancy. 1977. *The Bonds of Womanhood: "Woman's Sphere" in New England, 1780–1835.* New Haven: Yale University Press.

Crawford, J., S. Kippax, J. Onyx, U. Gault, and P. Benton. 1992. *Emotion and Gender: Constructing Meaning from Memory.* London: Sage.

Daniels, Arlene Kaplan. 1985. "Good Times and Good Works: The Place of Sociability in the Work of Women Volunteers." *Social Problems* 32 (4): 363–374.

Darwin, Charles. [1872] 1955. *Expression of Emotions in Man and Animals.* New York: Philosophical Library.

Davis, Kingsley, and W. Moore. 1945. "Some Principles of Stratification." *American Sociological Review* 10: 242–249.

Dawkins, Richard. 1978. *The Selfish Gene.* New York: Oxford University Press.

deMause, Lloyd. 1975. "Our Forebears Made Childhood a Nightmare." *Psychology Today* 8 (11): 85–87.

Demo, David H. 1992. "The Self-Concept over Time: Research Issues and Directions." *Annual Review of Sociology* 18: 303–326.

Denzin, Norman. 1984. *On Understanding Emotions.* San Francisco: Josey-Bass.

De Rougement, Denis. 1983. *Love in the Western World.* Rev. ed. M. Belgion, trans. Princeton: Princeton University Press.

DeSousa, Ronald. 1987. *The Rationality of Emotion.* Cambridge: MIT Press.

Doody, Margaret Anne. 1996. *The True Story of the Novel.* New Brunswick: Rutgers University Press.

Durkheim, Emile. [1893] 1933. *The Division of Labor in Society.* New York: Free Press.

———. [1897] 1951. *Suicide.* John A. Spaulding and George Simpson, trans. New York: Free Press.

———. [1912] 1954. *The Elementary Forms of the Religious Life.* J. W. Swain, trans. New York: Free Press.

———. 1961. *Moral Education.* New York: Free Press.

Eckhart, Meister. 1941. *Meister Eckhart, a Modern Translation.* Raymond Bernard Blakney, trans. New York: Harper.

Eisenstadt, S. N., and L. Roniger. 1984. *Patrons, Clients, and Friends: Interpersonal Relations and the Structure of Trust in Society.* New York: Cambridge University Press.

Ekeh, Peter Palmer. 1974. *Social Exchange Theory: The Two Traditions.* Cambridge: Harvard University Press.

Ekman, Paul. 1994. "All Emotions Are Basic." In *The Nature of Emotion: Fundamental Questions,* ed. Paul Ekman and Richard J. Davidson, pp. 15–19. New York: Oxford University Press.

Ekman, Paul, and Richard J. Davidson. 1994. *The Nature of Emotion: Fundamental Questions.* New York: Oxford University Press.

Elias, Norbert. 1978. *The Civilizing Process: A History of Manners.* New York: Urizen Books.

Ellis, Caroline. 1991. "Sociological Introspection and Emotional Experience." *Symbolic Interaction* 14 (1): 23–50.

Elshtain, Jean Bethke. 1981. *Public Man, Private Woman: Women in Social and Political Thought.* Princeton: Princeton University Press.

Emerson, Ralph Waldo. [1865 and 1896] 1921. "Compensation" and "Friendship." In *Essays: First Series.* Boston: Houghton Mifflin.

Engels, Friedrich. [1884] 1972. *The Origin of the Family, Private Property and the State.* E. Leacock, ed. New York: International.

Erikson, Kai T. 1976. *Everything in Its Path: Destruction of Community in the Buffalo Creek Flood.* New York: Simon and Schuster.

Etzioni, Amitai. 1987. *The Moral Dimension: Toward a New Economics.* New York: Free Press.

Eyer, Diane E. 1993. *Mother-Infant Bonding: A Scientific Fiction.* New Haven: Yale University Press.

Federal Glass Ceiling Commission. 1995. "Good for Business: Making Full Use of the Nation's Human Capital." *WIN News* 21, no. 2 (Spring): 71–72.

Felice, Lawrence G. 1981. "Black Student Dropout Behavior: Disengagement from School Rejection and Racial Discrimination." *Journal of Negro Education* 50, no. 4 (Fall): 415–424.

Ferguson, Frances. 1992. *Solitude and the Sublime: Romanticism and the Aesthetics of Individualism.* New York: Routledge.

Fichte, Johann Gottlieb. 1889. *The Science of Rights.* A. E. Kroeger, trans. London: Trubner.

Fiedler, L. 1966. *Love and Death in the American Novel.* New York: Dell.

Flax, Jane. 1987. "PostModernism and Gender Relations in Feminist Theory." *Signs: Journal of Women in Culture and Society* 12 (4): 621–643.

Ford, Boris, ed. 1964. *The Pelican Guide to English Literature.* Vol. 7, *The Modern Age.* Hammondsworth: Penguin Books.

Forster, E. M. 1936. "Notes on English Character." In *Abinger Harvest.* New York: Harcourt Brace Jovanovich.

Foucault, Michael. 1977. *Discipline and Punish: The Birth of the Prison.* Alan Sheridan, trans. New York: Pantheon.

Fowlkes, Martha. 1983. "Katie's Place: Women's Work, Professional Work, and Social Reform." In *Research in the Interweave of Social Roles: Jobs and Families,* vol. 3, pp. 143–159. Greenwich, Conn.: JAI Press.

Fox, Greer Litton. 1977. " 'Nice Girl': Social Control of Women through a Value Construct." *Signs: Journal of Women in Culture and Society* 2 (4): 805–817.

Franks, David D. 1989. "Power and Role-Taking: A Social Behaviorist's Synthesis of Kemper's Power and Status Model." In *The Sociology of Emotions: Original Essays and Research Papers,* ed. David D. Franks and E. Doyle McCarthy, pp. 153–177. Greenwich, Conn.: JAI Press.

———. 1991. "Mead and Dewey's Theory of Emotion and Contemporary Constructionism." *Journal of Mental Imagery* 15, nos. 1–2 (Spring): 63–166.

Franks, David D., and Gecas, Viktor. 1992. *Social Perspectives on Emotion.* Greenwich, Conn.: JAI Press.

Fréchet, Alex. [1979] 1982. *John Galsworthy: A Reassessment.* Denis Mahaffey, trans. Totowa, N.J.: Barnes and Noble Books.

Freud, Sigmund. 1926. "Inhibitions, Symptoms, and Anxiety." In *The Standard Edition of the Complete Psychological Works of Sigmund Freud,* ed. James Strachey, vol. 20, pp. 87–175. London: Hogarth Press.

———. 1961. *Civilization and Its Discontents.* James Strachey, trans. New York: Norton.

Friedan, Betty. 1963. *The Feminine Mystique.* New York: Norton.

Frost, Robert. [1930] 1984. "Education by Poetry: A Meditative Monologue." Amherst Alumni Council Address, November 15. In *Frost: Collected Poems, Prose, and Plays,* ed. Richard Poirier and Mark Richardson, pp. 717–728. New York: Library of America.

Gagnon, John. 1990. "The Self, Its Voices and Their Discord." Revision of a paper presented as "Conversations in the Self" at the 1990 Gregory Stone Symposium: The Sociology of Subjectivity, St. Petersburg Beach, Florida, January 27.

Galeano, Eduardo. 1991. *The Book of Embraces.* New York: Norton.

Galsworthy, John. 1922. *The Forsyte Saga.* London: William Heinemann.

Galt, William. 1943. "Our Mother Tongue: Etymological Implications of the Social Neurosis." *Psychoanalytic Review* 30, no. 3 (July): 241.

Gay, Peter. 1986. *The Bourgeois Experience: Victoria to Freud.* Vol. 2, *The Tender Passion.* New York: Oxford University Press.

Geary, Frank. 1925. *Land Tenure and Unemployment.* London: Allen and Unwin. Reprint, 1969, New York: Augustus M. Kelley.

Gergen, Kenneth J. 1991. *The Saturated Self.* New York: Basic Books.

Giddens, Anthony. 1991. *Modernity and Self-Identity: Self and Society in the Late Modern Age.* Oxford: Polity Press.

Gierke, Otto. 1938. "The Idea of Organization." In *Political Theories of the Middle Age,* trans. Fredric William Maitland, pp. 22-30. Cambridge: Cambridge University Press.

Gilligan, Carol. 1982. *In a Different Voice: Psychological Theory and Women's Development.* Cambridge: Harvard University Press.

Goffman, Erving. 1953. *Presentation of Self in Everyday Life.* Woodstock, N.Y.: Overlook Press.

———. 1956. "The Nature of Deference and Demeanor." *American Anthropologist* 58 (3): 473-499.

———. 1961. *Asylums: Essays on the Social Situation of Mental Patients and Other Inmates.* Garden City, N.Y.: Anchor.

———. 1963. *Stigma: Notes on the Management of Spoiled Identity.* New York: Aronson.

———. 1979. *Gender Advertisements.* New York: Harper Colophon Books.

Gordon, Steven L. 1981. "The Sociology of Sentiments and Emotion." In *Social Psychology: Sociological Perspectives,* ed. Morris Rosenberg and Ralph H. Turner, pp. 551-575. New York: Basic Books.

———. 1989. "Institutional and Impulsive Orientations in Selectively Appropriating Emotions to Self." In *The Sociology of Emotions: Original Essays and Research Papers,* ed. David D. Franks and E. Doyle McCarthy, pp. 115-136. Greenwich, Conn.: JAI Press.

Gould, Stephen Jay. 1981. *The Mismeasure of Man.* New York: Norton.

———. 1984. "Triumph of a Materialist." Review of *A Feeling for the Organism: The Life and Work of Barbara McClintock,* by Evelyn Fox Keller. *New York Review of Books* 31 (3-4): 58-71.

Gray, John. 1992. *Men Are from Mars, Women Are from Venus.* New York: HarperCollins.

Hamburg, David A. 1992. *Today's Children: Creating a Future for a Generation in Crisis.* New York: Times Books.

Haravin, Tamara K. 1982. *Family Time and Industrial Time.* Cambridge: Cambridge University Press.

Hardin, Garrett James. 1968. "The Tragedy of the Commons." *Science* 162 (December 13): 1243-1248.

———. 1974. "Living on a Lifeboat." *Bioscience* 24, no. 10 (October): 561-568.

———. 1977. *The Limits of Altruism: An Ecologist's View of Survival.* Bloomington: Indiana University Press.

Harré, Rom. 1986. "An Outline of the Social Constructionist Viewpoint." In *The*

Social Construction of Emotion, ed. Rom Harré, pp. 2–14. New York: Basil Blackwell.

Harré, Rom, ed. 1986. *The Social Construction of Emotion.* New York: Blackwell.

Harré, Rom, and Robert Finlay-Jones. 1986. "Emotion Talk across Times." In *The Social Construction of Emotion,* ed. Rom Harré, pp. 220–233. New York: Blackwell.

Harrison, Jim. 1990. "The Woman Lit by Fireflies." *New Yorker,* July 23, pp. 25–55.

Hartsock, Nancy C. M. 1983. *Money, Sex and Power: Toward a Feminist Historical Materialism.* New York: Longman.

Hassard, John, ed. 1990. *The Sociology of Time.* New York: St. Martin's.

Hegel, Georg Wilhelm Friedrich. 1977. *The Phenomenology of Mind.* A. V. Miller, trans. London: Oxford University Press.

Heilbroner, Robert L. 1991. *The Human Prospect: Looked At Again for the 1990s.* New York: Norton.

Heiss, Jerold. 1981. "Interactionist Theory and Emotions." In *The Social Psychology of Interaction,* ed. J. Heiss, pp. 288–302. Englewood Cliffs, N.J.: Prentice-Hall.

Hess, Beth B. 1985. "Aging Policies and Old Women: The Hidden Agenda." In *Gender and the Life Course,* ed. Alice S. Rossi, pp. 319–332. New York: Aldine.

Hesse, Hermann. [1920] 1960. *Aus einem Tagebuch des Jahres.* Zurich: Verlag der Arche.

———. 1951. *Siddhartha.* Hilda Rosner, trans. New York: New Directions.

———. 1974. *My Belief; Essays on Life and Art.* Theodore Ziolkowski, ed. Denver Lindley, trans. New York: Farrar, Straus and Giroux.

Hewitt, John P. 1989. *Dilemmas of the American Self.* Philadelphia: Temple University Press.

Hipple, Walter John, Jr. 1957. *The Beautiful, the Sublime, and the Picturesque in Eighteenth-Century British Aesthetic Theory.* Carbondale: Southern Illinois University Press.

Hirschman, Albert O. 1977. *The Passions and the Interests: Political Arguments for Capitalism before Its Triumph.* Princeton: Princeton University Press.

———. 1986. *Rival Views of Market Society and Other Recent Essays.* New York: Viking, Elizabeth Sifton Books.

Hobbes, Thomas. [1651] 1950. *Leviathan.* New York: Dutton.

Hochschild, Arlie Russell. 1975. "The Sociology of Feeling and Emotion: Selected Possibilities." In *Another Voice: Feminist Perspectives on Social Life and Social Science,* ed. M. Millman and R. M. Kanter, pp. 280–307. New York: Anchor.

———. 1979. "Emotion Work, Feeling Rules and Social Structure." *American Journal of Sociology* 85: 555–575.

———. 1983. *The Managed Heart: Commercialization of Human Feeling.* Berkeley: University of California Press.

———. 1989. *The Second Shift: Working Parents and the Revolution at Home.* New York: Viking.

Hogbin, Herbert Ian. 1932. "Polynesian Ceremonial Gift Exchange." *Oceana* 3: 13–39.

Homans, George C. 1950. *The Human Group.* New York: Harcourt Brace.

———. 1961. *Social Behavior: Its Elementary Forms.* New York: Harcourt, Brace and World.

Hunt, Morton. 1990. *The Compassionate Beast.* New York: William Morrow.

Hyde, Lewis. 1983. *The Gift: Imagination and the Erotic Life of Property.* New York: Vintage Books.

Ihering, Rudolph von. 1897. *The Evolution of the Aryan.* A. Drucker, trans. New York: Holt.

Inman, Mary L., and Robert S. Baron. 1976. "Influence of Prototypes on Perceptions of Prejudice." *Journal of Personality and Social Psychology* 70, no. 4 (April): 727–739.

Jacoby, Susan. 1983. *Wild Justice: The Evolution of Revenge.* New York: Harper.

Jacques, Eliot. 1990. "The Enigma of Time." In *The Sociology of Time,* ed. John Hassard, pp. 21–34. London: Macmillan.

James, William. [1950] 1981. *The Principles of Psychology.* New York: Dover Publications.

John of Salisbury. [1159] 1927. *The Statesman's Book: Selections from the Policraticus.* John Dickenson, trans. New York: Knopf.

Kanter, Rosabeth Moss. 1977. *Men and Women of the Corporation.* New York: Basic Books.

Kaplowitz, Stan A., Clifford L. Broman, and Wei Chen. 1992. "Perceptions of Social Facts about Blacks and Whites: Their Relationship to Race of Perceiver and to Racial Attitudes." Paper delivered to the meetings of the American Sociological Association, Pittsburgh.

Kaun, David E. 1984. "The Economists' Theory of Ideology: Competing Views." *Economic and Industrial Democracy* 5: 29–50.

Kelman, Steven. 1987. *Making Public Policy: A Hopeful View of American Government.* New York: Basic Books.

Kemper, Theodore D. 1978. "Toward a Sociology of Emotions: Some Problems and Some Solutions." *American Sociologist* 13 (1): 30–41.

———. 1987. "How Many Emotions Are There?: Wedding the Social and Autonomic Components." *American Journal of Sociology* 93 (2): 263–289.

———. 1990. "Themes and Variations in the Sociology of Emotions." In *Research Agendas in the Sociology of Emotions,* pp. 3–23. Albany: State University of New York Press.

———. 1990. "Social Relations and Emotions: A Structural Approach." In *Research Agendas in the Sociology of Emotions,* pp. 207–237. Albany: State University of New York Press.

Kemper, Theodore D., ed. 1978. *A Social Interactional Theory of Emotions.* New York: Wiley.

———. 1990. *Research Agendas in the Sociology of Emotions.* Albany: State University of New York Press.

Kemper, Theodore D., and Randall Collins. 1990. "Dimensions of Microinteraction." *American Journal of Sociology* 96 (1): 32–68.

Koestler, Arthur. [1942] 1946. "The Yogi and the Commissar." In *The Yogi and the Commissar,* by Arthur Koestler, pp. 3–14. New York: Macmillan.

Kohn, Alfie. 1986. *No Contest: The Case against Competition.* Boston: Houghton Mifflin.

———. 1990. *The Brighter Side of Human Nature: Altruism and Empathy in Everyday Life.* New York: Basic Books.

Kong, Dolores. 1996. "Daughter of China." *Boston Globe Magazine,* June 2, p. 20.

Lakoff, George, and Mark Johnson. 1980. *Metaphors We Live By.* Chicago: Chicago University Press.

Landes, David S. 1983. *Revolution in Time: Clocks and the Making of the Modern World.* Cambridge: Harvard University Press, Belknap Press.

———. 1986. Review of *How the West Grew Rich: The Economic Transformation of the Industrial World,* by Nathan Rosenberg and L. E. Birdzell, Jr. *New York Review of Books,* May 29, p. 47.

Langman, Lauren. 1992. "The Nation and the Self: Toward a Social Psychology of Nationalism." Paper presented at the meeting of the American Sociological Association, Pittsburgh.

Lapierre, Dominique. 1985. *The City of Joy.* Garden City, N.Y.: Doubleday.

Lasch, Christopher. 1979. *The Culture of Narcissism.* New York: Norton.

———. 1984. *The Minimal Self.* New York: Norton.

Lawrence, D. H. 1936. *Phoenix: The Posthumous Papers of D. H. Lawrence.* London: Heinemann.

———. 1966. *Selected Essays.* Harmondsworth, England: Penguin.

LeBon, Gustav. 1879. "Recherches anatomiques et mathématiques sur les lois des variations du volume du cerveau et sur leurs relations avec l'intelligence." *Revue d'anthropologie,* 2nd ser., 2: 27–104.

Lehmann, Jennifer M. 1994. *Durkheim and Women.* Lincoln: University of Nebraska Press.

Le Roux, Johann. 1996. "Street Children in South Africa: Findings from Interviews on the Background of Street Children in Pretoria, South Africa." *Adolescence* 31, no. 122 (Summer): 423–431.

Lévi-Strauss, Claude. [1949] 1969. *The Elementary Structures of Kinship.* James Harle Bell, John Richard von Sturmer, and Rodney Needham, trans. Boston: Beacon Press.

Lewontin, Richard C., Steven Rose, and Leon J. Kamin. 1984. *Not in Our Genes: Biology, Ideology, and Human Nature.* New York: Pantheon.

Linton, Ralph. 1936. *The Study of Man: An Introduction.* New York: F. Appleton.

Lofland, Lyn H. 1985. "The Social Shaping of Emotion: The Case of Grief." *Symbolic Interaction* 8 (2): 171–190.

Lopata, Helena Znaniecki. 1976. "Review Essay: Sociology." *Signs: Journal of Women in Culture and Society* 2 (Autumn): 165–176.

Lopata, Helena Znaniecki, and Barrie Thorne. 1978. "On the Term 'Sex Roles.'" *Signs: Journal of Women in Culture and Society* 4 (Spring): 718–721.

Lowe, George D., and Robert R. Smith. 1987. "Gender, Marital Status, and Mental Well Being: A Retest of Bernard's His and Her Marriages." *Sociological Spectrum* 7 (4): 301–307.

Lyons, John O. 1978. *The Invention of the Self: The Hinge of Consciousness in the Eighteenth Century.* Carbondale: Southern Illinois University Press.

MacPherson, C. B. 1962. *The Political Theory of Possessive Individualism: Hobbes to Locke.* London: Oxford University Press.

———. 1965. "Hobbes's Bourgeois Man." In *Hobbes Studies,* ed. K. C. Brown, pp. 169–183. Cambridge: Harvard University Press.

Maine, Henry Sumner. [1861] 1960. *Ancient Law: Its Connection with the Early History of Society, and Its Relations to Modern Ideas.* Rev. ed. New York: Dutton.

Malcolm, Janet. 1981. *Psycho-Analysis: The Impossible Profession.* New York: Knopf.

Malinowski, Bronislaw. 1922. *Argonauts of the Western Pacific.* London: George Routledge and Sons.

Mann, Thomas. [1948] 1969. "Introduction." In *Damian,* by Hermann Hesse, pp. v-xi. New York: Bantam.

Manu. 1869. *Institutes of Hindu Law; or, the Ordinances of Menu, According to the Gloss of Cullúca: Comprising the Indian System of Duties, Religious and Civil.* William Jones, trans. London: Allen.

Marcuse, Herbert. 1986. *One Dimensional Man: Studies in the Ideology of Advanced Industrial Society.* London: Ark Paperbacks.

Margolis, Diane Rothbard. 1979. "The Invisible Hands: Sex Roles and the Division of Labor in Two Local Political Parties." *Social Problems* 26: 314-324.

———. 1979. *The Managers: Corporate Life in America.* New York: Morrow.

———. 1985. "Redefining the Situation: Negotiations on the Meaning of 'Woman.'" *Social Problems* 32 (April): 333-347.

———. 1986. "Bargaining, Negotiating and Their Social Contexts: The Case of Organizations of Women in the Public Service." *Research in Politics and Society* 2: 267-281.

———. 1992. "Women's Work, Care-Giving and Two Traditions in Social Welfare." *Mid-American Review of Sociology* 16, no. 1 (Winter): 29-43.

Margolis, Howard. 1982. *Selfishness, Altruism, and Rationality.* Cambridge: Cambridge University Press.

Marshall, Thomas H. 1965. *Class, Citizenship and Social Development.* New York: Anchor.

Martin, Jane Roland. 1985. *Reclaiming a Conversation: The Ideal of the Educated Woman.* New Haven: Yale University Press.

Martin, W. 1971. "Seduced and Abandoned in the New World: The Image of Women in American Fiction." In *Women in Sexist Society,* ed. V. Gornick and B. K. Moran. New York: Basic Books.

Martindale, Don. 1981. *The Nature and Types of Sociological Theory.* 2nd ed. Prospect Heights, Ill.: Waveland Press.

Marx, Karl. [1867] 1967. *Capital: A Critique of Political Economy.* Samuel Moore and Edward Aveling, trans. New York: International Publishers.

Mauss, Marcel. [1923-1924] 1967. *The Gift: Forms and Functions of Exchange in Archaic Societies.* Ian Cunnison, trans. New York: Norton.

———. 1985. "A Category of the Human Mind: The Notion of Person; the Notion of Self." In *The Category of the Person,* ed. Michael Carrithers, Steven Collins, and Steven Lukes, pp. 1-25. Cambridge: Cambridge University Press.

McCarthy, E. Doyle. 1989. "Emotions Are Social Things." In *Research Agendas in the Sociology of Emotions,* ed. David D. Franks and E. Doyle McCarthy, pp. 51-72. Albany: State University of New York Press.

McCloskey, H. J. 1963. "The State as an Organism, as a Person, and as an End in Itself." *Philosophical Review* 72: 306-325.

McKinsey, Elizabeth. *Niagara Falls: Icon of the American Sublime.* Cambridge: Cambridge University Press.

Mead, George H. [1934] 1962. *Mind, Self, and Society: From the Standpoint of a Social Behaviorist.* Charles W. Morris, ed. Chicago: University of Chicago Press.

Mead, Margaret. 1935. *Sex and Temperament in Three Primitive Societies.* New York: Morrow.

Merchant, Carolyn. 1980. *The Death of Nature: Women, Ecology and the Scientific Revolution.* San Francisco: Harper and Row.

Merton, Robert King. 1951. *Social Policy and Social Research in Housing.* Vols. 1 & 2. New York: Journal of Social Issues.

———. 1957. *Social Theory and Social Structure.* Glencoe, Ill.: Free Press.

Meyerhoff, Hans. 1955. *Time in Literature.* Berkeley: University of California Press.

Miller, Jean Baker. 1976. *Toward a New Psychology of Women.* Boston: Beacon Press.

Mills, C. Wright. 1939. "Language, Logic, and Culture." *American Sociological Review* 4 (October): 670–680.

———. 1940. "Situated Actions and Vocabularies of Motive." *American Sociological Review* 5 (December): 904–913.

———. 1959. *The Sociological Imagination.* New York: Oxford University Press.

Monk, Samuel H. 1960. *The Sublime: A Study of Critical Theories in Eighteenth Century England.* Ann Arbor: University of Michigan Press.

Montaigne, Michel de. 1937. *Complete Works: Essays, Travel Journal, Letters.* Donald M. Frame, trans. Stanford: Stanford University Press.

Mookherjee, Mararsh N. 1994. "Mental Well-Being, Gender and Marital Status." Paper delivered at the meeting of the International Sociological Association, Bielefeld, Germany.

Moore, Helen A., and David R. Johnson. 1982. "A Re-Examination of Teacher Discrimination: Evidence of Sex and Ethnic Segmentation." Paper delivered to the meeting of the American Sociological Association.

Moore, W. E. 1963. *Time and Society.* New York: Wiley.

Morsbach, H., and W. J. Tyler. 1986. "A Japanese Emotion: *Amae.*" In *The Social Construction of Emotion,* ed. Rom Harré, pp. 289–307. New York: Blackwell.

Mumford, Lewis. 1961. *The City in History: Its Origins, Its Transformations, and Its Prospects.* New York: Harcourt, Brace and World.

Naylor, Gloria. [1980] 1982. *The Women of Brewster Place.* New York: Penguin.

Neal, Sister Marie Augusta. 1982. "Commitment to Altruism in Sociological Analysis." *Sociological Analysis* 43 (1): 1–22.

Nietzsche, F. 1970. *Thus Spake Zarathustra.* In *The Portable Nietzsche,* ed. and trans. W. Kaufmann. New York: Viking.

Nussbaum, Martha Craven. 1990. *Love's Knowledge: Essays on Philosophy and Literature.* Oxford: Oxford University Press.

O'Connor, Frank. 1954. "Guests of the Nation." In *More Stories by Frank O'Connor.* New York: Knopf.

Olson, Mancur, Jr. 1965. *The Logic of Collective Action.* Cambridge: Harvard University Press.

Otten, Anna, ed. 1977. *Hesse Companion.* Albuquerque: University of New Mexico Press.

Paglia, Camille. [1990] 1991. *Sexual Personae.* New York: Vintage Books.

Parsons, Talcott. 1951. *The Social System.* New York: Free Press.

———. 1966. "A Revised Analytical Approach to the Theory of Social Stratification." In *Class, Status and Power: A Reader in Social Stratification,* ed. R. Bendix and Seymour Martin Lipset. Glencoe, Ill.: Free Press.

Perinbanayagam, R. S. 1989. "Signifying Emotions." In *The Sociology of Emotions: Original Essays and Research Papers,* ed. David D. Franks and E. Doyle McCarthy, pp. 73–92. Greenwich, Conn.: JAI Press.

Persig, Robert. 1974. *Zen and the Art of Motorcycle Maintenance: An Inquiry into Values.* New York: Morrow.

Peters, Richard S. 1962. Introduction to *Body, Man, Citizen: Selections from Thomas Hobbes,* ed. Richard S. Peters. New York: Collier.

Phelps, Edmund S., ed. 1975. *Altruism, Morality and Economic Theory.* New York: Russell Sage.

Polanyi, Karl. 1944. *The Great Transformation.* New York: Rinehart.

Pope, Alexander. 1950. *An Essay on Man.* Maynard Neal, ed. Twickenham edition. London: Methuen.

Porcino, Jane. 1985. "Testimony before the New York State Governor's Task Force on Aging." Albany, N.Y.

Porter, Marilyn, and Alice Kessler-Harris. 1982. *Out to Work: A History of Wage-Earning Women in the United States.* New York: Oxford University Press.

Radcliffe-Brown, A. R. 1965. *Structure and Function in Primitive Society.* New York: Free Press.

Redfield, Robert. 1947. "The Folk Society." *American Journal of Sociology* 52 (4): 293–308.

Reich, Walter. 1979. "Grigorenko Gets a Second Opinion." *New York Times Magazine,* May 13, p. 18.

———. 1983. "The World of Soviet Psychiatry." *New York Times Magazine,* January 30, pp. 20–50.

Reiss, Ira L. 1980. *Family Systems in America.* New York: Holt, Rinehart and Winston.

Rogow, Arnold A. 1986. *Thomas Hobbes: Radical in the Service of Reaction.* New York: Norton.

Rorty, Amélie, ed. 1980. *Explaining Emotions.* Berkeley: University of California Press.

Rosenberg, Nathan, and L. E. Birdzell, Jr. *How the West Grew Rich: The Economic Transformation of the Industrial World.* New York: Basic Books.

Ruddick, Sarah. 1989. *Maternal Thinking: Toward a Politics of Peace.* New York: Ballantine Books.

Russett, Cynthia Eagle. 1989. *Sexual Science: The Victorian Construction of Womanhood.* Cambridge: Harvard University Press.

Ryan, William. 1971. *Blaming the Victim.* New York: Pantheon.

Sahlins, Marshall. 1972. *Stone Age Economics.* Chicago: Aldine-Atherton.

Scheff, Thomas. 1974. "The Labelling Theory of Mental Illness." *American Sociological Review* 39 (June): 444–452.

———. 1990. *Microsociology: Discourse, Emotion, and Social Structure.* Chicago: University of Chicago Press.

Schelling, Thomas. 1984. *Choice and Consequence.* Cambridge: Harvard University Press.

Scherer, K. R., H. G. Wallbott, and A. B. Summerfield, eds. 1986. *Experiencing Emotion: A Cross-Cultural Study.* Cambridge: Cambridge University Press.

Schurmann, Reiner. 1978. *Meister Eckhart, Mystic and Philosopher.* Bloomington: Indiana University Press.

Scott-James, R. A. 1951. *Fifty Years of English Literature, 1900-1950.* London: Longmans.

Sen, Amartya. 1977. "Rational Fools: A Critique of the Behavioral Foundations of Economic Theory." *Philosophy and Public Affairs* 6, no. 4 (Summer): 317–344.

Sennett, Richard, and Jonathan Cobb. 1972. *The Hidden Injuries of Class.* New York: Knopf.

Shaver, P. R., S. Wu, and J. Schwartz. 1992. "Cross-Cultural Similarities and Differences in Emotion and Its Representation: A Prototype Approach." In *Emotion: Review of Personality and Social Psychology,* ed. Margaret S. Clark, pp. 175–212. New York: Sage.

Shaw, Leroy R. 1957. "Time and the Structure of Hermann Hesse's *Siddhartha.*" *Symposium* 11 (Fall): 201–224.

Shott, S. 1979. "Emotions and Social Life: A Symbolic Interactionist Analysis." *American Journal of Sociology* 84: 1317–1334.

Shweder, Richard. "You're Not Sick, You're Just in Love." In *The Nature of Emotion: Fundamental Questions,* ed. Paul Ekman and Richard J. Davidson, pp. 32–44. New York: Oxford University Press.

Shweder, Richard, and Robert LeVine, eds. 1984. *Culture Theory: Essays of the Mind, Self, and Emotion.* Cambridge: Cambridge University Press.

Silko, Leslie Marmon, and James Wright. 1985. *The Delicacy and Strength of Lace.* Anne Wright, ed. Saint Paul: Greywolf Press.

Simmel, Georg. [1903] 1950. "Faithfulness and Gratitude." In *The Sociology of Georg Simmel,* ed. and trans. Kurt H. Wolff, pp. 379–395. New York: Free Press.

Sjoo, Monica, and Barbara Mor. 1987. *The Great Cosmic Mother: Rediscovering the Religion of the Earth.* San Francisco: Harper and Row.

Smith, Adam. [1776] 1976. *An Inquiry into the Nature and Causes of the Wealth of Nations.* Oxford: Clarendon Press.

———. [1779] 1976. *The Theory of Moral Sentiments.* Oxford: Clarendon Press.

Sorokin, Pitirim A. 1927. *Social Mobility.* New York: Harper.

Starhawk. 1987. *Truth or Dare: Encounters with Power, Authority and Mystery.* San Francisco: Harper and Row.

Stauffer, Donald A. 1930. *English Biography before 1700.* Cambridge: Harvard University Press.

Sternlicht, Stanford. 1987. *John Galsworthy.* Boston: G. K. Hall, Twayne Publishers.

Stevens, Earl K., and H. Ray Stevens. 1980. *John Galsworthy: An Annotated Bibliography of Writings about Himself.* De Kalb: Northern Illinois University Press.

Stewart, James B. 1983. *The Partners: Inside America's Most Powerful Law Firms.* New York: Simon and Schuster.

Strathern, Marilyn. 1988. *The Gender of the Gift: Problems with Women and Problems with Society in Melanesia.* Berkeley: University of California Press.

Strauss, Anselm L. 1969. *Mirrors and Masks: The Search For Identity.* San Francisco: Sociology Press.

Strauss, Leo. 1965. "On the Spirit of Hobbes's Political Philosophy." In *Hobbes Studies,* ed. K. C. Brown, pp. 1–30. Cambridge: Harvard University Press.

Swanson, Guy E. 1985. "The Powers and Capabilities of Selves: Social and Collective Approaches." *Journal for the Theory of Social Behavior* 15: 331–354.

———. 1990. "On the Motives and Motivation of Selves." In *Research Agendas in the Sociology of Emotions,* ed. David D. Franks and E. Doyle McCarthy, pp. 3–32. Albany: State University of New York Press.

Swidler, Ann. 1986. "Culture in Action: Symbols and Strategies." *American Sociological Review* 51: 273–286.

Tannen, Deborah. 1990. *You Just Don't Understand: Women and Men in Conversation.* New York: Ballentine.

Taylor, Charles. 1989. *Sources of the Self: The Making of the Modern Identity.* Cambridge: Harvard University Press.

Tchekov, Anton. 1930. *The Cherry Orchard.* Constance Garnett, trans. In *The Plays of Anton Tchekov,* pp. 59–115. New York: Modern Library.

Tec, Nechama. 1982. *Dry Tears: The Story of a Lost Childhood.* Westport, Conn.: Wildcat.

————. 1986. *When Light Pierced the Darkness: Christian Rescue of Jews in Nazi-Occupied Poland.* New York: Oxford University Press.

Thoits, Peggy A. 1989. "The Sociology of Emotions." *Annual Review of Sociology* 15: 317–342.

Thomas, Keith. 1965. "The Social Origins of Hobbes's Political Thought." In *Hobbes Studies,* ed. K. C. Brown, pp. 185–236. Cambridge: Harvard University Press.

Titmuss, Richard. 1971. *The Gift Relationship: From Human Blood to Social Policy.* New York: Pantheon.

Tocqueville, Alexis de. 1969. *Democracy in America.* J. P. Mayer, ed. George Lawrence, trans. New York: Harper and Row.

Tonnies, Ferdinand. [1887] 1963. *Gemeinschaft und Gesellschaft: Community and Society.* Charles P. Loomis, ed. and trans. New York: Harper and Row.

Tuan, Yi-Fu. 1982. *Segmented Worlds and Self: Group Life and Individual Consciousness.* Minneapolis: University of Minnesota Press.

Turnbull, Colin M. 1972. *The Mountain People.* New York: Simon and Schuster.

Turner, Ralph H. 1976. "The Real Self: From Institution to Impulse." *American Journal of Sociology* 81: 989–1016.

Turner, Victor. 1982. *From Ritual to Theatre: The Human Seriousness of Play.* New York: Performing Arts Journal Publications.

Ullmann, Walter. 1966. *The Individual and Society in the Middle Ages.* Baltimore: Johns Hopkins University Press.

U.S. Congress. 1966. Civil Rights: Hearing before Subcommittee No. 5 of the Committee on the Judiciary. House of Representatives. 89th Congress, Second Session. May 4, 5, 10, 11, 12, 17, 18, 19, 24, and 25. Serial no. 16.

Veblen, Thorstein [1899] 1961. *Theory of the Leisure Class.* New York: Modern Library.

Ward, Gordon Lloyd, and Robert Throop. 1989. "The Dewey-Mead Analysis of Emotions." *Social Science Journal* 26 (4): 465–479.

Washington, Booker T. 1965. *Up From Slavery: An Autobiography.* New York: Dodd, Mead.

Watkins, W. N. 1986. "Philosophy and Politics in Hobbes." *Philosophical Quarterly* 5, no. 19 (1955): 125–146.

Watson, John. *Behaviorism* [1924] 1925. New York: Norton.

Watt, Ian P. 1957. *Rise of the Novel: Studies in Defoe, Richardson, and Fielding.* Berkeley: University of California Press.

Weber, Max. 1952. *Ancient Judaism*. Hans H. Gerth and Don Martindale, ed. and trans. New York: Free Press.

————. 1958. *The Protestant Ethic and the Spirit of Capitalism*. Talcott Parsons, trans. New York: Charles Scribner's Sons.

Weigert, Andrew J. 1991. *Mixed Emotions: Certain Steps toward Understanding Ambivalence*. Albany: State University of New York Press.

Weiner, Annette B. 1976. *Women of Value, Men of Renown: New Perspectives in Trobriand Exchange*. Austin: University of Texas Press.

Weiskel, Thomas. 1976. *The Romantic Sublime: Studies in the Structure and Psychology of Transcendence*. Baltimore: Johns Hopkins University Press.

Weldon, T. D. 1947. *States and Morals: A Study in Political Conflicts*. New York: McGraw-Hill.

Westen, Drew. 1985. *Self and Society: Narcissism, Collectivism, and the Development of Morals*. Cambridge: Cambridge University Press.

Whyte, Martin King. 1978. *The Status of Women in Preindustrial Societies*. Princeton: Princeton University Press.

Wiegert, Andrew J. 1991. *Mixed Emotions: Certain Steps toward Understanding Ambivalence*. Albany: State University of New York Press.

Wikse, John R. 1977. *About Possession: The Self as Private Property*. University Park: Pennsylvania State University Press.

Williams, Trevor. 1976. "Teacher Prophecies and the Inheritance of Inequality." *Sociology of Education* 49, no. 3 (July): 223–236.

Wilson, Edward Osborne. 1975. *Sociobiology*. Cambridge: Harvard University Press, Belknap Press.

Wityak, Nancy L., and Ruth A. Wallace. 1981. "Durkheim's Non-Social Facts about Primitives and Women." *Sociological Inquiry* 51 (1): 61–67.

Woolf, Virginia. [1925] 1929. "Modern Fiction." In *The Common Reader*, pp. 184–195. London: Hogarth Press.

————. 1966. "Mr. Bennett and Mrs. Brown." In *Collected Essays*, vol. 1, ed. Leonard Woolf, pp. 327–330. London: Hogarth Press.

Zborowski, Mark, and Elizabeth Herzog. [1952] 1965. *Life Is with People: The Culture of the Shtetl*. New York: Schocken Books.

Zelizer, Viviana. 1985. *Pricing the Priceless Child: The Changing Value of Children*. New York: Basic Books.

Zerubavel, Eviatar. 1979. " 'Private-Time and Public-Time': The Temporal Structure of Social Accessibility and Professional Commitments." *Social Forces* 58: 38–58.

————. 1985. *The Seven Day Circle: The History and Meaning of the Week*. New York: Free Press.

Ziolkowski, Theodore. 1966. *Hermann Hesse*. New York: Columbia University Press.

————. 1970. "Siddhartha: The Hidden Landscape of the Soul." In *Hesse Companion*, ed. Anna Otten, pp. 101–157. Frankfurt: Suhrkamp.

————. 1977. *Disenchanted Images: A Literary Iconology*. Princeton: Princeton University Press.

Index